신흥교역국의 통관환경 연구

필리핀

한국조세재정연구원

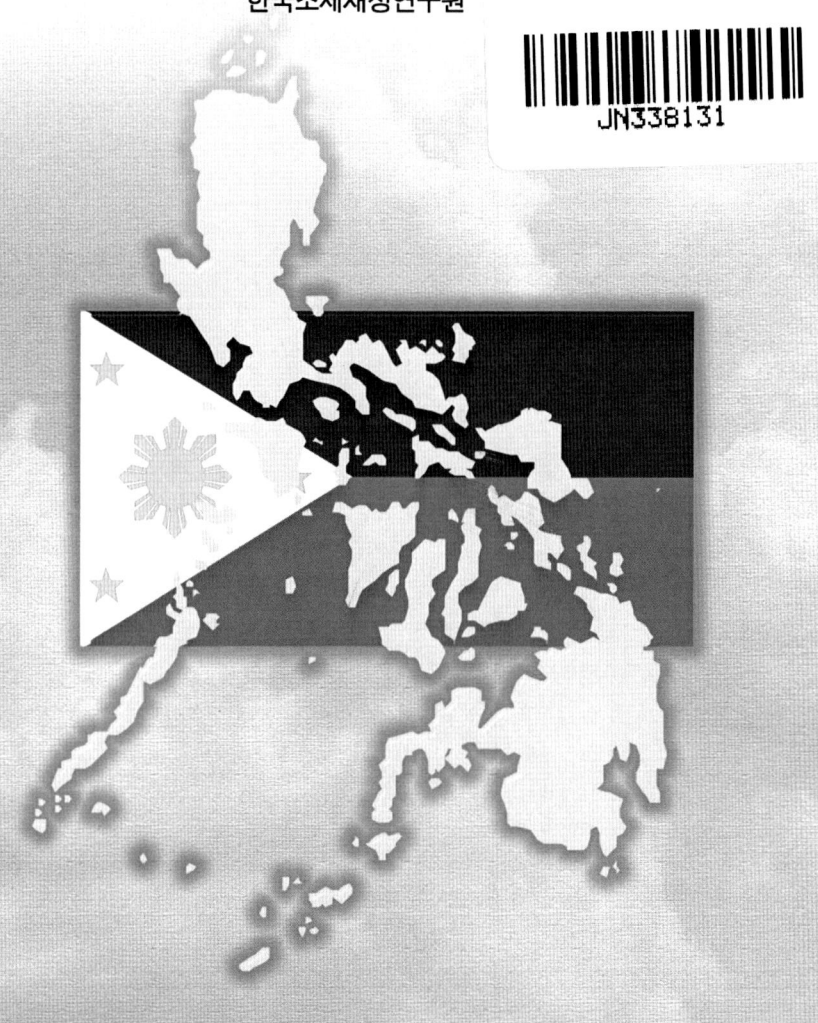

2014년 11월 15일 1판 1쇄 인쇄
2014년 11월 15일 1판 1쇄 발행

지 은 이　세법연구센터 / 한국조세재정연구원
발 행 인　이헌숙
표　　 지　김학용
발 행 처　생각쉼표 & 주)휴먼컬처아리랑
　　　　　서울특별시 영등포구 여의도동 45-13 코오롱포레스텔 309
전　　 화　070) 8866 - 2220 FAX • 02) 784-4111
등록번호　제 2009 - 000008호
등록일자　2009년 12월 29일

www.휴먼컬처아리랑.kr
ISBN 979-11-5565-100-1

신흥교역국의 통관환경 연구

필리핀

한국조세재정연구원

※ 본 보고서는 필리핀 관세제도의 대부분을 담기 위해서 노력하였으나 지면의 부족 및 시간상의 제약으로 인해 부족한 부분이 있다.

또한 가급적 최신의 내용을 수록하기 위하여 노력하였지만, 사회·경제 상황에 따라 세제에 변화가 빈번하여, 가장 최신의 내용을 본 보고서에 반영하는 데에는 한계가 있었다.

따라서 본 보고서는 필리핀의 관세에 내한 최소한의 길라잡이임을 밝히며, 보나 정확하고 구체적인 사항은 필리핀 관세국 및 재무부의 출판물 및 홈페이지와 관련 법령을 참조할 것을 권장함. 특히 민감한 사안에 대하여는 반드시 관련 법령을 통해 확인할 필요가 있으며, 불명확한 부분에 대해서는 관련 관세전문가의 도움을 받을 것을 강조하고자 한다.

본 보고서의 내용은 저자들의 개인적인 의견이며, 한국조세연구원의 공식적인 견해와 무관함을 밝혀 둔다.

목 차

I. 개 관 ··· 7
  1. 일반 개황 ·· 7
  2. 경제 개황 ·· 8
    가. 필리핀의 주요 경제 지표 ·· 8
    나. 필리핀의 수출입 동향 ··· 9
    다. 필리핀의 외국인 투자 동향 ·· 12
  3. 우리나라와 필리핀의 교역관계 ·· 15
  4. 필리핀의 자유무역협정(FTA, Free Trade Agreement) 현황 ········ 18
    가. 아세안자유무역협정(ASEAN Free Trade Area, AFTA) ·············· 18
    나. 한-ASEAN 자유무역협정(Korea-ASEAN Free Trade Agreement, AKFTA) ········ 19
    다. 필리핀-일본 경제동반자 협정(JPEPA) ································· 21
    라. 중-아세안 자유무역 협정(China-ASEAN Free Trade Agreement) ·············· 22

II. 외국의 통상환경 보고서 ·· 23
  1. World Bank의 『Doing Business 2011』 ····································· 23
  2. 미국 국별 무역장벽 보고서(National Trade Estimate Report on Foreign Trade Barriers: NTE 보고서) ·· 25
    가. 필리핀의 관세 구조 및 세관 통관 ····································· 25
    나. 품목별 이슈 ·· 26

III. 필리핀의 통관 환경 ··· 28
  1. 통관 행정 조직 ··· 28
    가. 필리핀 관세국(Bureau of Customs) ······································ 28
    나. 필리핀 통상산업부(The Department of Trade and Industry of Philippines) ···· 30

다. 필리핀 관세위원회(Tariff Commission of the Philippines) ·················· 32
　2. 필리핀의 통관 환경 ··· 32
　　　가. 관세 및 내국세 ··· 32
　　　나. 수입인증제도 ·· 35
　　　다. 수입규제제도 ·· 37
　3. 필리핀의 수입 통관 절차 ·· 41
　4. 필리핀의 수출 통관 절차 ·· 47

Ⅳ. 통관 절차별 고려 사항 ··· 50
　1. 수입신고 전 서류 준비 단계 ·· 51
　2. 수입신고/심사 검사 ·· 56
　3. 관세 납부 ··· 59
　4. 신고 수리 및 물품 반출 ··· 61

참고문헌 ··· 65

부 록 ··· 66
　부록 Ⅰ. 비즈니스 팁 ·· 66
　부록 Ⅱ. 주요 유관 기관 정보 ··· 70
　부록 Ⅲ. Executive Orders ·· 73
　부록 Ⅳ. TARIFF AND CUSTOMS CODE OF THE PHILIPPINES (TCCP) ············· 82

표 목차

〈표 Ⅰ-1〉 필리핀의 주요 경제 지표 ·· 9
〈표 Ⅰ-2〉 최근 필리핀 수·출입 동향 ·· 10
〈표 Ⅰ-3〉 필리핀 국가별 수·출입 실적(2010) ····································· 11
〈표 Ⅰ-4〉 필리핀 주요 수입 품목 및 금액 ·· 12
〈표 Ⅰ-5〉 필리핀 4대 투자 유치기관 합산 연도별 외국인 투자 실적 ····· 13
〈표 Ⅰ-6〉 국가별 대(對)필리핀 투자 순위 ·· 14
〈표 Ⅰ-7〉 분야별 대(對)필리핀 외국인 투자 동향 ····························· 15
〈표 Ⅰ-8〉 한-필 수출입동향 ·· 16
〈표 Ⅰ-9〉 최근 대(對)필리핀 10대 수출 품목 ··································· 17
〈표 Ⅰ-10〉 최근 대(對)필리핀 10대 수입 품목 ································· 18
〈표 Ⅰ-11〉 한-아세안 상품협정의 품목별 관세 인하 내역 ················· 20

〈표 Ⅱ-1〉 『Doing Business 2011』 필리핀의 무역 분야 순위 비교 ········ 24
〈표 Ⅱ-2〉 『Doing Business 2011』 단계별 수출입 소요기간(2010) ········ 24

〈표 Ⅲ-1〉 약품 수출 시 등록 신청의 요구 사항 ································ 37
〈표 Ⅲ-2〉 필리핀의 수입 관리 품목 리스트 ····································· 39
〈표 Ⅲ-3〉 필리핀의 수입 금지 품목 ·· 41

〈표 Ⅳ-1〉 필리핀 통관 절차별 고려 사항 ·· 50
〈표 Ⅳ-2〉 필리핀 수입 통관 시 추가서류 요구 품목 ························ 55

그림 목차

[그림 Ⅲ-1] 필리핀 관세국 기구도·· 28

Ⅰ. 개 관

1. 일반 개황[1]

☐ 필리핀의 정식 명칭은 필리핀공화국(Republic of the Philippines)이며 공화제를 정치체제로 택하고 있음
  ○ 마닐라가 수도이며, 현재 필리핀의 지방 행정구역은 주, 시, 군, 바랑가이(barangay)로 구성. 각 행정지역에는 행정자치 장(長)과 부장(副長), 의원이 있으며 바랑가이에는 바랑가이 장(長)과 위원회 위원이 있음
  ○ 1989년 '공화국법 제 6766호'에 의거, 지방자치를 위하여 무슬림 지역인 민다나오와 코르디예라를 자치지역으로 선정함
  ○ 1991년 지방자치법(Local Government Code)이 제정되어 중앙정부로부터 조세권을 비롯한 일부 권한을 양도받았음

☐ 1565년부터 에스파니아에 정복 당하여 지배를 받다가 1898년 독립을 선언하였으나 에스파니아-미국 전쟁의 결과로 미국의 지배를 받음. 1943년 일본이 점령하였으나 1945년 미국의 탈환 후 독립
  ○ 현재 말레이시아 사바주(州)를 둘러싼 영유권 갈등, 스프라틀리 군도(Spratly Islands)를 둘러싼 베트남·말레이시아·중국·타이완과 영토 분쟁을 겪고 있음

☐ 지리적으로 적도의 약간 북쪽에 위치, 아시아 대륙 남동쪽의 서태평양에 산재하는 7,107 개의 섬들로 구성되어 있으며 북부 루손섬, 중부의 수천 개의 섬인 비사얀제도, 남부 지역의 민다나오섬으로 구분됨
  ○ 면적은 한반도의 1.3배에 달하는 30만 400㎢에 달하며 필리핀해(海), 셀레베스해,

---
[1] 주필한국대사관: http://embassy_philippines.mofat.go.kr, 『필리핀 개황』 2011.5 참조

남중국해의 경계를 이루며 타이완섬과 보르네오섬, 셀레베스섬 사이에 위치함
- ○ 고온 다습한 아열대성 기후(연평균 27℃)로 크게 건기(12~4월)와 우기(5~11월)로 나뉘고 태풍·지진·화산 분화 등 자연재해가 빈발함

□ 필리핀의 인구는 약 9,400만명(2010년 추정)이며 말레이계가 주된 인종이고 중국, 미국, 스페인계 혼혈이 다수 존재함
- ○ 필리핀의 주요 종교는 카톨릭(80.9%), 이슬람교(5%), 기독교(4.5%) 등임

2. 경제 개황

가. 필리핀의 주요 경제 지표[2)]

□ 필리핀의 경제 성장률은 2009년 글로벌 금융위기 여파로 1.1%의 저성장에 머물렀으나 2010년에는 34년 만의 최고치인 7.3%를 달성함
- ○ 2011년 1/4분기 GDP 성장률은 정부 지출 감소와 세계 교역량 둔화로 4.9%를 기록하여 2010년 4/4분기의 7.1%보다 하락함

□ 2011년 1/4분기 평균 물가상승률은 4.1%로 전년 동기의 4.2%보다는 조금 낮은 수준을 기록하였으나 2011~12년까지 지속적인 상승세를 기록할 전망임
- ○ 필리핀 중앙은행은 2011년도 물가상승률을 3~5% 내에서 관리하는 것을 목표로 함

□ 필리핀은 1천만명에 달하는 해외 근로자(Overseas Foreign Workers, OFW)의 송금을 기반으로 하는 소비 중심 경제구조를 형성함
- ○ OFW 송금액은 2009년 171억달러, 2010년 187억달러로 필리핀 GDP의 12~13%를 차지함

---

2) 주필한국대사관,『필리핀 경제동향』2011.7 참조
　　OIS 해외진출정보시스템 〉국가별 정보 〉 필리핀 〉 경제동향 및 전망 참조

□ 필리핀 페소(peso)를 통화로 사용하고 있으며, 2011년 1/4분기 평균 환율은 달러당 43.8페소로 지난 동기 달러당 43.63페소보다 약세를 기록함

□ 풍부한 자연자원(매장량 세계 8위), 영어 사용, 저렴한 인건비 등을 강점으로 가지고 있으나, 제조업이 취약하여 공산품을 대부분 수입에 의존하고 있으며 3차산업인 서비스업이 GDP의 50% 이상을 차지하고 있음

〈표 Ⅰ-1〉 필리핀의 주요 경제 지표

구분	2007	2008	2009	2010
GDP 성장률(%)	7.2	3.7	1.1	7.3
GDP(억달러)	1440.43	1674.79	1609.91	1815.08
1인당 GDP(달러)	1623.82	1851.47	1745.6	1930.66
소비자물가(%)	2.8	9.3	3.2	3.8
실업률(%)	7.3	7.4	7.5	7.3
해외근로자 송금액 (억달러)	103	164	171	187.6
연평균 환율(달러: 페소)	46.55	44.47	47.64	45.11
외환보유고(억달러)	337.5	360.4	442.4	623.7

자료: OIS 해외진출 정보 시스템, 「필리핀의 주요 경제 지표」

나. 필리핀의 수출입 동향

□ 2011년 1~4월까지 수출은 165억달러, 수입은 211억달러로 46억달러의 무역 적자를 기록함
  ○ 수출입 및 교역액은 전년 동기 대비 각각 10.9%, 22.9%, 16.8%의 양호한 증가세를 보임

□ 필리핀 중앙은행(Bangko Sentral NG Philipinas, BSP)[3])에 따르면, 2010년 수출은 514 억달러로 2009년의 383억달러보다 34.2% 증가하였으며, 수입액은 547억달러로 2009

년의 430억달러보다 27.2% 급증함
- ○ 교역 증가량은 2009년의 급감에서 벗어나 예년 수준을 회복한 정도로 2010년의 전체 교역량은 증가하였으나 무역수지는 33억달러의 적자를 기록함

〈표 Ⅰ-2〉 최근 필리핀 수·출입 동향

(단위: 억달러, %)

구분	2007	2008	2009	2010	2011(1~4)
수출(증감률)	495(6.4)	490(-1.0)	383(-21.8)	514(34.2)	165(10.9)
수입(증감률)	577(8.4)	566(-1.9)	430(-24.0)	547(27.2)	211(22.9)
무역수지	-8.4	-76	-47	-33	-46

자료: 필리핀 통계청(National Statistic Office of Philippines, NSO); 필리핀 중앙은행(Bangko Sentral NG Philipinas, BSP)

☐ 원유, 곡물, 공산품의 대부분을 수입에 의존하며, 매년 발생하는 수십억달러의 무역 적자를 해외에 진출한 근로자(OFWs, Overseas Filipino Workers)의 송금액으로 충당함
- ○ 2010년 OFWs 송금액은 188억달러로 당해 필리핀 GDP의 약 10%를 차지하고 수출액의 약 40%를 차지함. 해당 금액은 매년 5~10%가량 증가 추세를 보임

☐ 미국, 일본을 비롯한 10대 교역대상국과의 교역 비중이 전체의 75%를 차지하며, 2011년 1~4월 사이의 대(對)일본 수출이 27억달러로 전체 수출의 16.5%를 차지함
- ○ 이어 미국이 23.9억달러로 14.5%, 중국이 18.9억달러로 11.5%를 차지함. 한국은 7.6억달러를 기록하여 수출 비중으로는 총량의 4.6%, 순위로는 6위임

☐ 2010년 기준 필리핀의 국가별 수출 금액은 일본이 78억달러로 총액의 15.2%를 차지함
- ○ 이어 미국이 74.9억달러로 14.6%, 싱가포르가 73.3억달러로 14.3%를 차지함. 한국은 22.3억달러를 기록하여 순위로는 8위, 수출 비중으로는 총량의 4.3%를 차지함

---

3) 필리핀 중앙은행(Bangko Sentral NG Philipinas, BSP) 해당 링크: http://www.bsp.gov.ph

□ 필리핀의 국가별 수입 금액은 수출과 마찬가지로 일본으로부터의 수입이 가장 많은 67.5억달러로 전체 수입액 547억달러 중 12.3%를 차지함
  ○ 미국이 58.6억달러로 10.7%, 싱가포르가 51.8억달러로 9.5%, 한국으로부터의 수입은 38.5억달러로 총수입의 7%로 순위로는 6위를 기록함

〈표 Ⅰ-3〉 필리핀 국가별 수·출입 실적 (2010)

(단위: 백만달러, %)

순위	수출 대상 국가	수출금액	증감률	수입 대상 국가	수입금액	증감률
1	일본	7,826	26.33	일본	6,747	26.3
2	미국	7,491	11.19	미국	5,859	14.52
3	싱가포르	7,331	196.32	싱가포르	5,184	39.13
4	중국	5,701	94.64	중국	4,608	21.07
5	홍콩	4,333	34.9	태국	3,866	57.73

자료: 필리핀 중앙은행(BSP); KOTRA/OIS 해외 진출 정보 시스템

□ 필리핀의 주요 수출 품목은 총량의 60%를 차지하는 전기전자, 반도체이며, 이외에 의류(주로 고급 브랜드 제품 봉제), 구리(동남아 2대 광물 부국), 목제품/가구 등이 주요 품목임
  ○ 전자/반도체의 경우 TI, 삼성전자, 산요, 아남, 인텔 등 다국적 전자회사가 다수 진출하고 있으며 이들 기업과 협력한 부품의 수입, 반제품 및 완제품 제조 수출 산업이 발달함
  ○ 2011.1~4월 현재 전기전자/반도체의 수출 비중은 다소 줄어들고 코코넛 오일과 의류 수출 비중이 증가하는 추세임

□ 필리핀의 주요 수입 품목은 전자/반도체용 중간재 수입 비중이 가장 높고 이외에 원유, 기계, 철강 등 자본재의 수입 비중이 상대적으로 높은 편임

<표 I-4> 필리핀 주요 수입 품목 및 금액

(단위: 백만달러, %)

순위	2010년			2011년 (1~4월)		
	수입 품목	수입 금액	비중	수입 품목	수입 금액	비중
1	전자, 반도체	14,492	26.5	전자, 반도체	5,990	28.4
2	원유, 연료	9,530	17.4	원유, 연료	4,217	20
3	운송장비	3,429	6.3	운송장비	1,010	4.8
4	산업용 기계	2,483	4.5	산업용 기계	953	4.5
5	데이터 처리기기	2,385	4.4	유·무기화학물	597	2.8
6	곡식류	2,200	4	플라스틱원료	546	2.6
7	유·무기 화학물	1,377	2.5	데이터 처리기기	507	2.4
8	철강	1,221	2.2	철강	469	2.2
9	플라스틱 원료	1,177	2.2	통신장비	414	2
10	통신장비	1,177	2.2	곡식류	356	1.7
	총액	54,720	100	총액	21,109	100

자료: 필리핀 통계청(NSO)

다. 필리핀의 외국인 투자 동향

□ 필리핀의 외국인 투자유치실적은 필리핀의 4대 투자유치 기관의 실적을 합산하여 필리핀의 통상산업부(Department of Trade and Industry, DTI)나 투자위원회(Board of Investment, BOI)에서 발표함
  ○ 필리핀은 ① 투자위원회(BOI), ② 경제자유구역청(PEZA, Philippine Economic Zone Authority), ③ 수빅자유구역관리청(Subic Bay Metropolitan Authority, SBMA), ④ 클락개발공사(Clark Development Corporation, CDC)의 4대 투자유치 기관 보유함
  ○ 2011년 1분기의 필리핀 FDI는 전년 대비 53% 감소한 220억페소(약 5.2억달러)임
    - 투자위원회가 발표한 필리핀의 2010년 투자유치 실적은 약 1,960억페소로 전년 대비 약 61% 상승함

〈표 Ⅰ-5〉 필리핀 4대 투자 유치기관 합산 연도별 외국인 투자 실적

(단위: 백만페소)

투자유치기관	2007	2008	2009	2010
투자위원회 (BOI)	102,281.7	93,551.6	10,396.9	22,328.5
클락개발공사 (CDC)	1,462.4	9,243.0	4,535.5	26,249.8
경제자유구역청 (PEZA)	87,375.6	70,355.1	103,421.3	142,167.4
수빅자유구역관리청 (SBMA)	22,963.1	9,531.2	3,462.2	5,322.9
합계	214,082.8	182,680.9	121,815.9	196,068.6

자료: 필리핀 투자위원회(BOI); 필리핀 중앙은행; OIS 해외진출정보

□ 필리핀의 국가별 외국인 투자 실적을 보면 2010년 일본이 583억페소로 전체의 29.8%를 차지하고 네덜란드가 18.8%, 한국이 15.9%, 스위스가 6.9%로 나타남

□ 우리나라의 대(對)필리핀 투자실적은 2010년 311억페소를 기록하여 투자국 순위 3위에 랭크됨
　○ 우리나라의 대(對)필리핀 투자순위 변화 추이는 2006년 6위, 2007년 2위, 2008년에서 2011년 1분기까지 3위를 기록함
　○ 2010년 네덜란드의 투자가 필리핀의 2대 정유사인 Shell에 대한 투자임을 감안, 실질적으로는 우리나라가 일본에 이어 실질적으로는 2대 투자국 지위임

□ 필리핀 통계청이 집계한 2011년 1분기 기준 대(對)필리핀 투자 순위로는 미국이 전체 투자 비중의 30.6%로 1위, 이어 일본이 21.5%, 우리나라가 17.5%, 대만이 6.1%, 싱가포르가 3.7%를 차지함
　○ 미국의 대(對)필리핀 투자는 67억페소로, 전년 동기보다 121% 증가하였으며, 일본은 47억페소를 기록하여 전년 동기 대비 54%가 감소됨
　　- 우리나라는 38억페소로 전년 동기 대비 84% 감소액을 보임

<표 I-6> 국가별 대(對)필리핀 투자 순위

(단위: 백만페소, %)

순위	2010			2011.1분기			
	국가	투자금액	비중	국가	투자금액	비중	전년 동기 대비 증가율
1	일본	58,333	29.8	미국	6,744	30.6	121
2	네덜란드	36,784	18.8	일본	4,729	21.5	-54
3	한국	31,182	15.9	한국	3,844	17.5	-84
4	스위스	13,557	6.9	대만	1,345	6.1	939
5	미국	13,159	6.7	싱가포르	824	3.7	-85
6	케이맨 제도	10,638	5.4	인도	428	1.9	190.3
7	버진 군도	7,654	3.9	홍콩	316	1.4	13,556
8	싱가포르	7,283	3.7	영국	315	1.4	-49
9	인도	1,857	0.9	스위스	281	1.3	-39
10	대만	1,506	0.8	호주	246	1.1	-49
	총계	196,068.60	100	총계	22,022	100	-52.8

자료: NSCB, 주필 한국대사관,「투자진출동향」(2011); BOI; 필리핀 중앙은행(OIS 2010)

□ 분야별 투자순위로는 제조업, 개인서비스, 전기·가스·수도, 광산개발, 금융·부동산, 농업 등이 높은 순위를 기록함
  ○ 2011년 1분기 역시 전자/반도체 중심의 제조업이 전체 FDI의 76%를 차지하고 이외 개인서비스가 8%, 부동산이 7%, 정보통신기술 분야가 5%를 차지하여 이들 4개 분야가 필리핀 전체 투자 유치금액의 96%를 차지함
  ○ 전년 대비 증가율 면에서는 정보통신기술 분야, 숙박/요식업, 부동산 순으로 크게 증가하였고 운송/저장, 교역/도소매, 농업, 제조 등은 50% 이상 감소세를 보임
  ○ 특징적인 것은 전력, 기업업무 외주(Business Process Outsourcing, BPO)[4] 투자가 크게 늘고 있음
    - 전력의 경우 필리핀의 전력난으로 인한 높은 전기료, 민영화 움직임, 재생에너지 개발 등이 반영됨

---

4) KOTRA, Global Window 해외투자속보「필리핀, BPO 산업 동향 및 콜센터 설립 혜택」, 2008

- 기업업무 외주(BOP) 부문은 영미 계열의 대기업들의 진출 확대로 필리핀의 대표적인 서비스 산업으로 자리잡고 있음

〈표 Ⅰ-7〉 분야별 대(對)필리핀 외국인 투자 동향

(단위: 백만페소, %)

순위	2010			2011.1분기			
	분야	금액	비중	분야	금액	비중	전년 대비 증가율
1	제조	162,908	83	제조	16,752	76	-61
2	전기/가스/수도	8,467	4.3	개인서비스(BOP)	1,808	8	21
3	개인서비스(BOP)	7,316	3.7	부동산	1,467	7	265
4	광산개발	6,075	3.1	정보통신기술	1,097	5	1,578
5	부동산	4,274	2.2	농업	294	1	-73
6	숙박/요식업	2,180	1.1	관산개발	288	1	-
7	농업	1,218	0.6	전기/가스/수도	184	1	13
8	정보통신(ICT)	1,175	0.6	숙박/요식업	47	0	349
9	운송/저장	813	0.4	행정/국방/치안	24	0	-
10	금융	693	0.4	전문/과학 기술 서비스	23	0	236
	총 FDI 유입액	196,069	100	총FDI 유입액	22,022	100	

자료: National Statistic Coordination Board, 주필리핀 한국 대사관

3. 우리나라와 필리핀의 교역관계

☐ 관세청에 따르면, 2010년 기준 우리나라의 대(對)필리핀 수출시장 순위는 17위, 수입시장 순위는 27위이며 2011.1~5월 기준 수출 순위는 3위 하락한 20위, 수입 순위는 27위를 유지함

☐ 한·필 무역수지는 2011년 1~5월 집계 기준으로 전년 대비 42.6% 증가한 12.8억달러

를 기록하였으며 2010년 기준으로는 2008~2009년에 걸친 적자에서 전년 대비 22.7% 증가한 23.5억달러의 흑자를 기록함
○ 2011년 1~5월 기준 수출금액은 전년 대비 21.9% 상승한 43.6억달러, 수입금액은 전년 대비 8.9% 상승한 15.6억달러를 기록함
○ 2010년 기준 우리나라의 대(對)필리핀 수출은 전년 대비 27.8% 증가한 58.4억달러, 수입은 31.5% 증가한 34.9억달러를 기록함

〈표 Ⅰ-8〉 한-필 수출입동향

(단위: 백만달러, %)

구분	2006	2007	2008	2009	2010	2011(1~5)
	금액	금액	금액	금액	금액	금액
수출 (증감률)	3,931 (22.0)	4,420 (12.9)	5,016 (13.5)	4,567 (-9.0)	5,838 (27.8)	2,835 (21.9)
수입 (증감률)	2,187 (4.3)	2,438 (11.5)	3,099 (27.1)	2,652 (-14.4)	3,488 (31.5)	1,560 (8.9)
수지 (증감률)	1,744 (96.2)	1,982 (13.6)	1,917 (-3.3)	1,916 (-0.1)	2,350 (22.7)	1,275 (42.6)
총계	6,118 (10.5)	6,858 (12.0)	8,115 (18.3)	7,219 (-11.0)	9,326 (29.2)	4,395 (16.9)

자료: 대한민국 관세청

☐ 2010년 기준 우리나라가 필리핀에 수출하는 주요 품목은 반도체, 석유제품, 자동차, 철강판, 정밀 화학원료 등이며, 2010년 총수출액은 전년 대비 27.8% 증가한 58.37억 달러를 기록함

☐ 관세청에 따르면, 2011.1~5월 기준, 대(對)필리핀의 10대 수출 품목이 차지하는 금액은 총수출 실적의 67.8%임
○ 주요 수출 품목은 전기전자/반도체, 석유제품, 정밀화학, 자동차, 철강, 동제품 등 중간재 및 산업재이며 기타 정밀화학, 동제품, 수동 부품, 합성수지 등의 수출량이 호조를 보임
- 반도체 수출 금액의 경우 세계 IT산업의 경기 부진으로 2011.1~5월 기준 전년

대비 15.1% 감소됨
- 철강의 경우 2009년 경제 위기로 수출금액이 급감했으나 2010년 76.7%의 증가율을 기록하여 예년 수준을 회복하였음. 필리핀 건설경기 활황과 국내 투자 기업 수요가 수출 증가 요인임

〈표 Ⅰ-9〉 최근 대(對)필리핀 10대 수출 품목

(단위: 천달러, %)

순위	2010년			2011년(1월~10월)		
	품목명	금액	전년 대비 증가율	품목명	금액	전년 대비 증가율
1	반도체	1,852,053	63.6	반도체	1,255,659	21
2	석유제품	536,077	-31.3	원유	501,867	237.6
3	자동차	330,588	73.1	동제품	331,727	-10.5
4	철강판	247,508	76.7	곡실류	257,177	25.6
5	정밀화학원료	245,408	61.4	컴퓨터	138,406	27.7
6	동제품	240,590	99.3	수동부품	128,643	38.2
7	수동부품	226,654	63.2	기호식품	89,226	11.8
8	합성수지	139,245	22.1	동광	83,375	129.8
9	기타기계류	103,069	60.6	식물성물질	60,079	22.2
10	편직물	94,429	31.1	평판디스플레이 및 센서	57,120	-12.5
	총 계	5,837,983	27.8	총 계	3,488,104	31.6

주: MTI 3단위 기준
자료: 한국무역협회 무역통계

□ 2010년 기준 우리나라가 필리핀에서 수입하는 주요 품목은 반도체, 원유, 동제품, 곡실류, 컴퓨터 순이며 2010년 총수입액은 전년 대비 31.6% 증가한 33.88억달러를 기록함

□ 2011년 1~5월 기준, 대(對)필리핀의 10대 수입 품목 금액의 합계는 총수입금액의 81.4%에 달함
 ○ 주요 수입 품목은 전체 수입의 36%를 차지하는 반도체, 원유, 곡실류, 동제품, 동

광 등 1차 제품 및 컴퓨터, 평판디스플레이 등 현지 다국적기업이 생산하는 IT 제품임

〈표 Ⅰ-10〉 최근 대(對)필리핀 10대 수입 품목

(단위: 천달러, %)

순위	2010년			2011년(1월~10월)		
	품목명	금액	전년 대비 증가율	품목명	금액	전년 대비 증가율
1	반도체	1,255,659	21	반도체	945,435	-10.7
2	원유	501,867	237.6	원유	587,126	43.2
3	동제품	331,727	-10.5	곡실류	249,085	13
4	곡실류	257,177	25.6	동제품	193,931	-29
5	컴퓨터	138,406	27.7	동광	190,495	150.3
6	수동부품	128,643	38.2	수동부품	114,252	8.9
7	기호식품	89,226	11.8	기호식품	88,093	19.5
8	동광	83,375	129.8	컴퓨터	60,651	-50.3
9	식물성물질	60,079	22.2	기구부품	50,410	16.7
10	평판디스플레이 및 센서	57,120	-12.5	식물성물질	41,395	-17.5
	총계	3,488,104	31.6	총계	3,084,461	5.8

주: MTI 3단위 기준
자료: 한국무역협회 무역통계

4. 필리핀의 자유무역협정(FTA, Free Trade Agreement) 현황

가. 아세안자유무역협정(ASEAN Free Trade Area, AFTA)

□ 2003년 ASEAN 회원국은 관세 인하/철폐를 바탕으로 무역거래 자유화를 통해 블록경제체제를 활성화할 목적으로 회원국 간의 자유무역지대를 창설하였음

  ○ 참가국은 10개국으로 싱가포르, 태국, 말레이시아, 인도네시아, 필리핀, 베트남,

브루나이, 라오스, 미얀마, 캄보디아임

□ ASEAN 경제장관회의에서 공동유효특혜관세협정[5]과 아세안자유무역협정(AFTA)이 정식 조인되었으며 1993년 1월부터 정식 개시되었음
  ○ 1992년 1월 싱가포르에서 개최된 제4차 ASEAN 정상회담에서 정식으로 아세안자유무역협정(AFTA)을 합의하였음
    - 회원국들은 '싱가포르 선언(Singapore Declaration of 1992)'을 채택하고, 'ASEAN 경제협력 증진을 위한 기본협정'[6]에 서명하였음
  ○ 1999년 11월 필리핀에서 열린 제3차 ASEAN 비공식 정상회담에서 기존 6개 회원국은 최종 2010년까지, 후발 가입국은 2015년까지 역내관세를 철폐하기로 합의함

나. 한-ASEAN 자유무역협정(Korea-ASEAN Free Trade Agreement, AKFTA)[7]

□ ASEAN 회원국 정부와 한국 간의 포괄적 경제협력(ASEAN-Korea Free Trade Area, AKFTA)에 관한 기본협정이 2010년 1월에 발효되었음[8]
  ○ 수입 상품에 부과되는 관세 인하 및 철폐에 대한 조항이 상품무역협정 제3조 및 2개의 부속서에 기술됨[9]
    - 상품무역협정상 필리핀의 ① 일반 품목은 전자 부품, 자동차 부품, 석유 제품, 철강 등이며, ② 민감 품목으로 분류된 것은 오리, 고등어, 야자수, 소시지, 신발류 등이고 ③ 초민감 품목은 닭, 돼지, 양배추, 마늘, 플라스틱제 의류 등임
  ○ 벼, 사탕수수당, 시동 전동기, 와이어링 세트 등은 양허 제외 품목으로 분류되었고 쌀, 쇠고기, 돼지고기, 닭고기, 민어, 조기, 고추류 등 108개 초민감 품목도 양허 대상에서 제외되었음

---

[5] Agreement on the Common Effective Preferential Tariff Scheme for ASEAN Free Trade Area, CEPT 협정)
[6] Framework Agreement on Enhancing ASEAN Economic Coorperation
[7] OIS 해외진출 정보 시스템〉 국가정보〉 필리핀〉 자유무역 협정 체결 현황
[8] OIS 해외진출 정보 시스템〉 필리핀 비즈니스 커뮤니티〉 해외 투자 뉴스레터 No. 14
[9] 외교통상부 자유무역협정사이트(www.fta.go.kr) 관세 인하 및 철폐 활용 내용 참조.

○ 협정 발효에 따라, 필리핀에서 수입되는 원유, 천연가스 등 11,559개 품목에 대한 관세가 즉시 철폐되고 냉동쥐치(10%), 해바라기씨유(10%), 주스(50%) 등 504개 품목은 2010년부터 0%의 세율이 적용됨
○ 우리나라의 수출품도 특혜관세 혜택을 받아 협정발효 즉시 일반 품목군(전체 품목의 90%)의 50%에 해당하는 우리 상품의 관세가 0~5%로 인하되고, 2012년 1월 1일까지 일반 품목군의 모든 관세가 철폐될 예정임

□ 필리핀 정부는 한-아세안 FTA 협정 이행을 위한 행정명령(EO632) 및 한-아세안 FTA 상품협정 추가 이행을 위한 이행법령(EO812)을 발효함[10]
○ 필리핀 관세청은 EO812를 통해 2009~2012년에 걸쳐 매4년 간 관세율을 부속서로 발표하고 한-아세안 신규 FTA 관세율 표를 일반에 배포함
- EO812에 따르면 필리핀 측은 일반 품목의 경우 2009년 1월부터 90% 이상 품목에 대해 관세를 철폐하고 2010년까지 95%, 2012년 1월부터 100%까지 철폐하도록 되어 있음
- 이외 전체 품목의 7% 수준인 민감 품목의 경우 2016년까지 전체 품목의 5% 이하로 감축될 전망이며, 초민감 품목(전체 품목의 3%)에 대해서는 다양한 관세 인하 방법을 제시할 예정임

〈표 Ⅰ-11〉 한-아세안 상품협정의 품목별 관세 인하 내역

한국 → 필리핀수출	발효즉시 일반품목군(전체 품목의 90% 이상)의 50%에 해당하는 품목 관세가 0~5%로 삭감 - CD Player(15 → 8%), 골프카트(20 → 10%), 블라우스(15 → 8%), 담배(10 → 5%), 사과, 배(5 → 3%), 밧데리(15 → 8%), 폴리에스터 직물(5 → 3%) 등
필리핀 → 한국 수출	- 원유(3%), 천연가스(3%), 초콜릿(8%), 담배(40%), 밧데리(8%), 캔뚜껑(8%), 폴리에스터직물(8%) 등 11,559개 품목 관세 즉시 철폐 - 냉동쥐치(10%), 혼합주스(50%), 해바라기씨유(10%) 등 2010년부터 0% 적용

자료: 마닐라 KBC

---

[10] KOTRA 〉마닐라 KBC 〉필리핀 진출기업의 한-아세안(필리핀 편) FTA 활용하기

□ 한-아세안 FTA 서비스협정은 2007년 11월 한-아세안 정상회의를 통해 서명되었으며 2009년 5월에 발효됨
  ○ 서비스 협정은 건설, 인프라, 금융, 통신, 운송 등 서비스 분야 자유화(상업적 주재 즉 지분 제한, 국경 간 거래, 자연인 주재, 해외소비 관련사항)에 관한 규정임

□ 한-아세안 FTA 투자협정은 2009년 6월에 서명되었으며 필리핀 측은 2007년 11월 대통령의 승인으로 관련 법안을 통과시켰음
  ○ 본 협정은 양국 투자자의 일반적 대우, 투명성 제고, 투자자-국가 간 분쟁해결 절차 등을 규정하고 있으며 세부 양허계획(분야별 자유화 계획)은 5년 내 완료하기로 합의함

□ 한국 기업들은 한-아세안 FTA에 따른 광산 개발 서비스 개방을 통해 필리핀의 광물자원 개발 분야에 대한 진출 기반을 마련하였으며, 레스토랑, 호텔업, 레저(여행) 사업의 개방으로 필리핀 관광 분야에서 혜택을 볼 수 있을 것으로 전망됨
  ○ 기존에는 호텔업 및 여행 사업에 대한 외국인 지분이 40%로 제한되었으나 한-아세안 FTA 승인 후에는 100%로 외국인 순수 자본으로 운영이 가능함

다. 필리핀-일본 경제동반자 협정(JPEPA)

□ 일본과 필리핀 간의 자유무역 협정(Japan-Philippines Economic Partnership Agreement, JPEPA)이 2008년 12월에 발효되었음
  ○ 필리핀은 일본에서 수입되는 산업용품(Industrial Goods), 철강(Iron and Steel), 자동차 및 자동차 부품, 전기·전자 제품 및 관련 부품, 섬유, 의류, 과일(포도, 배)에 대해 부과되는 수입 관세를 향후 10년 내에 삭감 또는 폐지할 예정임
  ○ 필리핀의 자동차/전자산업에 직접 투자하는 일본 투자자에게 비FTA 협정국과 차별화되는 혜택(Incentive)을 제공함
  ○ 일본 정부는 필리핀 간호사 및 간호간병인의 일본 진출을 허용하고 필리핀산 농·수·축산물(협정 품목), 가공 식품 및 기타 부산물에 대한 관세를 최대 10년 내에

단계적으로 삭감·폐지할 예정임

□ 필리핀과 일본 간의 경제동반자협정은 필리핀 시장에서 일본 자동차·철강 등의 수출 경쟁력을 제고시킬 것으로 예상됨에 따라, 한국 제품과의 경쟁이 더 치열해질 것으로 전망됨

라. 중-아세안 자유무역 협정(China-ASEAN Free Trade Agreement)

□ 중국과 아세안 간의 FTA는 2010년 1월1일부터 발효되어 유럽연합(EU), 북미자유무역지대(NAFTA)에 이어 세계에서 세 번째로 큰 자유무역지대가 출범하였음
  ○ 아세안은 중국과 전체 교역품목의 90%에 달하는 7,000여 개 품목에 대해 상호 무관세를 적용하였음
    - 한국과 중국의 무관세 대상 품목이 상당 부분 겹쳐 아세안 시장에서의 양국 간 수출경쟁이 치열해질 것으로 전망됨

□ 필리핀은 현재 외국과의 교역 확대를 촉진하기 위해 추가적인 자유무역협정(FTA)을 추진중에 있으며 대상 국가는 미국, 대만, 베트남, 유럽연합(EU) 등임
  ○ 필리핀은 대만과의 협정을 통해 중국에 투자하려는 대만 기업을 필리핀으로 유치하는 것을 목표하고 있음
  ○ 필리핀은 EU를 상대로 2010년 6월 브뤼셀에서 상호우호 협정(Partnership Cooperation Agreement, PCA)을 체결하기로 합의

Ⅱ. 외국의 통상환경 보고서

1. World Bank의 『Doing Business 2011』

□ 세계은행(The World Bank)은 2004년부터 매년 '사업하기 좋은 나라(Ease of doing business)' 순위를 다양한 부문에 걸쳐 조사하여 『Doing Business』라는 보고서명으로 발표하고 있음
  - ○ 2011년에 발간된 당해 보고서는 2010년 한 해 동안 183개국에 대하여 부문별로 조사·평가한 내용을 수록함
  - ○ 『Doing Business 2011』 보고서상 순위를 결정하기 위하여 조사된 분야는 사업 개시, 건설허가, 재산권 등록, 신용취득, 투자자보호, 세금 납부, 무역, 계약 이행 및 폐업 등 9개의 지표임
  - ○ 2011년 보고서에 따르면, 종합적인 '사업의 용이성(Ease of Doing Business)'에 있어 싱가포르가 1위를 차지하였으며, 우리나라는 16위에 랭크되었음

□ 필리핀은 전반적인 사업의 용이성에 있어 전체 조사국인 183국 중 전년도보다 2순위 하락한 148위에 올랐으며, 부문별 주요 지표 중 무역 분야(Trading Across Borders)에서는 전년도보다 7순위 상승한 61위를 기록함
  - ○ 당해 보고서의 무역 분야 순위는 수출입에 필요한 서류의 개수와 수출입 소요 일수 및 소요 비용 등을 산출하여 순위를 정하고 있으며, 필요서류가 적고 수출입 소요 기일이 짧을수록 더욱 높은 순위에 오르는 형식임

〈표 Ⅱ-1〉『Doing Business 2011』 필리핀의 무역 분야 순위 비교

구분	필리핀	East Asia & Pacific	OECD	인도네시아	한국
수출필요서류(개수)	8	6.4	4.4	5	3
수출소요시간(일)	15	22.7	10.9	20	8
수출소요비용(달러/컨테이너)	675	889.8	1,058.7	704	790
수입필요서류(개수)	8	6.9	4.9	6	3
수입소요시간(일)	14	24.1	11.4	27	7
수입소요비용(US$/컨테이너)	730	934.7	1,106.3	660	790
무역분야 순위	61	-	-	47	8

자료: The World Bank, 『Doing Business』 2011 RANK

○ 필리핀에서의 해상 수출 비용은 컨테이너당[11] 약 675달러가 소요되는 것으로 조사되었으며, 수출에 필요한 서류는 8가지이고, 서류 준비를 비롯하여 수출 통관 및 국내 운송, 항만에서의 업무를 포함, 수출에 총 15일이 소요되는 것으로 조사되었음
○ 해상 수입에 있어서 컨테이너당 약 730달러가 소요되며, 수입에 필요한 서류는 8가지이고, 서류 준비를 포함한 수입통관 및 국내 운송, 항만 업무를 포함하여 총 14일이 소요됨

〈표 Ⅱ-2〉『Doing Business 2011』 단계별 수출입 소요기간(2010)

(단위: 일, 달러)

단계별 수출소요 기간(비용)		단계별 수입소요 기간(비용)	
수출서류준비	8(150)	수입서류 준비	8(170)
통관	2(85)	통관	2(185)
항만업무	3(270)	항만업무	3(200)
내륙운송	2(170)	내륙운송	1(175)
총소요시간	15	총소요시간	14

---

11) 20피트 컨테이너(TEU) 만재 화물 기준이며, 위험물 또는 군수품 등이 아니라는 가정하에 금액을 산정함

□ 2010년 필리핀은 전자결제와 세관신고서 제출 기능을 추가한 전자통관시스템(electronic customs systems)의 기능 향상을 통해 무역에 소요되는 비용과 시간을 절감함

2. 미국 국별 무역장벽 보고서(National Trade Estimate Report on Foreign Trade Barriers: NTE 보고서)

가. 필리핀의 관세 구조 및 세관 통관

□ 국별 무역장벽보고서[12]는 1974년 통상법(Trade Act of 1974) 제181조에 근거하여 미국 무역대표부(USTR)가 작성, 매년 3월 말 의회에 제출하는 연례보고서임
  ○ 이 보고서는 미국 업계의 의견과 해외 주재 미국 대사관의 보고서와 관련 정부 부처의 의견 등을 기초로 작성됨
  ○ 2011년 보고서는 미국의 62개 주요 교역국 및 경제권의 무역과 투자 장벽에 대해 포괄적으로 기술하고 있음[13]

□ 미국 무역대표부(USTR)의 국별 무역장벽보고서는 부패구조가 필리핀의 최대 무역투자 장벽임을 언급함
  ○ 필리핀에 진출한 기업들은 현지에서의 차별적인 관세 부과, 세관 통관 및 법원의 판결 등에서 자의적인 법률 해석 등을 통해 불이익을 받고 있음을 언급함

□ 2010년 필리핀 단순 평균 양허 관세율(simple average bound tariff)은 25.44%, 단순 평균 실행 관세율(simple average applied Tariff)은 6.82%로 전체 관세 품목의 6%가량에 15% 이상의 관세율을 적용함

---

12) 자료원: 2011 NTE(http://www.ustr.gov), The Philippine Star 등 주요 언론 KOTRA & globalwindow.org
13) 2010년부터 SPS(동식물 위생 및 검역) 및 TBT(무역에 대한 기술 장벽) 관련 사안은 NTE 보고서와 별도로 발표하고 있음

□ 모든 농산물과 비농산물의 3분의 2는 양허 관세를 적용받으며 비적용 품목으로는 자동차, 화학제품, 플라스틱, 식물성 섬유, 신발류, 헤드기어, 어류, 종이 제품 등이 있음

□ 화학 폐기물, 모터사이클, 자동차 및 부품과 같은 일부 품목은 최대 30%에 달하는 높은 관세를 징수하며 관세할당제에 해당하는 농산물은 30~65%가량의 높은 관세(in-quota Tariffs)가 적용됨
   ○ 설탕 관세는 65%로 가장 높고, 그다음으로 쌀이 50%의 고관세율을 적용받음

□ 가금류, 돼지, 감자, 커피, 커피 추출물 등도 관세할당제를 적용받으며 육류 및 기타 잡육, 소시지, 육류 조제품, 양배추, 당근, 마니옥(카사바), 고구마, 동물용 사료(개·고양이 사료를 제외)는 30~45%의 관세가 적용됨

□ 아세안(ASEAN) 회원국 간에는 설탕(38%), 쌀(40%)과 같은 민감 품목을 제외한 모든 품목은 ASEAN 자유무역협정에 따라 99%의 무관세가 적용됨

□ 필리핀은 2010년 6월 세계관세기구의 개정 교토의정서에 동의하였으나 의정서 조항에 맞도록 국내 관세 및 세관법(Tariff and Customs Code)의 개정이 필요함

나. 품목별 이슈

□ 필리핀 정부는 차체 무게에 따라 승용차는 30%, 화물차 20~30%, 승합차 15~20%가량의 수입 관세를 적용하며 자동차, 모터사이클 완제품에 대해서는 여전히 농산물 이외의 품목 가운데서는 가장 높은 관세를 부과함
   ○ 특정 국가들은 ASEAN 자유무역협정과 일본-필리핀 경제 파트너십 협정(JEPEPA)에 따라 자동차 수입 시 특혜 관세 혜택이 있음

□ 2010년 4월 아로요 대통령은 국내 자동차 생산을 촉진하고 지역 수출에 박차를 가하기 위한 자동차 개발프로그램(MVDP; Motor Vehicle Development Program)을 수정

하는 대통령령을 발표함
- ㅇ 필리핀 국내의 자동차 조립 생산 촉진을 위해 자동차 부품 수입 관세는 낮게 조정 되었으며 면세품목인 대체 연료 차량을 제외하고, MVDP 등록자가 수입하는 모든 CKD(completely knocked-down)에는 1%의 관세를 적용함
  - 일본과 아세안 회원국 간에는 CKD에 대해 완전 무관세를 적용함

□ 검증된 CBU(Completely Built Units) 수출업자는 수입 관세나 수입된 완제품 검증에 활용되는 수출 신용을 얻을 수 있으며, 이 시스템으로 적용되는 관세율을 10%까지 낮출 수 있음
- ㅇ 수입차에 대해 12%의 부가세를 부과하고 자동차 가격에 따른 누진세와 소비세를 부과하며 수정된 정책에서도 중고차 수입 금지를 고수함

□ 필리핀은 증류주 제품별로 각기 다른 관세율을 적용함
- ㅇ 설탕, 야자나무 등 필리핀 내 생산 원료로 주조된 증류주는 낮은 관세율을 적용받고(2009년 1ℓ당 13.59페소) 수입 증류주에는 10~40배가량 높은 관세를 부과함

□ 필리핀은 옥수수, 돼지고기, 가금류 등 15개 농축산물에 대해 Minimum Access Volume(MAV) 시스템으로 잘 알려진 자율관세할당(Tariff Rate Quota, TRQ) 제도를 실시함

□ 2002년 이후 쿼터 외의 닭고기 수입에 대한 특별 세이프가드 조치를 유지하여 쿼터 외 관세를 2배로 확대했음
- ㅇ 필리핀 농림부는 2009년의 태풍으로 인해 일시적으로 닭고기 8000MT에 특별 세이프가드 조치를 해제해 2009년과 2010년의 가금류 수입량을 증대시킨 바 있음

□ 필리핀 정부는 세이프가드 조치를 통해 세라믹 바닥제품과 벽타일, 유리제품, 스틸 앵글바(steel angle bars), 판지 등에 수입 관세를 부과하는 규제조치를 운영함

Ⅲ. 필리핀의 통관 환경

1. 통관 행정 조직

가. 필리핀 관세국(Bureau of Customs)

[그림 Ⅲ-1] 필리핀 관세국 기구도

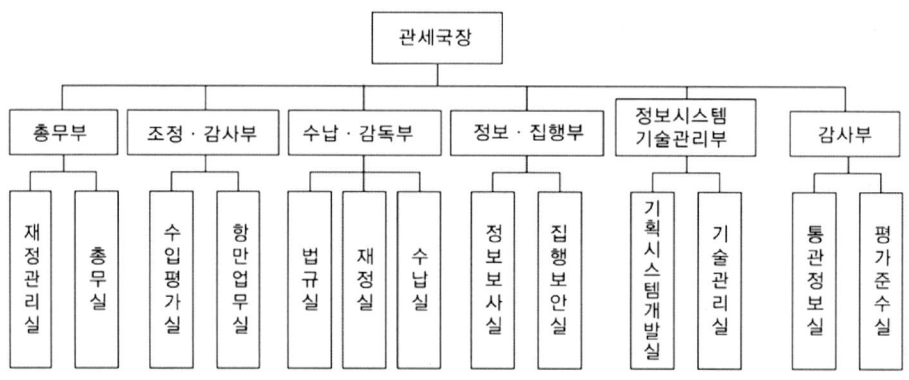

□ 필리핀에서 우리나라 관세청의 기능을 수행하는 기관의 공식명칭은 필리핀 관세국(Bureau of Customs)[14]이며 필리핀 재무부(Department of Finance)에 속하여 세입업무(Revenue Operation Group)를 수행함
　○ 수입물품에 대한 관세 및 제세의 징수를 비롯하여 각종 화물의 입출항 관리, 밀수행위의 방지, 수출 산업의 지원, 필리핀 관세법의 적용, 국제 무역상의 편의 증진 등의 임무를 수행함[15]

---

14) 필리핀 관세국, http://www.customs.gov.ph/
15) 필리핀 관세국 업무 소개 해당 링크: http://www.customs.gov.ph/about.php

□ 관세국장(the Customs Commissioner)을 중심으로 총무부, 조정/감사부, 수납/감독부, 정보/집행부, 정보시스템/기술 관리부 등의 중앙부처와 행정구역별 15개 지역 세관(Collecting Districts)으로 구성됨

□ 총무부(Internal Administration Group)는 관세국장을 대변하고 관세국 내부 행정업무를 담당하며 산하에 재정 관리실(Financial Management Office)과 총무실(Human Resources Management Division)을 둠

□ 조정·감사부(Assessment and Operations Coordination Group)는 ① 수입 상품의 가치에 대한 정보를 수집하고 발표하며, ② 평가 관리, 수출품의 최종처리, 창고업무/운영 지원, 경매 및 처분 활동 등을 관할하며 관련 규정을 검토함
  ○ 조정·감사부 산하에는 수입평가실(Import & Assessment Service)과 항만업무실(Port Operation Service)이 있음
    - 수입평가실 산하에는 평가·분류과(Valuation & Classification Division), 분석감시과(Assessment Coordination & Monitoring Division), 보세조정과(Warehouse Coordination & Monitoring Division)가 소속됨
    - 항만업무실 산하에는 경매·화물처분과(Auction & Cargo Disposal Monitoring Division), 수출조정과(Export Coordination Division), 항만업무 조정과(Port Operations Coordination Division)가 소속됨

□ 수납·감독부(Revenue Collection Monitoring Group)는 세입회계, 통계 수집 및 분석, 담보 등에 대한 업무를 담당하고 산하에 법규실(Legal Service), 재정실(Financial Service), 수납실(Collection Service)을 둠

□ 정보부와 집행부(Intelligence and Enforcement Group)는 필리핀 세관과 경제활동 등에 관한 정보를 수집하고 내부 감사와 경찰권 발동을 담당함

□ 정보시스템 및 기술관리부(Management Information System and Technology

Group)는 관세청의 IT설비 및 업무를 관리함

□ 필리핀에서는 세관이 'Collecting Districts'라는 명칭으로 운용되고 있으며, 항구도시를 중심으로 지역 사무소로 설치·운영되고 있음
  ○ 필리핀은 행정구역상 17개 지역(Region)으로 나뉘어져 있는데, 2011년 현재 이 중 12개 지역에 총 15개의 세관을 두고 있으며, 2개 사무소(Cagayan, Bataan)는 추가 신설중에 있음
  ○ 세관은 수출입 물품의 통관과 관리 감독, 국제 우편물 관리, 업무 등을 수행함
    - NCR(National Capital Region)내에 Manila항 세관, Manila 국제 컨테이너항 세관, Ninoy Aquino 국제공항세관의 3개 세관이 있음
    - 이 외에 San Fernando항 세관, Subic항 세관, Clark항 세관, Batangas항 세관, Legazpi항 세관, Iloilo항 세관, Cebu항 세관, Tacloban항 세관, Zamboanga항 세관, Cagayan de Oro항 세관, Davao항 세관, Surigao항 세관이 있음

나. 필리핀 통상산업부(The Department of Trade and Industry of Philippines)

□ 필리핀 통상산업부(the Department of Trade and Industry of Philippines, DTI)[16] 산하의 International Trade Group(ITG)은 9개 세부 부서로 구성되어 수출입 통관 절차 및 수입 규제 품목 등을 관리하고 있으며 수출입자 등록 서비스 등을 담당함
  ○ Bureau of Export Trade Promotion(BETP)의 경우 수출 지원 업무를 담당함
    - Trade Information and Assistance Group(TIAG), Market Strategy and Consultancy Group(MSCG), Product Research and Strategy Group (PRSG)의 기능 조직들로 구성되어 있음
  ○ Bureau of Import Services(BIS)는 수입 관련 업무를 지원하고 수입규제 품목/민감 품목 등의 수입절차를 관리하며 덤핑, 상계관세, 긴급수입 제한조치 등에 대한 조사를 담당함
    - 자율 수입 품목의 수입량(import level) 및 가격 관리, 수입량의 예측 및 통계 분

---
16) 필리핀 통상산업부 해당링크: http://www.dti.gov.ph/splash.php

석, 필리핀 관세 체계 분석, 수입거래 관리 등을 담당함
- 무역구제에 대한 결정 및 해당 물품 관련 수출업자 지원 담당
- 중고차의 수입에 대한 법률 및 규정을 제안하고 반포함
- 수입 허가증(Certificate of Authority to Import, CAI) 발급/특정 프로그램을 기반으로 한 중고차 수입에 관한 허가증을 발급함
- 수입 관련 데이터 생성, 연간 필리핀 수입에 대한 보고, 수입 절차에 관한 정보를 제공함
- 필리핀 관세국(BOC) 및 외교부(Department of Foreign Affairs, DFA), Foreign Trade Service(FTSC) 등과 함께 수입물품 가격 입증 업무 및 수출거래 가치에 대한 정보 관리를 담당함
- 필리핀 관세국(BOC) 및 각 산업부문들과 협력하여 계정 분류 오류 및 가격 저평가(undervaluation) 관리 등을 담당하며 외국의 물품 공급자 및 수입자의 이의제기 사항에 대한 관리 등을 담당함

○ Bureau of International Trade Relations(BITR)는 필리핀이 체결한 자유 무역 협정 및 국가 간의 투자협상 업무를 담당함

○ Center for International Trade Expositions and Missions(CITEM)은 통상산업부의 수출 진흥 기관으로 무역박람회, 특별 전시회 등의 국내외 활동을 통해 필리핀 제품을 홍보함
- 섬유 부문의 무역 지원을 위해 Garments and Textile Industry Development Office(GTIDO)를 산하 기관으로 두고 있음

○ Foreign Trade Service Corps(FTSC)을 통해 필리핀의 무역투자 부문을 지원하고 해외 파견 상무 참사관(commercial counselors)을 통해 필리핀의 무역회사와 외국 투자자들을 연계함

○ 그 외 통상산업부(DTI) 산하에는 International Coffee Organization Certifying Agency(ICOCA), Product Development and Design Center of the Philippines (PDDCP), Philippine Trade Training Center(PTTC), E-Commerce Office (ECO) 부서 등이 있음

다. 필리핀 관세위원회(Tariff Commission of the Philippines)

□ 필리핀 관세위원회(Tariff Commission of the Philippines, TC)는 필리핀의 행정 및 입법 기관을 대상으로 관세 및 관련 주제에 관한 자문을 제공함
  ○ 본 기관은 필리핀의 무역구제에 관한 심의를 담당하여 필리핀의 산업 경쟁력과 소비자 복지에 기여하는 것을 목적으로 함
  ○ 필리핀의 관세 및 세관법(Tariff and Customs Code of the Philippines, TCCP)에 근거한 관세위원회의 주요 역할
    - 필리핀 관세/세관법을 집행하고 관리함
    - 필리핀 관세 정책을 개발하고 관련 정부기관에 이에 대한 자문을 제공함
    - 덤핑 및 보조금과 같은 불공정 무역 관행에 대해 조사하고 심의함
    - 긴급수입 제한조치에 관하여 조사하고 관련 정부기관에 자문을 제공함

2. 필리핀의 통관 환경

가. 관세 및 내국세

□ 필리핀 관세위원회(TC)는 관세/세관법에 근거하여 관세율 정보와 수출입 관련 서류 양식, 한-ASEAN FTA 관련 법령 및 행정 명령(Executive Order), 관세 분류 코드 등의 정보를 제공함

□ 필리핀의 상품 분류는 HS 시스템을 따르며 자체 상품 분류 코드로 SITC[17] 방식을 원용한 PSCC 코드[18]도 사용함

---

17) SITC, Standard International Trade Classification:
   1938년 국제연맹에서 무역통계의 국제적 비교를 위하여 제정된 상품 분류방식을 말한다. 1963년에 개정되었으며 약 45,000개 품목을 1,312개의 기본항목, 177개의 group, 625개의 sub group, 56개의 division, 10개의 section으로 구분하고 있다

18) Philippine Standard Commodity Classification(PSCC) http://www.nscb.gov.ph/csd/pscc1.asp

○ 필리핀은 아세안 국가 간 교역 증진을 위해 2003년 아세안 관세코드(AHTN; ASEAN Harmonized System of Tariff Nomenclature)[19]를 채택함

□ 관세위원회를 통해 품목 분류 번호(AHTN)[20]와 원산지 선정 요건을 확인한 후 수출입하고자 하는 상품이 협정 관세율의 혜택을 받을 수 있는지 판별함
 ○ 우리나라의 경우 2008년 1월부로 한-ASEAN 상품 협정이 발효되어 2010년까지 한·필 양국 간 교역품목의 90%에 대한 관세가 철폐되었고 2016년까지는 대부분 품목에 대한 관세가 철폐 또는 인하될 예정임[21]

□ 필리핀 관세위원회(TC)에서 한-ASEAN FTA 관련 행정명령(Executive Order), EO 52, EO 895, EO 812, EO 639, EO 638 등을 확인함[22]
 ○ 한-아세안 자유무역협정(AKFTA) 관련 행정명령 EO 812는 일반 품목 관세 삭감 규정을 명시하고 EO 638은 민감 품목 관세를 양허를 규정함

□ 우리나라 관세청 FTA포탈[23]을 통해 한국과 필리핀 간의 협정세율 적용 품목, 상대국 세율, 원산지 기준 등을 확인할 수 있음
 ○ 원산지 증명서(Certificate of Origin, C/O)의 경우 통일서식 'Form AK'를 사용하며 대한상공회의소[24] 또는 FTA포털의 유니패스를 통해 신청 가능함

□ 필리핀은 수입물품에 관세 및 부가세(12%), 물품에 따른 특별소비세/물품세 등의 내국세를 부과하고 있으며, 물품에 따라 상계관세도 부과될 수 있음

---

19) '아세안 관세코드'는 아세안 10개 회원국이 공동으로 사용하게 될 1만 700개의 품목분류 코드를 말하며, 회원국들은 상호 수출품에 대해 8자리 또는 10자리의 관세분류 코드를 사용
20) AFTA상의 관세율 및 품목 번호 확인방법: http://www.tariffcommission.gov.ph/AHTN_(TARIFF)_BOOK.htm
21) 외교통상부, 『2010 외국의 통상환경』
22) 각 행정명령 내용은 부록 Ⅲ 참조
 관세위원회 행정명령 관련 링크: http://www.tariffcommission.gov.ph/executiv1.html
23) 대한민국 관세청 FTA 포탈 해당 링크: http://fta.customs.go.kr
24) 대한상공회의소 원산지 증명서 관련 링크: http://cert.korcham.net/certweb

○ 필리핀의 최혜국 관세율은 일반적으로 0~30% 사이임
○ 관세: FOB Value + 운임 + 보험(통상FOB기준 × 4%) = CIF 마닐라 × 관세율
○ 관세율이 10%일 때 관세평가 대상으로서의 수출 가격 예시:
  - Export Value (FOB) 100달러
  - Freight (운임) 5달러
  - Insurance (통상 FOB 기준 × 4%) 4달러
  - Dutiable Value 109달러
  - Rate of Duty 10%
  - Duty Amount (최종금액) 10.9달러

□ 부가가치세는 각종 서비스와 수입품(수입품은 수입 시 납부)을 포함한 제품 판매 대금에 대해 12%가 적용됨
  ○ 부가세: CIF 마닐라 + 수입관세 + 마닐라 항만 비용 = 마닐라 Landed 비용 × 12%
  ○ 필리핀 국세청 관련법[25])에 따라 부가세가 면세되는 수입 품목은 식품용이 아닌 농산품, 수산품, 임산품, 일반 소비용 가축, 비료, 종자, 동물용 사료 등임
  ○ 부가가치세와 더불어 물품세(excise tax)를 부과하는 품목은 알코올, 담배, 석유제품, 광물자원, 보석류, 향수, 자동차, 영화필름

□ 특별소비세[26])는, 특정 품목의 국내 소비 또는 수입 시 부가세에 더해서 발생하는 내국세로 광물, 석유제품, 자동차, 주류, 담배, 화장품 등에 대해 발생함

□ 필리핀은 옥수수, 돼지고기, 가금류 등 15개 농축산물에 대해 자율관세할당(Tariff Rate Quota, TRQ) 제도를 실시하며 관세율은 20~25%임

---

25) BIR; Bureau of Internal Revenue, National Internal Revenue Code of 1997, Republic Act No. 8424 (http://www.chanrobles.com/legal6.htm)
26) 특소세 관련법 관련 정보 (http://www.bir.gov.ph/taxcode/2005.htm)

나. 수입인증제도

☐ 필리핀의 표준화 및 인증은 해당 업종의 제품과 관련된 필리핀 정부 유관 기관 및 국제공인기관(ISO, IEC)에서 전적으로 관여함
  ○ 현지에서 인지도 및 효용성이 높은 국제 인증으로는 ISO9001이 있으며, 이외에도 각각의 분야에 필요한 국제 인증을 요구함

☐ 표준화 및 인증이 필요한 제품은 필리핀 규격(PS: Philippine Standard) 조항에 의거, 필리핀 통상산업부(DTI)의 표준청(Bureau of Philippine Standard, BPS)에서 제공하는 ICC(Import Commodity Clearance) 마크 획득이 필요함
  ○ ICC 인증 필요 서류:
    - ICC 인증 신청서 원본과 공증된 3장의 사본, 선하증권, 제품리스트, 송장(Invoice), DTI 및 증권거래위원회(SEC)에 수입자로 등록한 등록 서류, 표준규격 인증서(ISO 등 국제 표준) 등이 있음
  ○ ICC 인증서 획득을 위해서는 다음의 네 가지 중 한 가지 요건에 해당되어야 함
    - 필리핀 표준청(BPS)의 제품 테스트는 없었으나, ISO9001:2000을 소유하고 있는 경우
    - 필리핀 표준청(BPS)의 제품 테스트와 ISO9001:2000을 소유하고 있는 경우
    - 수입 허가제도의 수입관리 대상 제외 품목으로 필리핀 표준청(BPS)의 제품 테스트와 ISO9001:2000을 소유하지 않고 있는 경우
    - 필리핀 표준 규격과 안전 규격 마크(Safety Certification)가 있는 경우

☐ 표준화 인증은 전기·전자, 기계, 섬유, 화학 분야에서 이루어지고 있으며 생산자의 제품의 질을 판단하기보다는 현지 시장에서의 사용 가능 여부와 자국민 경제 및 건강에 미칠 영향력 등을 기준으로 판단함
  ○ 전기/전자, 석유/화학공업 및 건축/건설의 경우는 표준 규격 조건과 함께, 제품별 사용 목적에 따라 세부적으로 분류된 동종 민간단체의 규격 조건을 준수해야 함
    - 일반적인 전자제품 수입 시, TUV Rheinland Philippines Inc.[27]에 테스트를 받

은 후 이를 필리핀 통상산업부(DTI)에 제출하여 수입물품 허가서(ICC)를 획득한 후 기타 수입 절차에 따른 업무를 추진함

- 중고 가전제품의 경우 필리핀 환경자원부(DENR, Department of Environment and Natural Resources)로부터 Environmental Clearance Certificate를 발급받고 정확한 Invoice Value 책정을 위해 선적지의 필리핀 대사관으로부터 Authentication of Commercial Invoice를 추가 발급받아야 함

☐ 섬유직물, 기성복, 의류, 액세서리 등에 대해서는 라벨링이 의무화되어 있으므로 수출입자의 세심한 주의가 필요함

☐ 식품 및 의약품의 경우에는 식품의약국의 성분 및 효능 테스트 통과가 필요하며 주재국에 약품을 수출하기 위해선 필리핀 식약청에 사전 허가를 받아야 함

---

27) TUV Rheinland Philippines Inc. www.tuv.com/ph

〈표 Ⅲ-1〉 약품 수출 시 등록 신청의 요구 사항

식약청 사전 허가 시 필요한 서류
- BD #1 s. 2002에 규정된 등록 지원서 작성
- 약품 등록 서식 첨부/참조(개정판)
- 모라토리엄 제어 대상 증명서
- 과거 RSN에 해당되어 승인 불가 통보한 서신 사본(재신청의 경우)
- 제조업자, 무역업자, 분배자 간의 서명 날인된 계약서 사본

수입, 수출업자, 도매업자에 요구되는 사항
- A.O. 54 규정에 명시된 제품 등록 증명서 원본 제출
- 제품 출처가 명기된 제조업자, 무역업자, 분배자, 수입업자의 LTO 사본
- 추가 서류: 금지/통제 약품의 경우(DDB에서 발행된 허가증)

기준 복용량과 제조법
- 약품에 사용된 원재료의 technical 내역서
- 주요 원재료에 대한 분석표
- 공급자(제조업자)에 의한 원재료 분석
- 제조업체의 완제품 분석
- 완제품에 대한 technical data(기술 검사서)
- 완제품에 대한 분석표(1회분의 견본 제출)
- 제조 공정 내역서, 생산 장비, 추출 견본, 품질 검사 및 포장 공정 설명 내역서
- 효능을 분석/검사한 데이터 자료 e.g. 색층 분석
 (비공식적인 포뮬러라면 분석/테스트 결과 첨부)

안정성 시험(Stability Studies)
- Accelerated (최초 신청)-1 batch at 3 elevated temperature
- Long Term(갱신)-3 batches
- In-Use(개조된 제품)
- 1 batch at 30 oC and 2 oC -8 oC/ 3 batches at 30 oC and 2 oC -8 oC

시중에 유통되고 있는 상태의 샘플, 상용화 상태의 견본(유효기간이 1년 이상)

라벨의 재질
- 고유색상이 지정된 label 도안 및 실물 각 3매
- Bioavailability / Bioequivalence Studies (for Rifampicin)

다. 수입규제제도

□ 수입물품은 수입허가/규제/금지품목으로 분류되며 통관되며 수입규제는 원칙적으로 모든 수입을 자유롭게 허용하는 Negative System을 채택함

□ 수입규제에는 수입금지 품목, 수입수량 제한, 수입절차상의 제한[28] 등이 있음
  ○ 수입절차상의 제한은 수입관리대상 품목을 선정하여 품목별로 해당 정부기구의 승인을 거쳐 관련 라이선스/품질인증마크/품목별 인증서 등을 획득한 후에 공인 은행을 통해 부과된 세금을 지불하는 방식임
    - 특정 품목에 대한 수입 허가권(license) 제도를 통해 수입 허가권을 보유한 일부 회사만 수입을 허용함
  ○ 수입관리 품목 관련 승인 기관:
    - ATO: Air Transportation Office
    - BTI: Bureau of Plant Industry
    - BFAD : Bureau of Food and Drugs
    - BIR : Bureau of Internal Revenue
    - BOI : Board of Investment
    - BPI : Bureau of Plant Industry
    - BRAR : Bureau of Fisheries & Aquatic Resources
    - CAB : Civil Aeronautics Board
    - DDB : Dangerous Drugs Board
    - DENR : Dept. of Environment & Natural Resources
    - ERB : Energy Regulatory Board
    - MARINA : Maritime Industry Authority
    - NBI : National Bureau of Investigation
    - NTA : National Tobacco Authority
    - NTC : National Telecommunications Commission
    - PNP-FEO : PNP Firearms and Explosives Office
    - PNRI : Phil. Nuclear Research Institute

---

[28] 외교통상부, 『외국의 통상환경 2010』

〈표 Ⅲ-2〉 필리핀의 수입 관리 품목 리스트

품목	관련 기관
Acetic anhydride	DDB
쌀, 옥수수	NFA
Sodium Cyanide	BFAD
Chlorofluorocarbon	BFAD
Penicillin, derivatives	BFAD
정제석유제품	ERB
석탄	ERB
컬러복사기	NBI & Cash Dept. of Central Bank
폭약용 화공약품	PNP-FEO
양파, 마늘, 감자, 양배추(종자용)	Bureau of Plant Industry
농약	Fertilizer & Pesticide Authority
중고 자동차 부품	BIS
중고 타이어	DTI
달러화로 결제하지 않는 중고차 수입	BIS
정부기관의 컴퓨터 및 주변기기 (연간 200만페소 초과 시)	Nat'l Computer Center
방사능물질	PNRI
필리핀 통화의 합법적 입찰	BSP
금화, 구리, 니켈 등 각종 주화용 빈 동전, 지폐	BSP
국내에서 충분히 생산되는 농산물 - 옥수수, 가금류/돈육 및 그 제품, 쇠고기 제외 육류 및 그 제품	NFA, BAI
휴대전화 단말기, 전화수신기 등 모든 통신기기	NTC
중고컴퓨터	DENR
냉장고, 냉동고, 에어컨용 프레온 가스	DENR
신선 과일 및 채소류	BPI
신선 및 냉동 어류	BFAR
동물용 사료	BAI
가공 식품류 및 약품	BFAD
PVC resin	BOI
Cigarettes & other Tobacco Products	NTA, DENR, BIR
화장품	BFAD
수의약품	BFAD, BAI
보트 및 각종 선박	MARINA
각종 항공기	ATO
컴퓨터(모뎀 장착된 것)	NTC

자료: OIS 해외 진출 정보 시스템) 필리핀 편) 수입 규제

□ 필리핀은 수출국가에도 동등한 규제가 가능하도록 한 국제무역기구 (WTO)의 규정과 기준을 감안, 민감 품목과 고도 민감 품목으로 분류된 농산물 분야를 제외하고는 수입규제와 관련된 사안들이 많지는 않은 편임
  ○ 필리핀에서 가장 취약한 농업부문에서는 고율 관세, 쿼터 및 비관세 장벽 형성 등의 보호조치가 이루어지고 있음
    - 쌀에 대한 총량규제, 설탕생산 및 처리과정에 대한 고도의 규제, 쌀 및 옥수수 등에 대한 가격지지 정책 등이 주요한 내용임
  ○ 특히 민감품목(sensitive items)에 대해서는 Minimum Access Volume (MAV) 정책에 의거한 규제정책을 시행하고 있으며 이며 관세율은 20~25%에 이르고 있음
    - 대상품목: 옥수수, 설탕, 돼지고기, 가금류, 커피, 커피추출물 등

□ 자국 산업 피해 방지를 이유로 제조업이 어느 정도 활성화된 분야를 중심으로 특정 품목에 세이프 가드 발동을 요청하는 경우가 발생함
  ○ 필리핀의 수입규제 근거 법령인 Anti-Dumping Law/Safeguards Law (RA 8800)를 적용하여 필리핀 무역산업부(DTI) 및 관세위원회(TC)[29]에서 특정 제품의 수입을 제한함
    - 수입규제 사례로는 2008년 봉강(Angle Bar Industry)에 대해서 세이프가드 조치 발동을 요청하는 제소가 이루어졌으며, 필리핀의 판지 산업(Testliner Board Industry) 부문에서도 판지에 대해 제소, 수입 규제를 실시하였음

□ 필리핀 정부예산으로 조달하는 물품의 입찰에 순수한 외국 업체(제조업자, 공급업체, 중개업체 등)의 참여는 불가능, 필리핀인의 투자비율이 60% 이상인 합작법인을 설립하여야만 입찰 참여가 가능함

□ 필리핀은 제반 국내법에 근거하여 공공위생, 안전 및 보건상 필요하다고 판단되는 물품을 수출입 금지함

---

29) 필리핀 관세위원회 사이트 해당 링크: http://www.tariffcommission.gov.ph

<표 Ⅲ-3> 필리핀의 수입 금지 품목

수입 금지 품목
- 양파, 감자, 마늘, 양배추 등 농산품 (종자용 제외) - 성인용 제품/재료 - 중고 의류 및 넝마 - 장난감 총 - 폭약 및 총기, 무기류 및 부품 (특별히 승인된 건 제외) - 내란 선동 등의 불온한 내용을 담고 있는 서적, 생명의 위협, 신체에 해악을 주는 내용의 서적 - 불법 낙태용 도구 및 약품 등 - 도박용구, 카드, 기구 등 - 복권, 경마권 등 - 귀금속으로 제조된 예술품 - 불량 의약품 및 식품 - 마리화나 및 기타 마약 등 - 기타 법률에 의해 수입이 금지된 것 품목의 수출 가능성에 대해 확인 필요

자료: OIS 해외 진출 정보 시스템〉국가정보〉필리핀〉수입 규제

3. 필리핀의 수입 통관 절차

□ 수입업자는 필리핀 관세국(Bureau of Customs)의 고객등록시스템(Client Profile Registration System, CPRS)에 기업정보를 등록한 후[30] 관세국 산하의 정보조사업무 부서(Customs Intelligence Investigation Service, CIIS)를 통해 수입면허(Customs Accreditation Secretariat, CAS)를 획득해야 함

  ○ 필리핀의 수입면허(CAS)는 재무부가 발급하며, 이를 취득하기 위해서는 신청서, SEC 법인등기증, 재무제표, 소득세 납부실적, 각종 유틸리티 청구서 등을 구비해야 함

  ○ 수입업자는 필리핀 세관(BOC)에 1,500페소의 연간 등록비 및 500페소의 차후 갱신 비용(processing fee for subsequent updates of the registration)을 납부해야 함

  ○ 수입면허(CAS)의 취득은 통상 현지 업체 및 브로커를 통해 진행됨

  ○ 수입면허 신청 접수 후 서류 검토, 사업장 소재지 방문 실사, 최종 승인까지 보통 1

---

[30] OIS 해외진출 정보 시스템 〉 필리핀 비즈니스 커뮤니티 〉 해외 투자 뉴스레터 NO. 10

개월 정도가 소요되며 서류가 미비하거나 사업장 실사 후 추가조사가 필요한 경우는 더 오랜 시일이 소요됨
- ○ 수출입 면허 신청을 위한 구비서류
  - 신청서(Application Form)
  - 법인등기사본(Sec Certificate of Registration)/개인사업자등록증사본(Proof of Registration of DTI)
  - 회계사가 서명한 재무제표 사본(Audited Financial Statement)
  - 법인세 납부증명(Income Tax Return of the Company)
  - 각종 공과금 납부증명 (Proof of Utility Billing) 등

□ 수입자는 필리핀 통상산업부(DTI)의 BIS(the Bureau of Import Services)[31]를 통해 필리핀 수입 통관 절차 및 규제 내용을 확인할 수 있음

□ 필리핀 정부는 안전, 보안, 위생, 기타 국내 산업 보호 등의 이유로 일부 제품의 수입을 제한하거나 금지하고 있으므로 수입업무부서에 문의하여 해당 물품을 수입금지품목, 허용품목, 규제대상품목으로 구분해야 함
- ○ 수입 규제대상품목의 경우 해당 정부기구의 승인을 거쳐 수입규제품목 관련 라이선스/품질인증마크/품목별 인증서 등을 획득한 후에 공인은행(Authorizes Agent Bank, AAB)을 통해 부과된 세금을 납부해야 함

□ 필리핀의 수입 관리 대상 품목에 대한 빠른 업데이트가 이루어지고 있지 않으므로 사전에 수입업무부서(BIS)에 문의하여 정확히 확인해 둘 필요가 있음
- ○ 사전에 수입허가를 받아야 하는 품목의 경우 현지 세관에 도착된 이후에 수입 허가를 받아 서류를 제출할 경우 '수입 허가를 사전에 받지 않은' 사례에 해당되어 30%의 벌금이 부과될 수 있음

□ 수입자는 해당 물품이 한-ASEAN FTA 관세 양허대상 품목인지 여부를 확인해야 함

---

31) 필리핀 통상산업부 해당 링크: http://www.dti.gov.ph/dti/index.php?p=196

- ○ 한국 정부의 FTA포털이나 필리핀 관세위원회의 관세관련 법령을 통해 물품의 HS Code, 협정세율 및 원산지 기준을 확인할 수 있음
- ○ 필리핀은 관세위원회 사이트(Tariff Commission of Philippines)[32])에 게재한 행정명령을 통하여 한-ASEAN FTA의 관세양허를 규정하며 관련 법령은 EO52(2011), EO895(2010), EO812(2009), EO638(2007) 등이 있음[33])

□ 수입물품은 단순 소비재인 경우와 단순 소비재가 아닌 경우로 나뉘어 통관이 진행되며, 단순소비재가 아닌 물품의 경우에는 다시 보세공장용(Customs Bonded Manufacturing Warehouse, CBMW)과 보세공장용이 아닌 물품으로 나뉘어 통관이 이루어짐[34])
- ○ 수입물품이 단순소비재인 경우 증명서가 첨부된 소비재 반입 신청서를 EPD(Entry Processing Division)에 제출하고 소비재 수입증명서와 확인서를 FED(Formal Entry Division)에 제출하는 절차를 거쳐 물품 반출을 완료함
- ○ 수입물품이 단순소비재가 아닌 경우에는 보세공장용인 경우와 보세공장용이 아닌 경우로 나뉘어 통관이 진행됨
  - 단순소비재는 아니나 보세공장용일 경우에는 필리핀 관세국에 보세 반입을 신청하여 물품을 반출하고, 단순소비재가 아니며 보세공장용도 아닐 경우에는 FED(Formal Entry Division)의 특별수송허가(Special Permit to Transfer, SPT)를 받아 물품을 반출함
- ○ 필리핀의 보세공장은 수출을 위한 가공무역을 진행하여 국제수지의 개선과 고용 증대, 국내 생산시설의 가동률을 높이기 위해 설립되었으며 진출 기업에 관세 혜택이 부여됨
  - 외국원자재를 수입·사용함에 있어 복잡한 통관 절차를 필요로 하지 않으며, 관세에 상당한 담보물을 공탁하지 않고도 관세가 유보된 상태에서 가공 제품을

---

32) 필리핀 관세위원회 해당 링크: www.tariffcommission.gov.ph
33) 관련 행정명령(Executive Order)의 내용은 부록 Ⅲ을 참조
34) FTA 종합지원 포털〉체결국 통관 절차〉필리핀 해당 링크: http://www.ftahub.go.kr/kr/apply/costoms/03/index0211.jsp

만들어 수출할 수 있음. 단, 보세공장에서 가공된 제품이 국내 타 지역에 유입되는 경우는 이를 수입품으로 보아 관세가 부과됨
 - 복잡한 사무절차와 금리의 부담을 받지 않는다는 점에서 큰 이점이 있으나 관세행정권의 확보 차원에서 세관의 관리와 감독을 받아야 함

☐ 수입자는 공인은행(Authorizes Agent Bank, AAB)을 통해 신용장을 개설하고 은행에서 세관 앞 출고 허가서를 발행함

☐ 필리핀의 통관 관련 정부부처가 연계된 단일 통관 창구(National Single Window)사이트35)를 통해 수입신고가 이루어지며, 세관 시스템에 수입화물 정보를 입력한 후 출력하여 세관에 수입통관 프로세스를 진행함
 ○ 수입신고 시 제출할 필수서류는 선하증권, 화물운송장, 상업송장, 견적송장, 포장명세서 등이 있으며 필요시 수입규제품목 관련 라이선스/품질인증마크/품목별 인증을 제출해야 함
 ○ 수입신고서는 수입자, 하물인수자(consignee), 어음소유자(holder of the bill)에 의해 서명되어야 하며, 서명은 개인 또는 회사, 기업의 책임자 또는 허가를 받은 통관대행업자(customs broker) 등에 의해 이루어짐

☐ 수입 허용품목과 관련 정부기관 인증을 거친 수입 규제 품목의 수입신고서는 필리핀 세관에서 신속통관(supper green lane)과 일반통관(ordinary green lane) 등으로 분류되어 통관됨
 ○ Supper Green Lane은 우수 수입업자를 대상으로 화물 도착 전에 전자서류로 통관을 신청, 물품 도착 후 추가 서류 및 실제 검사 없이 통관을 진행하는 제도임
  - 그 외 수입업체들은 세관에서 수입통관을 진행 할 경우에 Red Lane(전수검사), Yellow Lane(추가 서류검사), Green Lane(서류검사)으로 분리되어 수입 통관됨
 ○ 신속통관(supper green lane) 제도에 의한 통관 절차 과정
  - 전자 통관 신고서(electronic entry declaration)를 작성하고 필리핀 관세청의

---

35) Phil. National Single Window 해당 링크: www.nsw.gov.ph/faqs

ACOS(authorized customs operation system)의 전자문서교환(electronic data interchange)을 통해 상기 신고서를 제출함
- 신고서를 심사하고 전자 처리된 세금/관세 등을 전송함
- 공인은행(AAB)에 ACOS 평가에 따른 세금/관세를 지불함
- Customs Authorization Payment system에 지불한 세금에 대한 서류를 전송함
- 전자상으로 세금과 지불액이 맞는지 정산 후 화물 방출 가능(cargo release message) 서류를 보세창고 운영인에게 전송하여 이를 기반으로 수입자에게 화물을 전달함
- 위의 과정이 화물을 실은 선박의 도착 이전에 이루어질 경우 화물을 선박에서 바로 트럭으로 이동할 수 있음

☐ 보세구역으로 물품을 반입할 시 국내 신용장, 은행지불보증, 보세창고어음, 물품이 보세구역에서 반출될 때 지불되어야 할 세금, 관세, 다른 요금들에 각각 상응하는 보증이 필요함
  ○ 적법하게 보세구역으로 들어온 물품의 장치기간의 경우 통관 항에 도착한 날짜로부터 최대 1년 동안 장치될 수 있음
  ○ 공공 보세창고나 개인 보세창고의 사용료는 수입자와 창고 운영인 사이에서 결정되나, 이러한 사용료는 세관원에 의해 지정된 관습적인 보세창고의 이용료를 초과할 수 없음

☐ 보세구역에 들어온 물품이 운송 화물 목록에 의해 필리핀의 다른 구역으로 즉시 운송될 경우, 물품은 검사 또는 평가 없이 운송되며 세관원의 대리로 임명된 수탁인의 승인 아래 국내 신용장, 은행지불보증 채권 등을 담보로 운송됨

☐ 수입자는 수입 관련 자료를 수입일로부터 3년간 보관해야 하며, 관세국은 수입업자의 세관규칙 준수 여부를 확인하기 위하여 수입 완료 후 3년간 수입자가 보관한 서류를 검사할 수 있음

□ 필리핀 세관은 수입물품을 대상으로 세관검사(customs inspection), 관세분류(tariff classification), 관세평가(appraisement) 등을 진행하며, 수입에 따르는 각종 세금, 관세 및 기타 요금을 부과함
  ○ 세관원은 물품의 패키지가 세관에 수입신고 내용, 송장, 여타 다른 문서의 내용과 일치하는지 확인하고 필요시에 샘플검사를 진행함
  ○ 세관원은 모든 합리적인 방법을 동원하여 물품의 가격이나 가치를 평가하며 송장, 선서진술서, 제조원 등의 보고서 등을 조사함

□ 세관원은 관세에 상응하는 담보(국내선하증권, 은행지불보증, 채권 등)나 관세의 납부를 확인한 후 신고를 수리함
  ○ 수입자는 수입하기 전에 수입신고서를 공인은행(AAB)에 제출하여야 하며 세관을 통해 부과된 세금을 동 은행에 제출해야 함
  ○ 필리핀의 과세가격은 거래가격을 기초한 국내 인도가격에 의해 결정되며 수입물품에는 관세, 부가세(12%), 특소세(excise tax), 물품세 등이 부과됨
    - 특소세 부과 대상 품목은 광물, 석유제품, 자동차, 주류, 담배, 화장품 등임

□ 세관원은 검사받지 않은 물품의 경우 신속하고 빠른 운송을 위해 현금 보증으로 국내 선하증권, 은행지불보증, 채권에 상당하는 금액을 요구할 수 있고, 금액은 세금·관세 또는 다른 지불해야 할 요금의 100%임
  ○ 현금 보증금이 지불 되지 않았을 경우, 세금, 관세, 다른 지불 요금 등이 지급될 때까지 물품 운송이 보류됨

□ 관세는 수입된 물품이 소비를 위해 국내 시장으로 반입되기 이전에 처리되어야 하며, 세관은 OLRS(on-line release system)를 통해 은행으로부터 관세 납부 사실을 통보받으면 수입자에게 화물을 양도함

□ 보세공장에서 제조, 가공된 물품은 보세상태에서 직접 수출이 가능하며 적법한 절차에 따라 세금이 면제됨

○ 수출을 위해 제조, 가공되는 보세공장의 수입된 물품들은 보세공장으로 들어온 날짜부터 9개월 내에 사용되어야 하며, 충분한 사유가 있을 시 세관장의 허락하에 완료일로부터 3개월까지 사용기한의 연장이 가능함
  - 허용 기간 내에 사용되지 않은 제조를 위한 수입물품은 그 물품에 상응하는 세금을 납부하여야 함
○ 필리핀 관세국 관세표(TCCP) Section 106에 의한 관세 환급 품목
  - 선박 운항용 연료, 도시가스 생산과 전력 생산용 원유 및 역청, 석유나 석유류에 대한 관세 환급, 재무부 장관 승인이 있을 경우 관세 환급 또는 관세 환급 예정액만큼의 세액공제보증서(tax credit)를 발행함

□ 투자위원회(BOI)와 경제자유구역청(PEZA)에 등록된 업체의 경우 행정명령(Executive Order 226, Omnibus Investment Act)에 의거하여 관세 면제 등의 세금 혜택을 부여함

4. 필리핀의 수출 통관 절차36)

□ 수출자는 필리핀 통상산업부(DTI)나 증권거래위원회(Exchange Commission, SEC)에 등록하고 거래하게 될 도시, 지방자치단체, 국세청(Bureau of Internal Revenue, BIR) 등에도 등록하여 수출 물품이 통관될 수 있도록 준비해야 함
  ○ 모든 수출자들은 국세청(BIR) 등록 시 제공되는 고유의 납세등록번호(taxpayer identification number, TIN)를 통관 과정에서 사용하여야 함

□ 수출업자는 외국인 구매자에게 견적송장을 보내어 무역을 확정시킨 후 외국인 구매자가 사인한 견적송장을 다시 돌려받음

□ 수출업자는 공인은행(AAB)을 통하여 신용장, 대금지급인환증(document against

---

36) 필리핀 통상산업부(DTI) 〉 수출업무부서 해당 링크: http://www.dti.gov.ph/dti/index.php?p=223

payment), 인수인도조건(document against acceptance), 당좌계정(open account), 상품인도결제(cash against document), 가지급(prepayment advance), 회사 간 당좌계정(intercompany open account), 전신환(telegraphic transfer) 등을 통해 대금을 지급받음

☐ 수출업자는 물품 운송 준비 완료 후 수출 신고서(export declaration form)를 작성해야 하며 수출 신고서를 추가 서류들과 세관에 제출하고 세관의 AL(Authority to Load)에서 검사함
  ○ 수출통관 서류 샘플은 BETP(Bureau of Export Trade Promotion), DTI Provincial offices, BOC Processing Units, OSEDCs(One-Stop Export Documentation Center), PHILEXPORT offices 등에서 얻을 수 있으며 수출규제 품목의 경우 관련 정부기관의 승인을 획득해야 함
  ○ 수출통관 필수 서류는 선하증권/항공화물운송장, 상업송장/견적송장(TIN 기재), 포장명세서 등이며 특정 물품의 경우 추가 서류를 세관에 제출해야 함
  ○ 사전수출 승인 품목의 경우 관련 수출 승인 서류를 미리 준비해야 하며 특정 품목 수출 시 품목별로 개별 인증기관의 허가를 획득해야 함
    - 코코넛을 수출하려면 필리핀의 PCA(Philippine Coconut Authority)에 등록해야 하며 필리핀산 돌이나 나무 등을 수출할 경우 해당 품목의 수출 승인을 별도로 획득해야 함
    - 한국으로 수출 시 포장단위로 나무로 만들어진 팔레트를 사용하게 되면 모든 나무 팔레트가 검역(fumigation)을 받아야만 한국의 세관에서 별도의 과태료 없이 통관이 가능함

☐ 필리핀 수출입 통관은 특별한 하자가 없는 한 2일에서 3일이 소요됨
  ○ 대부분의 선하증권은 Surrender 처리하여 한국에서 선하증권 원본 없이도 사본만으로 실시간 통관이 가능함(원본 없이도 수출자가 Surrender 해주면 수입업자가 원본 없이도 물건을 찾아감)
  ○ 전시회 등 일시적인 수입물품을 반출할 경우 수출신고서, 상업송장, 포장명세서,

선하증권, 입국증명서 원본을 세관에 제출해야 함

□ 수출 제품 생산을 위해 수입된 자본재의 관세 환급을 위해서는 수출제품의 제조 및 생산에 실제 사용된 수입자재의 수량(분량) 및 가격과 실제 납부한 관세를 서류상으로 입증해야 함
  ○ 관세 환급 또는 관세 환급 예정액에 대한 세액공제 보증서는 기납부 관세의 100%를 초과할 수 없음
    - 필리핀 경제개발청(NEDA, 관세청 관할 부처)에서 자재 수입 당시 해당 자재가 필리핀 내에서 생산되고 있지 않거나 경쟁력 있는 자재가 아님을 입증해야 함
  ○ 수입된 자재는 수입일로부터 1년 안에 완제품으로 수출되어야 하고 수출 후 6개월 안에 해당 관세 환급 혹은 세액공제 보증서를 청구해야 함

□ 필리핀에서 수출을 하는 경우 수출통관 면장을 처리하는 관세사에게 지급하는 Brokerage Fee는 Import Brokerage Fee의 50%만 지급됨

Ⅳ. 통관 절차별 고려 사항

〈표 Ⅳ-1〉 필리핀 통관 절차별 고려 사항

단계	유의 사항
1. 신고 전 서류준비	○ 해당 물품이 필리핀 내 수입이 가능한 제품인지 확인해야 함 　- BOC(Bureau of Customs), AAB(Authorizes Agent Bank)에 문의 ○ 수입관리 대상 품목의 정리·발표가 늦으므로 관세국(BOC)의 Bureau of Import Service(BIS)에 문의 사전에 정확히 확인해야 함 ○ 수입규제 품목 수입 시 인증 과정이 복잡하고 다수의 증빙을 요구함 ○ 수입면허의 유효기간은 1년으로 매년 갱신이 필요함
2. 수입신고	○ FTA 양허품목 등에 대한 정보 부족으로 수입신고가 지연될 수 있음 ○ 품목분류 및 가격평가에 있어 세관별로 상이한 경우가 발생할 수 있음 ○ 수입신고 과정상 정상적 비용 외에 추가 비용 요구사례가 있음
3. 심사·검사	○ 일부 품목은 세관에 물품이 도착하기 전에 수입허가를 받아야 함 　- 도착 후 수입 허가를 받아 서류를 제출할 경우 벌금 부과 ○ C/O에 문제가 있다고 판단될 시 철저한 검증 서류 요구 　- 수입통관시 C/O 원본을 제출해야 함 　- 생산자와 수출자 정보가 다를 경우 추가 증빙을 요구함 　- 전자서명에 대한 이해 부족으로 통관 지연이 발생한 사례가 있음 ○ 특정 품목은 통관 시 추가서류 제출을 요구 통관 절차가 복잡함 　- 추가서류 요구 품목: 비료, 동물성 식품, 오토바이, 영화 및 TV 상품, 살충제, 식물/식물 생산물, 라디오 송신기, 무전기, 비디오 그램 등
4. 관세 납부	○ 신고가격과 거래가격이 다를 경우 신고가격에 대한 근거자료를 요구함 　- 제출된 자료를 근거로 세관에서 책정한 수입가격에 불복이 있을 경우 세관의 Tariff 부서에 이의를 제기할 수 있음 ○ 신규 반입 제품에 대해서 높은 관세를 부과하는 경향이 있음 ○ 6개의 민감 품목군은 최소 시장접근 정책(MAV)으로 규제되며 관세율은 20~25%임(옥수수, 설탕, 돼지고기, 가금류, 커피, 커피추출물 등)
5. 신고수리	○ 보세구역 반입물품은 통관 항 도착일로부터 최대 1년간 장치됨 ○ 개인 창고 사용료는 세관의 지정 보세창고 이용료를 초과할 수 없음 ○ 항만 사용료 및 컨테이너 종류별 운송비용이 비싼 편임 ○ 경제특구관리청 등록 요건 및 절차가 복잡함

1. 수입신고 전 서류 준비 단계

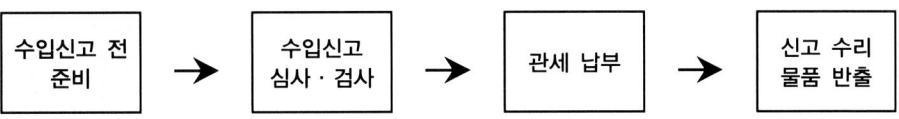

□ 수출입 통관을 진행하기 위해서는 수출입자 면허(CAS)를 획득해야 하며 통상산업부(DTI)의 CIIS(Customs Intelligence Investigation Service)상의 CPRS(Client Profile Registration System)에 기업정보를 사전 등록할 의무가 있음
  ○ 수출입자는 사전에 해당 물품의 품목 분류, 수출입 규제 품목 해당 여부 등을 파악해야 함
  ○ 필리핀 관세국에 의뢰하여 해당 수입 품목의 수입 규제/금지 여부를 확인하고 수입 규제 품목일 경우 해당 정부기관의 인증서를 발급받아야 함
  ○ 2008년부터 한국과 필리핀 양국의 상품부문에 대한 FTA가 시행되고 있으므로 각국 관세청에 문의하여 수입품목이 양허관세 적용 품목인지 확인해야 함

□ 수출입업자 간의 계약 조건이 결정될 경우 한국 수출업자는 마닐라 항에 물품이 도착할 때까지의 해상운임을 물류업체에 의뢰함

□ 필리핀의 수입업자는 물품이 마닐라 항에 도착한 후부터 수입통관 비용, 관세/세금 납부액, 창고 및 운송비용 등을 산정함

□ 통관 절차의 간소화를 위하여 수출입업자를 대상으로 단일 통관창구(National Single Window, NSW)가 운영중에 있음[37]
  ○ 수입자는 필리핀 정부부처가 연계된 단일 통관창구를 통해 수입신고를 진행하고 수입통관 서류 및 요건을 온라인으로 일괄 제출할 수 있음
    - 세관 시스템에 수입화물 정보를 입력하여 출력한 후 세관에 수입통관 프로세스

---
[37] 마닐라 KBC 보도 「필리핀, 수입통관 대폭 빨라진다」 2010. 3. 24

를 진행하는 형식임
- ○ 본 제도의 도입으로 인해 수입업체는 수입통관에 필요한 서류를 한 번만 관세국에 제출하거나 온라인으로 처리함
- ○ 수입업체가 관세국에 수입허가에 필요한 서류를 제출하는 것으로 수입신고 업무가 종료되며 접수기관(관세국)은 별다른 문제가 없을 경우 30분 내에 통관서류를 발급함
- ○ 단일 통관창구(National Single Window)를 통해 다음의 해당 10개 정부기관과 연결하여 업무를 처리함:
  - 투자청(Board of Investments)
  - 동물산업청(Bureau of Animal Industry)
  - 관세청(Bureau of Customs)
  - 식품의약청(Bureau of Food and Drugs)
  - 국세청(Bureau of Internal Revenue)
  - 식물산업청(Bureau of Plant Industry)
  - 제품표준청(Bureau of Product Standards)
  - 국립식품청(National Food Authority)
  - 필리핀경제구역청(Philippine Economic sZone Authority)
  - 설탕규제청(Sugar Regulatory Administration)

□ 해당 물품이 필리핀 내 수입 가능한 제품인지의 여부를 필리핀 관세국(Bureau of Customs, BOC)이나 공인은행(Authorizes Agent Bank, AAB)에 문의해야 함

□ 필리핀 시장에 대한 정보가 부족하므로 물품 거래 시 계약 요건을 사전에 분명하게 설정할 필요가 있음
- ○ 필리핀 현지 업체에 냉온수기를 수출한 국내 업체가 현지 업체에게 조건부 독점권을 부여하였으나 현지 업체가 불명확한 계약 내용을 빌미로 지속적인 독점권을 행사함으로써 현지 진출에 곤란을 겪은 사례가 존재 함

□ 품목 분류 코드가 아세안 국가별로 상이하므로 수입자가 필리핀 관세국(BOC)이나 관세위원회(TC) 사이트에 접촉하여 해당 물품이 한-ASEAN 자유 무역 협정의 양허관세율을 적용받을 수 있는 품목인지 확인해야 함
 ○ 품목 번호가 달라질 경우에는 원산지 결정 기준이 달라 협정 관세가 배제되고 추징이 발생될 수 있음
  - 자동차 부품을 여러 나라에 걸쳐 수출하는 경우 각 국가별로 품목번호가 상이하여 원산지 증명서 발행 및 원산지 결정기준 파악이 어려움

□ 수입자는 ASEAN 국가들을 대상으로 FTA 양허 및 원산지 결정 기준에 대한 충분한 정보를 수집할 필요가 있음
 ○ ASEAN 국가의 바이어가 FTA 원산지 증명서를 한국 국내 업체에 신청한 경우에도 관련 정보를 충분히 제공하지 못해 C/O 발급 준비에 어려움이 발생한 사례가 있음
 ○ 수출자 서명과 관련 명확한 규정의 부재로 기발급한 C/O를 정정 또는 재발급받는 사례가 있음
  - 예를 들어 해당국이 수출자의 친필 사인이나 도장만 인정된다고 규정한 경우, 우리나라의 전산시스템을 통한 원산지 증명서가 인정되지 않는 사례가 발생함

□ 현재 기관 발급 원산지 증명서의 경우 생산자와 수출자가 다를 경우 원산지 소명서를 제출하고 원산지 확인서를 제출해야 하므로 발급 절차의 간소화가 필요함
 ○ 원산지 증명서에는 단가 정보 등 기업의 영업비밀이 있어 공개가 곤란한 측면이 있음

□ 수입자는 원활한 통관 절차를 위하여 정확한 관세율 정보 확인 및 통관 법령 수집을 위해 노력해야 함
 ○ 관세율 정보는 양국 관세청 홈페이지에서 조회할 수 있으나 업데이트가 늦고 상호 불일치하는 경우도 발생할 수 있음

□ 필리핀 신규 진출 투자기업 중 수입면허(CAS)가 없는 경우 세관에서 통관 서류가 접

수되지 않는 것을 미리 숙지하지 못해 통관상의 어려움을 겪는 경우가 있으므로 CAS 면허를 필수적으로 취득해야 함
- ○ 필리핀에 신규 진출하는 업체 중 한국 및 제3국과 수출입 업무를 동반하는 기업은 CAS 관련 사항을 숙지하고 CAS 등록 기간을 고려하여 수출입 일정을 잡아야 함
- ○ CAS 면허의 유효기간은 1년으로 매년 갱신되어야 함
  - CAS 등록을 했다고 해서 모든 품목의 수출입이 가능한 것은 아니며 일부 특정 품목은 필리핀의 해당 주무부처로부터 별도의 사전 수출입 승인을 받아야 함 (예: 곡물/코코넛/수산물/의약품/식음료/화장품/광물 등)

□ 필리핀에 신규로 진출하는 일부 투자기업들은 필리핀 증권거래위원회(SEC)에 법인으로 등기하고 세무서(BIR)로부터 TIN No.만 받은 후 공장설비, 사무집기, 원자재 등의 수입을 서두르는 경우 있으나 CAS 면허가 없어 수입신고를 하지 못하는 경우가 있음
- ○ CAS 면허가 없어 통관서류 접수가 거부된 상황에서 이미 물품을 선적하고 수입대행업체를 찾아 B/L 등 선적서류를 수정하느라 불필요한 시간과 비용을 낭비하는 경우가 많음

□ 필리핀에 진출한 한국인이 통상 상용비자인 9G 비자를 받기 위해서는 AEP(Alien Employment) 등 10가지 이상의 구비서류를 제출하여야 함
- ○ 1999년부터 한인회가 9G 비자업무를 소정의 수수료를 받고 대행해 주고 있으나, AEP 취득 후 비자 발급에 약 2~3개월 소요됨

□ 수입자는 통관 시 필수 제출 서류 이외에도 공공 보건, 안전, 국가안보, 국제 협약 준수 및 지역 산업 보호를 위해 추가서류(Supporting Documentation)를 제출해야 하는 경우가 있음
- ○ 해당 서류는 수입 규제품목 관련 라이선스/품질인증마크/품목별 인증 등임

〈표 Ⅳ-2〉 필리핀 수입 통관 시 추가서류 요구 품목

해당품목	추가 제출 서류
Fertilizers	− Permit for Imported Fertilizer Product Registration − Permit for Experimental Use Permit for Fertilizer Efficacy Trial
Animal Product	− Veterinary Certificates (clean report of findings) − CITES Import Permit (Export Permit from shipper) for endangered species − Certificate of Product Registration
Motor Vehicles	− Permit to No-Dollar Importation of Used Motor Vehicle and Affidavit of Undertaking − Authority to Import Under EO 782 As Amended By EOs 354 and 361 (Used Trucks, Engines, special Purpose Vehicles) and Joint Affidavit of Undertaking − Permit for Spare Parts Importation (for Motorcycles and Motor Vehicles) and Affidavit
Movie/TV Products	− Import Permit (for Movie and TV Products)
Pesticides	− Registration of a Pesticide Active Ingredient − Registration of a Pesticide Product
Plants and Plant Products	− Permit to Import Plants and Plant Products − Plants and Plant Products derived from or that include GMO Genetically Modified materials are subject to permit control per AO2002. − Phytosanitary Certification
Radio Transmitter(s), Transceiver(s)	− Permit to Purchase/Possess Radio Transmitter(s),Transceiver(s)
Videograms (DVDs, Video-CDs, VHS Tapes)	− PermitforVideogramImportClearance

자료: OIS 해외진출 정보 시스템〉국가 정보〉필리핀〉수입 인증

2. 수입신고/심사 검사

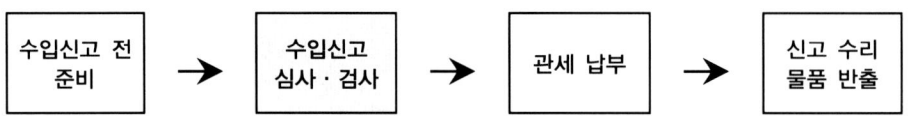

- □ 필리핀 세관은 수입신고 사항을 신속 통관(Super Green Lane)과 일반 통관(Ordinary Green lane)으로 나누어 처리함
  - ○ 신속 통관(Super Green Lane)의 경우 우수 인증 수입업체를 대상으로 화물 도착 전에 전자 서류로 통관을 신청하면 물품 도착 후 추가 서류 및 실제 검사 없이 통관을 진행할 수 있음
    - 그 외 수입 업체는 Red Lane(전수검사), Yellow Lane(추가 서류검사), Green Lane(서류검사)등으로 구분하여 통관됨

- □ 세관원은 물품의 가격을 평가하고 필요시에 샘플 검사를 진행하며 이 과정에서 송장, 선서 진술서, 제조원가 보고서 등을 조사함

- □ 필리핀에서의 수입통관은 수입허가품목/수입제한품목/수입금지품목으로 분류되어 이루어지며, 단순소비재인 경우와 단순소비재가 아닌 물품에 따라 수입 통관 절차가 달라지므로 필리핀 관세국(BOC)의 수입국(BIS)에 문의하여야 함

- □ FTA 적용 품목일 경우 마닐라 세관에 원산지 증명서를 제출해야 함
  - ○ 한국 관세청이나 상공회의소에서 AK FORM(원산지 증명서)을 발급받아 필리핀 세관에서 통관 시 수입신고 서류에 첨부해야 함

- □ 한-아세안 원산지 증명(C/O) 서류인 AK FORM 은 각 '란'마다 그 내용이 특정되어 있어, 상대국 수입자가 수입통관 시 필요한 내용을 추가하여 입력하기에 용이하지 않음

○ 원산지 증명서(C/O) FOB 가격란에 현지 화폐 단위로 기재해 줄 것을 요청하는 사례가 발생하였음

□ 필리핀 현지에서의 한-ASEAN 수출입 관련 전문 인력이 부족하여 통관이 지연되는 경우가 있으며 이를 해결하기 위해 주필리핀 한국대사관에 추가 전문 인력이 배치될 필요가 있음

□ 품목 분류 및 가격평가에 있어 필리핀 세관의 재량권이 적용되어 세관별로 품목 분류 및 가격평가 기준이 달라질 수 있고, 수입신고 과정상 관세 외 추가 비용이 발생할 수 있음

□ 업계의 필요에 따라 한-아세안 특혜관세 대상 품목을 명시한 자료 사본을 사용하고 있으나 자료의 정확성이 검증되지 않음
  ○ 한-아세안 FTA에서 시장개방 양허 대상으로 분류된 품목임에도 불구하고, 미양허 품목에 부과되는 기본세율을 적용하는 경우도 발생함

□ 원산지 검증 시 엄격한 입증서류를 요구하여 통관이 지연될 수 있음
  ○ C/O의 원본을 제출해야 하고 생산자와 수출자의 정보가 다를 경우 추가 증빙서류를 요구할 수 있음
  ○ 세 번 변경 시 원산지 기준을 적용함에도 상대국 세관의 검증 과정에서 생산 공정 세부내용, 원가자료 등을 요구하는 경우가 있음

□ 필리핀 현지 진출 업체 중 국내로부터 물품을 수입하면서 원산지 증명서(C/O)를 발급받았으나 필리핀 현지의 전자서명에 대한 이해 부족으로 통관 지연을 초래할 수 있음
  ○ 추후 서울세관에서 해당 기업의 C/O가 정상 발급된 것을 확인하면 필리핀이 한국의 관련 절차를 이해하고 정상처리해 주기로 약속함

□ 한국 관세청에서 발급한 한-아세안 FTA 원산지 증명서를 필리핀 관세국에 제출하였으나 동 증명서의 진위 여부가 문제시되어 통관이 지연된 사례가 발생하였음

□ 일반 상품과 달리 중고자동차는 사전 수입 승인품목으로 분류되어 필리핀 무역산업부의 BIS에서 사전 수입 승인을 받은 후 선적함[38]
   ○ 필리핀의 수입금지 대상 중고차는 12인승 이하의 승합차량(승용차 포함)임
      - 12인승을 초과하는 미니버스 및 일반 버스 등은 수입이 가능하며, 건설 중장비(지게차/포크레인/굴삭기/불도저/크레인/덤프트럭/믹서 트럭 등)도 수입 가능함

□ 사전 수입허가가 필요한 품목의 경우, 수입자가 현지 세관에 물품이 도착된 이후에 수입 허가 서류를 제출하면 '수입허가를 받지 않은' 사례에 해당되어 30%의 벌금이 부과될 수 있음

□ 필리핀 세관은 최근 국세청과 관세청 간의 합동조사 과정에서 화교기업이 보유한 600여 장의 위조 원산지 증명서(C/O)를 적발한 계기로, 수입업체가 제출하는 면세용 원산지 증명서의 위조 여부를 철저히 확인하도록 지시한 바 있음[39]
   ○ 2010년 필리핀이 체결한 각종 자유무역협정에 근거하여 면세 또는 감세 수입신고 된 건수는 54,000건으로 집계되었음
   ○ 원산지 증명서의 위조 또는 허위기재가 적발된 경우 관세 추징은 물론 밀수 혐의로 형사고발 조치되며, 의심되는 사안의 경우 기재 내용에 대한 정밀 조사와 함께 수출국 발급기관에 발급 사실에 대한 진위 여부 확인을 요청함
      - 관련 대상국은 중국, 일본, 한국, 호주, 뉴질랜드, 인도 등

---

38) OIS 해외진출 정보 시스템〉필리핀 해외투자 진출 정보 카페〉해외투자 뉴스레터 No. 12
39) OIS 해외진출 정보 시스템〉필리핀 비즈니스 커뮤니티〉해외투자 뉴스레터 No. 65 '필리핀 세관, FTA 원산지 증명서 철저 확인 지시'

3. 관세 납부

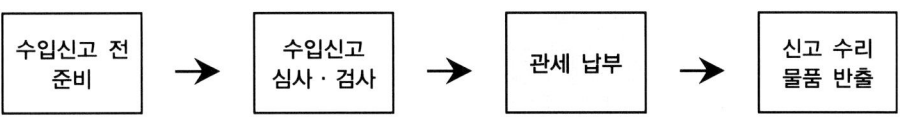

- 필리핀의 관세 및 부가세 납부 방식은 세관에 등록된 수입자 거래은행을 통해 계좌이체 방식으로 납부함
  - 세관원은 관세 상응 담보나 관세 납부를 확인한 후 수입신고를 수리하며 해당 담보의 경우 국내선하증권, 은행지불보증, 채권 등이 있음

- 필리핀의 최혜국(MFN) 관세율은 일반적으로 0~30% 사이이며, 필리핀 관세 및 세관법(TCCP)에 근거하여 자유무역협정 체결 여부에 따라 특혜관세율(preferential rate)이 적용됨

- 한-ASEAN 자유무역협정상의 양허관세를 적용할 경우에도 수입관세를 면제 또는 감면받을 수 있으나 12% 부가세는 필수적으로 납부해야 함
  - 부가세는 CIF Manila 가격에 수입 관세를 더한 금액의 12%임
  - 임시자유수입품목, 세관관세창고(Customs bonded warehouse)로 들어오는 품목, 특별법에 따라 수입된 품목 등과 같은 특정 수입품에 대한 관세를 면제함

- 수입업체와 브로커들은 수입 관련 기록을 수입 일자로부터 3년간 보관할 의무가 있음
  - 필리핀 관세국(Bureau of Customs)은 수입업체 및 브로커가 작성한 기록 문서에 대해 수입이 완료된 후 3년 안에 검사를 실시하여 세관 규칙 준수 여부를 확인할 권한을 지님

- 필리핀 세관에서 기존에 거래가 없던 신규반입 제품에 대해서 임의로 높은 관세를 부과하는 경우가 있어 사전에 관련 법규 및 관세율을 조사해야 함

□ 사후실사 시 원산지 판정에 오류가 있으면 수출자가 가산세를 부담해야 하며 원산지 판정 오류 시 가산세 부담 주체 기준이 분명하게 확립될 필요가 있음

□ 관세 환급에 관한 규정을 정해 놓고는 있으나 실제로 관세 환급을 받는 경우는 거의 없으며, Tax Credit을 발행하여 추후 관세 납부 시 이를 활용하여 보유한 Credit만큼 차감하는 것이 일반적임

□ 필리핀 관세청 관세표(TCCP: Tariff and Customs Code of the Philippines)의 Section 106항에서 관세환급(Drawback)에 관한 세부 사항을 설명함
  ○ 선박운항용 연료에 대한 관세 환급
    - 국제무역 혹은 연안무역에 이용되는 선박운항에 소요되는 오일에 부과된 수입 관세에 대해서는 부관된 관세의 99%를 초과하지 않는 한도 내에서 환급함
    - 재무부 장관의 승인이 있을 경우 관세 환급(현금) 혹은 관세 환급 예정금액 만큼의 세액공제보증서(Tax Credit)를 발행해 주도록 규정함

□ 도시가스 생산과 전력 생산에 사용되는 원유나 역청재(아스팔트원액)로부터 추출된 석유나 석유류에 대한 관세 환급 혜택이 있음
  ○ 전기업체나 가스업체가 아닌 기업이 원유나 역청제로부터 추출된 석유류를 수입한 후 전기/가스 생산업체에 동 제품을 그대로 판매하거나 가공하여 직접 혹은 간접적으로 판매한 경우에는 수입 시 부과된 관세의 50%를 환급함

□ 수출제품 생산을 위해 수입되는 자재에 대한 관세 환급에 해당되는 품목은 수출제품의 원료, 포장, 장식, 상표 부착 등에 사용된 자재에 한함
  ○ 수출용 자재에 대한 관세 환급은 실제 수출제품에 사용된 양 만큼에 대하여 관세 환급(현금) 혹은 관세 환급 예정금액 만큼의 세액공제보증서(Tax Credit)를 발행해 주도록 규정하였음

□ 환급 과정상에서 수출제품의 제조 및 생산에 실제 사용된 수입자재의 수량(분량) 및

가격과 실제 납부된 관세를 서류상으로 입증해야 함
- ○ 관세 환급(현금) 혹은 관세 환급 예정금액에 대한 세액공제 보증서(Tax Credit)는 자재 수입 시 납부된 관세의 100%를 초과할 수 없음
- ○ 수입자는 해당 자재가 필리핀에서 생산되고 있지 않거나 이에 대한 경쟁력 있는 대용 자재가 없다는 사실을 필리핀의 경제개발청(NEDA: National Economic and Development Authority)에서 확인받아야 함
- ○ 수입된 자재는 수입일로부터 1년 안에 제품으로 수출되어야 하고 수출 후 6개월 안에 해당 물품에 대한 관세 환급(현금) 혹은 세액공제 보증서(Tax Credit)를 청구해야함
- ○ 같은 수입자재로부터 2가지 혹은 그 이상의 수출제품이 만들어진 경우의 관세 환급에 대한 배분(할당)은 형평성에 기초하여 조정될 수 있음
  - 관세 환급 신청비는 건당 500페소로 하며 상황에 따라 변동될 수 있음

□ 필리핀 관세청의 관세표(TCCP: Tariff and Customs Code of the Philippines) Section 106 항에 근거하여 재무부 장관이 분할 관세 환급에 대한 규정과 시행에 대하여 공표할 수 있음

4. 신고 수리 및 물품 반출

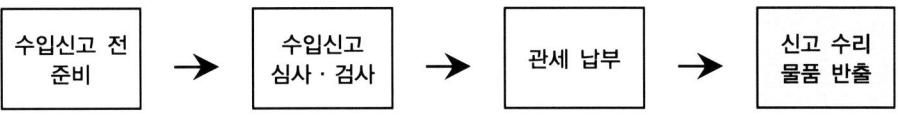

□ 세관은 OLRS(on-line release system)로 은행으로부터 관세 납부 사실을 통보받은 후에 수입자에게 화물을 양도함

□ 보세구역 반입물품은 통관 항 도착일로부터 최대 1년간 장치될 수 있으며 개인 창고

사용료는 세관 지정의 보세창고 이용료를 초과할 수 없음

□ 수입자는 마닐라 항만 및 해운사에 부두 사용료(Port Charge)를 납부해야 하며 통상 물류업체가 이를 대납하고 청구서에 일괄적으로 포함시킴
  ○ 필리핀 투자위원회(BOI)와 경제자유구역청(PEZA)에 등록된 업체들의 경우 EO226(Omnibus Investment Act)에 의거하여 자격요건이 충족되면 부두 사용료에 부과되는 부가세가 차감되며 THC(Terminal Handling Charge)라는 컨테이너 화물에 대해서만 부가세를 부과함

□ 자본재를 수입할 때 관세 면제 혜택을 받은 기업이 해당 자본재를 매각하게 될 경우 관세 회피의 여지가 있으므로 해당 기업이 5년 내에 면세품을 재판매할 경우에는 정상 관세의 2배를 납부해야 함
  ○ 필리핀 투자위원회(BOI) 등의 투자인센티브기관에 등록된 기업에 자본재를 매각할 경우 5년 내에 관세 면제 혜택을 받은 자본재 수입품을 재판매할 경우에도 관세 납부 의무가 면제될 수 있음

□ 필리핀의 3개 주요 세관은 마닐라 항구, NAIA 국제공항, 마닐라 국제 컨테이너항이 있음[40]
  ○ 마닐라 항구는 3개의 대표적인 항만인 North Harbor, South Harbor 및 그 사이에 위치한 MICT(Manila International Container Terminal)로 구성되어 있으며, 이들 3개 항만은 모두 필리핀 항만청(Philippine Ports Authority, PPA)의 소유임

□ 필리핀의 운송의 경우 마닐라 항을 중심으로 해운 운송이 이루어지나 마닐라 항의 정체가 심하고 물류비도 아시아에서 인도네시아와 함께 가장 높은 것으로 인식되고 있음
  ○ 다수의 항구에도 불구하고 높은 연한해운 비용과 낙후된 해운 시설 및 행정적인 측면이 문제점으로 지적되어 왔음

---

40) KOTRA〉Globalwindow〉해외진출정보〉투자속보 게제 정보〉필리핀 유망 산업별 투자환경 요약 발췌

○ 필리핀의 물류비는 전기요금과 함께 비즈니스 비용을 높이는 주요인으로 작용하며 높은 창고료와 내륙운송비가 부담으로 작용할 수 있음
○ 필리핀 국내 도서지역 간 해운비가 높으며 냉동식품류의 경우 내륙운송비가 해상운송비보다 높은 것으로 알려져 있음

□ 높은 보세창고비가 문제로 지적되고 있으며 필리핀 내 보세창고 설립을 위해서는 보세창고협의회인 ACOB의 동의가 있어야 하므로 이로 인해 보세창고 신규 오픈이 쉽지 않은 실정임
○ 필리핀의 보세창고료는 인도네시아와 더불어 비교적 높은 수준이며 보세창고 비는 3일 보관기준으로 100달러/CBM 정도임

□ 물품 도착 후 30일 내 통관 접수를 이행하지 않으면 벌금을 부과하며 이 경우 필리핀 세관은 수입자가 인수 의사가 없는 것으로 보고 물품을 압류 조치하게 되는데 이에 대한 압류를 해제(lifting of abandonment)하기 위해서는 시간과 비용이 소요됨
○ 기타의 사유로 물품을 반송해야 하는 경우에 복잡한 요건과 청구 비용 등으로 인해 불편을 초래할 수 있음

□ 세관 관행상 수입화물의 품질, 수출 또는 수입자의 계약 불이행 등의 사유로 필리핀 항구에 도착한 화물을 반송하고자 하는 경우 필리핀 세관이 반송을 승인하지 않고 관세, 부가세 납부와 함께 수입 통관한 후 반출하도록 유도하는 경우가 많음

□ 마닐라 항에서 수입자의 창고 혹은 공장까지의 육상 운송비용이 소요됨
○ 컨테이너 종류별로 화물의 무게에 따라 약간의 차등을 두어 지정된 육상운송비용이 발생하며 간혹 컨테이너 샤시 비용을 별도로 청구하기도 함
○ 마닐라 항에 도착한 화물은 Demmurage와 Storage 모두 통상 도착일을 포함하여 5일간의 Free Time이 주어짐
- Demmurage는 해당 컨테이너를 제공한 해운사에서 청구하는 금액이며 Storage는 마닐라 항만의 CY(컨테이너야드) Operator가 청구하는 금액임

□ 창고나 공장에 이송된 컨테이너는 즉시 화물을 꺼내고 반납해야 함
  ○ 이틀이 경과하면 해당 해운사에서 컨테이너 Detention Charge를 청구하게 되므로 주의해야 하며 이러한 경우 사전에 물류회사를 통해 해당 해운사와 합의한 후 컨테이너를 보관해야 함

참고문헌

외교통상부『외국의 통상환경 보고서 아·대양주』, 2010
USTR,『National Trade Estimate Report on Foreign Trade Barriers』, 2010
Worldbank,『Doing Business Report』, 2011

OIS 카페 필리핀 비즈니스 클럽, www.ois.go.kr
OIS 해외투자정보성공/실패 사례, www.ois.go.kr
마닐라 KBC, www.globalwindow.org
Board of Investments (BOI), www.boi.gov.ph
Department of Trade and Industry(DTI), www.dti.gov.ph
Business World, www.bworld.com.ph
Fedex 필리핀의 세계 통관정보, www.fedex.com〉customs tool

부록 Ⅰ. 비즈니스 팁

□ 필리핀에는 마닐라의 니노이아키노 국제공항(Ninoy Aquino International Airport, NAIA)을 비롯하여 국제공항이 전국 주요 지역에 소재하고 있음
  ○ 마닐라의 관문인 NAIA 1에 외자를 도입하여 NAIA 2, NAIA 3 등의 새로운 공항을 신축하였으며 필리핀 항공을 이용하는 경우 NAIA 2 터미널을 이용함

□ 마닐라 국제공항 입국 시에는 입국카드를 작성한 후 출입국 심사대를 통과하여 Arrival Gate를 통해 공항청사 건물로 나가면서 입국 카드 사본 1매와 수화물 티켓(통상 짐표로 호칭됨)을 제출해야 함
  ○ 출국할 경우 공항청사 건물에 입장할 때 X-ray 검색대를 통과해야 하는데 승객들이 몰리는 경우가 많고 공항 사정에 따라 20~30분을 기다릴 수 있기 때문에 항공기 출발 시간 기준 2시간 전까지 공항에 도착해야 함

□ 마닐라와 주요 도시 간의 비행시간은 서울 3.5시간, 동경 4시간, 상해 3.25시간, 대만 2시간, 홍콩 1.5시간, 방콕 3시간, 콸라룸푸르 3.5시간, 싱가포르 3시간 정도 소요됨

□ 필리핀에는 Manila, Cebu, Batangas, Zamboanga, Iloilo, Davao, San Fernando 등에 국제 항구가 있으며 운송비용은 도착지 및 계절에 따라 다르므로 제품 선적 시기에 맞춰 운송업체에 문의하는 것이 좋음

□ 필리핀 현지의 법인 혹은 개인 은행계좌 개설을 위해 필요한 요건[41]을 숙지해야 함
  ○ 필리핀 현지의 법인 은행계좌 개설을 위해서는 사무소(법인, 지사, 연락사무소, 지역본부 등)가 존재해야 하며, 개인의 경우 학생비자 이상 장기 체류 비자(관광비

---

[41] 필리핀 투자뉴스 67호 (11.04.30) ■ 투자진출 A to Z

자 제외)를 보유해야 함

☐ 현지 바이어가 국내업체에 대한 대금 결제를 거부할 경우 해당 바이어를 접촉하여 설득할 수 있는 방법이 용이하지 않음

☐ 필리핀은 공급자 우위의 시장인 측면이 있으며 의사결정이 일관적이지 않아 거래 제의를 할 경우에도 관심이 높지 않으면 답변을 하지 않는 경우가 많음
  ○ 수입업체 혹은 유통업체들이 자신들의 필요에 의해 추후 연락하는 형태를 취함

☐ 필리핀 수입 물품의 약 50% 정도가 대리점을 통해 수입되고 있으며, 에이전트나 유통업체들이 독점권을 요구하는 경우가 많음
  ○ 대리점은 해당 브랜드만을 취급하는 것이 아니고 여러 가지 상품 또는 경쟁 브랜드를 동시에 취급하고 있음

☐ 필리핀의 유통업체들은 재고 보유를 꺼려 물품을 소량으로 반복 구매하므로 신속한 배송이 중요함
  ○ 가구나 컴퓨터, 복사기 등을 구입하기 위해 가구점이나 사무용기기 판매점을 접촉해 보면 재고가 없는 경우가 많음
  ○ 재고가 있더라도 곧바로 예약금을 내고 예약을 하지 않으면 곧 다른 사람에게 판매가 되어 새로 수입품이나 제작품이 들어올 때까지 두세 달을 기다려야 하는 경우가 흔함

☐ 통상 4월(부활절), 12월(크리스마스, 연말 모임)에는 수입 상담이 거의 이루어지지 않고 의사 결정권을 지닌 기업주들이 해외 휴가를 즐기기 때문에 상담이 어려움

☐ 현지 상거래의 대부분을 장악하고 있는 화교상인들은 해외 거래선 구축 시 중국, 대만, 홍콩 등 중국계와의 거래를 선호함

□ 일반적으로 양복바지에 와이셔츠와 넥타이 착용이 정장으로 통용됨
　ㅇ 필리핀은 상하의 나라이므로 정장 상의를 생략하는 경우가 있으나 건물 내에서는 에어컨이 강하게 가동되므로 상담 장소에서 종일 상담하는 경우 상의를 준비하는 것이 좋음
　ㅇ 필리핀 전통의상인 바롱(Barong)을 입고 상담에 응하면 상대방에게 친밀감을 줄 수 있음

□ 친밀감 형성을 위하여 현지어인 '따갈로그어'를 일부 사용하는 것이 좋으나 단기간에 언어 습득이 쉽지 않은 어려움을 감안해 볼 때 간단한 인사 정도를 익히면 무난함
　ㅇ 상담자의 나이가 많거나 여성인 경우에는 상담자가 악수를 청하기 전까지 기다려야 함

□ 두터운 유대 관계가 형성되기 전에 고가의 선물을 주는 것은 거래에 악영향을 미칠 수 있으므로 한국의 전통차나 기념품 같은 부담 없는 선물하는 것이 바람직함
　ㅇ 한국 인삼에 대한 인식이 좋으며 현지 회사 사장 및 주요 간부의 비서와 상의해서 선물을 구입하는 것이 바람직함

□ 특별히 터부시되는 것은 없으나 언성을 높이는 것은 매우 모욕적인 일로 간주되므로 주의해야 하며, 필리핀 남부 민다나오 섬의 회교권에서는 회교율법에 의한 금기 사항이 존재함
　ㅇ 한국인들이 다소 급한 성격이라는 점에서 상대방에게 언성을 높일 만한 사안에 대해 화를 내는 등의 반응에도 현지인들이 의아하게 생각하거나 자존심에 상처를 받는 경우가 있음
　ㅇ 손가락이나 손으로 탁자를 두드리는 것은 여성에 대한 모욕의 의미가 될 수 있음

□ 자존심이 매우 강하므로 종업원이든 누구든 무시하는 태도를 보이지 않는 것이 좋음
　ㅇ 직원이 잘못을 했더라도 다른 사람들이 있는 공개석상에서 야단을 치면 모욕을 받는다고 생각하므로 다른 사람들이 없는 곳으로 불러 잘못을 지적해야 함

○ 최근 몇 년간 한국인 방문객들이 현지인들을 노골적으로 무시하거나 모욕적으로 대하는 사건들이 현지 언론에도 계속 보도된 바 있어 현지인들의 감정을 상하게 하지 않도록 유의해야 함
○ 유흥가에서 과격하게 행동하면 신변에 위협을 느낀 상대방이나 경비원들이 권총을 발사할 수도 있으며 현지법에 의해 엄격하게 다스려지게 되므로 무리한 행동을 하지 않는 것이 좋음

부록 Ⅱ. 주요 유관 기관 정보

■ 주 필리핀 대한민국 대사관

웹페이지	http://embassy_philippines.mofat.go.kr
주소	122 Upper McKinley Road, McKinley Town Center, Fort Bonifacio, Taguig city 1634, Philippines

■ 대사관

전화번호	(63-2) 856-9210
팩스번호	(63-2) 856-9008, 9019
이메일	philippines@mofat.go.kr

■ 영사과

전화번호	(63-2) 856-9210
팩스번호	(63-2) 856-9024
이메일	ph04@mofat.go.kr

■ 세부명예총영사관

주소	Mezzanine Floor, UC-ICTC Bldg., Gov. Cuenco Avenue Banilad, Cebu City
전화/팩스	(63-32) 231-6345

■ KOTRA 마닐라 무역관(KBC)

웹페이지	www.kotra.or.kr - 해외무역관 - 마닐라 무역관
주소	UNIT 1504, 15F, BDO Equitable Tower, 8751 Paseo de Roxas St., Makati Manila
전화번호	(63-2) 893-1183, 3244
팩스번호	(63-2) 817-3369
이메일	manila@kotra.or.kr

■ 한필상공회의소(Korean Chamber of Commerce Philippines)

웹페이지	http://www.kccp.ph/
주소	Korean Chamber of Commerce Philippines.,Unit 1104 Antel Corporate Centre, 121 Valero Street, Salcedo Village, Philippines
전화번호	(63-2) 885-7342
팩스번호	(63-2) 885-7343

■ 필리핀 무역산업부(Department of Trade and Industry)

웹페이지	http://www.dti.gov.ph
주소	385 Industry and Investments Bldg., Sen. Gil Puyat Ave., Makati City, Philippines 1200
전화번호	(63-2) 751-0384
팩스번호	(63-2) 895-6487

■ Board of Investments(BOI)

웹페이지	http://www.boi.gov.ph
주소	Industry and Investments Building 385 Senator Gil Puyat Avenue, Makati City 1200 Metro Manila, Philippines
전화번호	(63-2) 897-6682, (63-2) 890-9308
이메일	nerbac@boi.gov.ph

■ Bangko Sentral ng Pilipinas(BSP)

웹페이지	http://www.bsp.gov.ph
주소	Mabini St. cor. P. Ocampo St., Malate Manila, Philippines 1004
전화번호	(63-2) 708-7701
이메일	bspmail@bsp.gov.ph

■ Nat'l Food Authority(NFA)

웹페이지	http://www.nfa.gov.ph
주소	National Food Authority Department of Agriculture North Avenue, Diliman, Quezon City
전화번호	(63-2) 453-3900, (63-2) 981-3800
팩스번호	Fax No. (63-2) 453-3900
이메일	e-mailnfa@nfa.gov.ph

■ Nat'l Computer Center

웹페이지	http://www.ncc.gov.ph
주소	Commission on Information & Communications Technology C.P. Garcia Avenue, U.P. Diliman, Quezon City
전화번호	(63-2) 920-0101
팩스번호	(63-2) 920-7414

■ Nat'l Statistics Office

웹페이지	http://www.census.gov.ph
주소	Ramon Magsaysay Boulevard Sta. Mesa, Manila 1008 P. O. Box 779 PHILIPPINES
전화번호	(63-2) 716-0807 / (63-2) 713-7074
팩스번호	Fax: (63-2) 713-7073 / 715-6503
이메일	C.Ericta@census.gov.ph

부록 Ⅲ. Executive Orders

Executive Orders 52[1]:

Signed 5 August 2011/Published: 12 August 2011 Manila Bulletin

Temporary wavier of the reciprocal tariff treatment on certain articles to implement the agreement between the republic of the Republic of the Philippines and the Republic of Korea on the compensatory measure in relation to the delayed implementation of Philippine Tariff Concessions under the framework agreement on comprehensive economic cooperation among the governments of the member countries of the association of Southeast Asian Nations and the Republic of Korea.

WHEREAS, Paragraph 5 (b) (ii) of Annex 1 of the Agreement on Trade in Goods under the Framework Agreement on Comprehensive Economic Cooperation among the Governments of the Member Countries of the Association of Southeast Asian Nations and the Republic of Korea (AKFTA TIG Agreement) stipulates that ASEAN 6, which includes the Philippines, shall eliminate tariffs for at least 90% of the tariff lines placed in the Normal Track not later than 1 January 2009. Executive Order (EO) No. 812 (s.2009), which implements the said provision, took effect six (6) months behind schedule or on 07 July 2009;

WHEREAS, EO No.638 (s. 2007) grants reciprocal tariff treatment to products in the Sensitive Track of Parties to the AKFTA TIG Agreement;

WHEREAS, during its meeting on 17 May 2011, the National Economic and Development Authority (NEDA) Board approved the temporary waiver of reciprocal tariff treatment on certain articles as compensatory measure to the Republic of Korea;

WHEREAS, Note Verbale number 11 1953 dated 08 July 2011 issued by the Philippine Department of Foreign Affairs and Note Verbale Number KPH 2011-093-P dated 14 July 2011 issued by the Embassy of the Republic of Korea shall be regarded as constituting an

---

[1] 필리핀 관세위원회 해당링크: http://www.tariffcommission.gov.ph/EO%2052%20Annex.pdf

agreement between the two Governments to implement the compensation package; and,

WHEREAS, Section 402 of Presidential Decree No. 1464 or the Tariff and Customs Code of 1978, as amended, authorizes the President, upon the recommendation of NEDA, to modify import duties (including any necessary change in classification) and other import restrictions as are required or appropriate to carry out and promote foreign trade with other countries;

NOW, THEREFORE, I, BENIGNO SIMEON AQUINO III, President of the Republic of the Philippines, by virtue of the powers vested in me by law, do hereby order:

SECTION 1. Rates of Import Duty. The articles specifically listed in the Annex hereof, as classified under Section 104 of the Tariff and Customs Code of 1978, as amended, shall be imposed the AKFTA rate in accordance with the schedule indicated opposite each article for a period of twelve (12) months. The AKFTA rates so indicated shall be accorded to imports coming from parties to the AKFTA TIG agreement subject to qualification under the Rules of Origin as provided for in the said Agreement.

The nomenclature and the rates of import duty on tariff headings not enumerated and those listed but replaced by the symbol "X X X" shall remain in force and effect.

SECTION 2. Levy on Articles. Upon the effectivity of this Executive Order, all articles listed in the Annex which are entered and withdrawn from warehouses in the Philippines for consumption shall be levied the AKFTA rates of duty for twelve (12) months, thereafter, the reciprocal tariff treatment provided under EO No. 638 shall apply.

SECTION 3. Separability Clause. If any provision of this Executive Order is declared invalid or unconstitutional, the other provisions not affected thereby shall remain valid and subsisting.

SECTION 4. Repealing Clause. All orders, rules, regulations, and issuances, or parts thereof, which are inconsistent with this Executive Order, are hereby repealed, amended, or modified accordingly.

SECTION 5. Effectivity. This Executive Order shall take effect immediately upon publication in a newspaper of general circulation.

DONE, in the City of Manila, this 5th day of August, in the year of Our Lord, Two Thousand and Eleven.

By the President:(Sgd.) PAQUITO N. OCHOA, JR.
Executive Secretary

Executive Order 895

Signed:18 June 2010/Published: 30 June 2010 The Manila Times

Modifying the rate of import duty on refined coconut oil as provided for under the tariff and customs code, as amended, in order to implement the transfer from the sensitive track to the normal track category under the ASEAN-Korea Free Trade Area(AKFTA)

WHEREAS, the Agreement on Trade in Goods (TIG) under the Framework Agreement on Comprehensive Economic Cooperation Among the Governments of the Member Countries of the Association of the Southeast Asian Nations and the Republic of Korea (Framework Agreement) was signed on 24 August 2006 in Kuala Lumpur, Malaysia;

WHEREAS, Annex 2 paragraph 6 of the Framework Agreement under the AKFTA provides that:

"… any Party may unilaterally accelerate the tariff reduction and/or elimination for its tariff lines placed in the Sensitive Track at any time if it so wishes. Nothing in this Agreement shall prevent any Party from unilaterally transferring any tariff line from the Sensitive Track into the Normal Track at any time if it so wishes."

WHEREAS, an accelerated reduction of the preferential tariff rate on refined coconut oil shall allow domestic exporters to take full advantage of the benefits under the AKFTA;

WHEREAS, the National Economic and Development Authority (NEDA) Board approved on 25 May 2010 the transfer of refined coconut oil from the Sensitive Track to the Normal Track and the reduction of its AKFTA rate to zero;

WHEREAS, Section 402 of the Tariff and Customs Code of 1978 (Presidential Decree No. 1464), as amended, empowers the President of the Republic of the Philippines, upon the recommendation of the NEDA, to modify import duties for the promotion of foreign trade;

NOW, THEREFORE, I, GLORIA MACAPAGAL-ARROYO, President of the Republic of the Philippines, by virtue of the powers vested in me by law, do hereby order:

SECTION 1. The article specifically listed in the Annex (Article Transferred from Sensitive Track to the Normal Track Category under the AKFTA) hereof, shall be subject to the rates of import duty as indicated in Columns 4 to 6 of said Annex.

SECTION 2. The applicable rate shall be the AKFTA preferential tariff, subject to the submission of the proper Certificate of Origin (CO) Form AK. Pursuant to Section 1313(a) of the Tariff and Customs Code of the Philippines, as amended, the Tariff Commission may, upon request, issue tariff classification rulings to confirm the applicable rates of duty of particular products covered by this Executive Order.

SECTION 3. From the date of effectivity of this Executive Order, the article listed in the Annex entered into or withdrawn from warehouses in the Philippines for consumption shall be imposed the rate of duty therein prescribed subject to compliance with the Rules of Origin as provided for in Article 5 of the Agreement on TIG under the Framework Agreement.

SECTION 4. Nothing in this Executive Order shall preclude the Philippines from invoking its right of recourse to all trade remedy measures provided for in its law, the AKFTA Agreement and relevant international agreements as an effective device against import surges.

SECTION 5. The provisions of this Executive Order are hereby declared separable and in the event any of such provisions is declared invalid or unconstitutional, the other provisions, which are not affected thereby, remain in force and effect.

SECTION 6. All presidential issuances, administrative rules and regulations, or parts thereof, which are contrary to or inconsistent with this Executive Order are hereby revoked or modified accordingly.

SECTION 7. This Executive Order shall take effect fifteen (15) days following its complete publication in the Official Gazette or in a national newspaper of general circulation.

Done in the City of Manila, this 18th day of June, in the year of Our Lord, Two Thousand and Ten.

Signature of the President

By the President:

LEANDRO R. MENDOZA

Executive Secretary

ANNEX

Article transferred from sensitive track to the normal track categoty under the ASEAN-Korea Free Trade Agreement(AKFTA)

Hdg. No.	AHTN Code 2007	DESCRIPTION	Applicable AKTA Rate of Duty (%)		
			2010	Starting 01 January	
				2011	2012
(1)	(2)	(3)	(4)	(5)	(6)
15.13		Coconut (copra), palm kernel or babassu oil and fractions thereof, whether or not refined, but not chemically modified. - Coconut (copra) oil and its fractions:			
	1513.19	- - Other:			
	1513.19.20	- - - Refined oil	0	0	0

Executive Order No. 812[2]

Signed:15 June 2009/Published: 23 June 2009 The Manila Times

Modifying the rates of duty on certain imported articles as provided for under the tariff and customs code of 1978, as amended, in order to implement the commitment to reduce the tariff rates on ninety percent (90%) of the products in the normal track to zero with flexibility under the ASEAN-Korea Free Trade Area(AKFTA)

WHEREAS, Articles 1.3 and 2.1 of the Framework Agreement on Comprehensive Economic Cooperation (Framework Agreement) Between the Association of South East Asian Nations (ASEAN) and the Republic of Korea reflects the Parties' commitment to establish the ASEAN - Korea Free Trade Area covering Trade in Goods;

---

[2] 필리핀 관세위원회 해당링크:
http://www.tariffcommission.gov.ph/EO%20812%20akfta_annex_final_for_publication.pdf

WHEREAS, Article 3.2(a) of the Trade in Goods (TIG) Agreement of the Framework Agreement provides that tariff lines placed in the Normal Track by each Party shall have their respective applied MFN tariff rates gradually reduced and eliminated in accordance with the modalities set out in Annex 1 of the Agreement with the objective of achieving the targets prescribed in the threshold therein;

WHEREAS, the aforesaid Annex 1 Section 5(b) of the TIG Agreement provides that ASEAN 6 shall implement the following targets and thresholds: (ii) eliminate tariffs for at least 90% of the tariff lines placed in the Normal Track not later than 1 January 2009; (iii) eliminate all tariff lines by 2010 with flexibility on 5% of the total lines,or as listed in the agreed schedule, not later than 1 January 2012;

WHEREAS, the NEDA Board during its meeting on 31 March 2009 approved the grant of AKFTA rates of 0% on 90% of the products in the Normal Track with flexibility;

WHEREAS, Section 402 of the Tariff and Customs Code of 1978 (PD 1464), as amended, empowers the President of the Republic of the Philippines, upon the recommendation of the National Economic and Development Authority, to modify import duties to the promotion of foreign trade;

NOW, THEREFORE, I, GLORIA MACAPAGAL-ARROYO, President of the Republic of the Philippines, by virtue of the powers vested in me by law, do hereby order;

SECTION 1. The articles specifically listed in the Annex (Articles Granted Tariff Concession Under the Normal Track of the ASEAN – Korea Free Trade Area) hereof, as classified under Section 104 of the Tariff and Customs Code of 1978, as amended, shall be subject to the AKFTA rates in accordance with the schedule indicated in Columns 4-6 of the Annex. The AKFTA rates so indicated shall be accorded to imports coming from the parties of the Agreement on Trade in Goods of the Framework Agreement applying tariff concession to the same product pursuant to Article 3 of the Agreement on Trade in Goods of the Framework Agreement.

SECTION 2. For ASEAN 8 (i.e. Brunei Darussalam, Cambodia, Indonesia, Lao Peoples Democratic Republic, Malaysia, Myanmar, Singapore and Vietnam) the applicable rate shall be the AKFTA rate, subject to the submission of the proper Certificate of Origin, Form AK. The Tariff Commission pursuant to Section 1313(a) of the Tariff and Customs Code of the Philippines, as amended, may, upon request, issue tariff classification rulings to confirm the applicable rates of duty of particular products subject to this section.

SECTION 3. In the event that any subsequent change is made in the basic (MFN) Philippine rate of duty on any of the articles listed in the Annex to a rate lower than the rate prescribed in Columns 4-6 of the Annex, such article shall automatically be accorded the corresponding reduced duty.

SECTION 4. From the date of effectivity of this Order, all articles listed in the Annex entered into or withdrawn from warehouses in the Philippines for consumption shall be imposed the rates of duty therein prescribed subject to compliance with the Rules of Origin as provided for in Article 5 of the Agreement on Trade in Goods of the Framework Agreement.

SECTION 5. All Presidential issuances, administrative rules and regulations, or parts thereof, which are contrary to or inconsistent with this Executive Order are hereby revoked or modified accordingly.

SECTION 6. This Executive Order shall take effect fifteen (15) days following its complete publication in the official gazette or in a newspaper of general circulation in the Philippines.

Done in the City of Manila, this 15th day of June, in the year of Our Lord Two Thousand and Nine.

GLORIA MACAPAGAL ARROYO
By the President:
EDUARDO R. ERMITA
Executive Secretary

Executive Order 638[3)4)]

Signed: July 21, 2007/published: November 1, 2007 The Manila Times

Modifying the rates of duty on certain imported articles as provided under the tariff and customs code of 1978, as amended, in order to implement the commitment to grant reciprocal tariff rate treatment on tariff lines included in the sensitive track of the ASEAN-KOREA Free Trade Area(AKFTA)

WHEREAS, the Framework Agreement on Comprehensive Economic Cooperation (Framework Agreement) between the Association of South East Asian Nations (ASEAN) and

---

3) 필리핀 관세위원회 해당링크:
   http://www.tariffcommission.gov.ph/EO%20638%20appendix1_Senstive%20List_annexA_5.pdf
4) 필리핀 관세위원회 해당링크:
   http://www.tariffcommission.gov.ph/EO%20638%20AKFTA_HSL_AppendixII.pdf

Korea was signed by the Heads of Government/State of the ASEAN Member States and Korea on 13 December 2005 in Kuala Lumpur, Malaysia;

WHEREAS, Articles 1.3 and 2.1 of the Framework Agreement reflect the Parties' commitment to establish the ASEAN - Korea Free Trade Area (AKFTA) covering trade in goods by 2010 for ASEAN 6 and Korea, and by 2016 or 2018 for the newer ASEAN Member States;

WHEREAS, the Agreement on Trade in Goods of the Framework Agreement was signed by the Economic Ministers of the Parties on 24 August 2006 in Kuala Lumpur, Malaysia;

WHEREAS, Article 3(2)(b) of the Agreement on Trade in Goods of the Framework Agreement provides that tariff lines placed in the Sensitive Track by each Party shall have their respective applied MFN tariff rates reduced or eliminated within timeframes in accordance with the modalities set out in Annex 2 of the Agreement;

WHEREAS, the aforesaid Annex of the Agreement on Trade in Goods of the Framework Agreement provides that the reciprocal tariff rate treatment of tariff lines placed by an exporting Party in the Sensitive Track, excluding Group E, while the same tariff lines are placed by the importing party in the Normal Track, shall be governed by the following conditions: (a) the tariff rate for a tariff line placed by an exporting Party in the Sensitive Track, excluding Group E, must be at 10% or below and the exporting Party has given notification to that effect to the other Parties in order for that exporting Party to enjoy reciprocity; (b) the reciprocal tariff rate to be applied to a tariff rate of exporting Party's tariff line, or the Normal Track tariff rate of the same tariff line of an importing Party from whom reciprocity is sought, whichever is higher; (c) notwithstanding subparagraph (b), the importing party can, on its own discretion, apply its Normal Track tariff rate even if such rate is lower than the tariff rate of the exporting party; and (d) the reciprocal tariff rate to be applied to a tariff line placed by an exporting Party in the Sensitive Track shall in no case exceed the applied MFN rate of the same tariff line of an importing Party from whom reciprocity is sought.

WHEREAS, Section 402 of the Tariff and Customs Code of 1978 (PD 1464), as amended, empowers the President of the Republic of the Philippines, upon the recommendation of the National Economic and Development Authority, to modify import duties for the promotion of foreign trade;

NOW, THEREFORE, I, GLORIA MACAPAGAL-ARROYO, President of the Republic of the Philippines, by virtue of the powers vested in me by law, do hereby order:

SECTION 1. The products of the other Parties under their Sensitive Track in Annex "A" hereof, will be accorded reciprocal tariff treatment as governed by Paragraph 7 of Annex 2 of the Agreement on Trade in Goods after a notification has been received from the Party/Parties that the rates of duty of products in its Sensitive Track are at 10% and below. For confirmation of the products covered by this reciprocity rule, the Tariff Commission, upon request shall issue tariff classification rulings pursuant to Section 1313(a) of the Tariff and Customs Code, as amended.

SECTION 2. From the date of effectivity of this Order, all articles listed in Annex "A" entered into or withdrawn from warehouses in the Philippines for consumption shall be imposed the rates of duty therein prescribed subject to compliance with the Rules of Origin as provided for in Article 5 of the Agreement on Trade in Goods of the Framework Agreement.

SECTION 3. All presidential issuances, administrative rules and regulations, or parts thereof, which are contrary to or inconsistent with this Executive Order are hereby revoked or modified accordingly.

SECTION 4. This Executive Order shall take effect immediately following its complete publication in the Official Gazette or in a newspaper of general circulation in the Philippines.

Done in the City of Manila, this 21st day of July, in the year of Our Lord, Two Thousand and Seven.

부록 IV. TARIFF AND CUSTOMS CODE OF THE PHILIPPINES (TCCP)[5]

VOLUME I

TITLE 1. - IMPORT TARIFF

SEC. 100. Imported Articles Subject to Duty.

All articles, when imported from any foreign country into the Philippines, shall be subject to duty upon each importation, even though previously exported from the Philippines, except as otherwise specifically provided for in this Code or in other laws.

SEC. 101. Prohibited Importations.

The importation into the Philippines of the following articles is prohibited:
1. Dynamite, gunpowder, ammunitions and other explosives, firearms and weapons of war, and parts thereof, except when authorized by law.
2. Written or printed articles in any form containing any matter advocating or inciting treason, or rebellion, insurrection, sedition or subversion against the Government of the Philippines, or forcible resistance to any law of the Philippines, or containing any threat to take the life of, or inflict bodily harm upon any person in the Philippines.
3. Written or printed articles, negatives or cinematographic film, photographs, engravings, lithographs, objects, paintings, drawings or other representation of an obscene or immoral character.
4. Articles, instruments, drugs and substances designed, intended or adapted for producing unlawful abortion, or any printed matter which advertises or describes or gives directly or indirectly information where, how or by whom unlawful abortion is produced.
5. Roulette wheels, gambling outfits, loaded dice, marked cards, machines, apparatus or

---

5) http://www.tariffcommission.gov.ph/listof1.html

mechanical devices used in gambling or the distribution of money, cigars, cigarettes or other articles when such distribution is dependent on chance, including jackpot and pinball machines or similar contrivances, or parts thereof.

6. Lottery and sweepstakes tickets except those authorised by the Philippine Government, advertisements thereof, and lists of drawings therein.
7. Any article manufactured in w hole or in part of gold, silver or other precious metals or alloys thereof, the stamps, brands or marks or which do not indicate the actual fineness of quality of said metals or alloys.
8. Any adulterated or misbranded articles of food or any adulterated or misbranded drug in violation of the provisions of the "Food and Drugs Act ".
9. Marijuana, opium, poppies, coca leaves, heroin or any other narcotics or synthetic drugs which are or may hereafter be declared habit forming by the President of the Philippines, or any compound, manufactured salt, derivative, or preparation thereof, except when imported by the 2 Government of the Philippines or any person duly authorised by the Dangerous Drugs Board, for medicinal purposes only.
10. Opium pipes and parts thereof, of whatever material. All other articles and p arts thereof, the importation o f which i s prohibited by law o r rules and regulations issued by competent authority. (As amended by Presidential Decree No. 34)

SEC. 102. Abbreviations.

The following abbreviations used in this Code shall represent the terms indicated:
ad val. For ad valorem.
e.g. For exempli gratia meaning for example'.
i.e. For'id est' meaning 'that is'.
hd. For head. kg For kilogram.
kgs For kilograms.
I For litre.
g.w. For gross weight.
I.W. For legal weight.
n.w. For net weight.

SEC. 103. General Rules for the Interpretation of the Harmonized System.

Classification of goods in the Nomenclature shall be governed by the following principles:
1. The titles of Sections, Chapters and Sub -Chapters are provided for ease of reference only; for legal purposes, classification shall be determined according to the terms of the

headings and any relative Section or Chapter Notes and, provided such headings or Notes do not otherwise require, according to the following provisions.

2. (a) Any reference in a heading to an article shall be -taken to include a reference to that article incomplete or unfinished, provided that, as presented, the incomplete or unfinished article has the essential character of the complete or finished article. It shall also be taken to include a reference to that article complete or finished (or falling to be classified as complete or finished by virtue of this Rule), presented unassembled or disassembled.

(b) Any reference in a heading to a material or substance shall be taken to include a reference to mixtures or combinations of that material or substance with other materials or substances. Any reference to goods of a given material or substance shall be taken to include a reference to goods consisting wholly or partly of such material or substance. The classification of goods consisting of more than one material or substance shall be according to the principles of Rule 3.

When by application of Rule 2 (b) or for any other reason, goods are, prima facie, classifiable under two or more headings, classification shall be effected as follows:

a. The heading which provides the most specific description shall be preferred to headings providing a more general description. However, when two or more headings each refer to part only of the materials or substances contained in mixed or composite goods or to part only of the items in a set put up for retail sale, those headings are to be regarded as equally specific in relation to those goods, even if one of them gives a more complete or precise description of the goods.

b. Mixtures, composite goods consisting of different materials or made up of different components, and goods put up in sets for retail sale, which cannot be classified by reference to 3 (a), shall be classified as if they consisted of the material or component which gives them their essential character, insofar as this criterion is applicable.

c. When goods cannot be classified by reference to 3 (a) or 3 (b), they shall be classified under the heading which occurs last in numerical order among those which equally merit consideration.

1. Goods which cannot be classified in accordance with the above Rules shall be classified under the heading appropriate to the goods to which they are most akin.

2. In addition to the foregoing provisions, the following Rules shall apply in respect of the goods referred to therein:

a. Camera cases, musical instrument cases, gun cases, drawing instrument cases, necklace cases and similar containers, specially shaped or fitted to contain a specific article or set of articles, suitable for long -term use and presented with the articles for which they are intended, shall be classified with such articles when of a kind normally sold therewith. The Rule does not, however, apply to containers which give the whole its essential character; Subject to the provisions of the Rule 5 (a) above, packing materials and packing containers presented

3. For legal purposes, the classification of goods in the subheadings of a heading shall be determined according to the terms of those subheadings and any related Subheading Notes and, mutatis mutandis, to the above Rules, on the understanding that only subheadings at the same level are comparable. For the purposes of the Rule the relative Section and Chapter Notes also apply, unless the context otherwise requires.

SEC. 104. Rates of Import Duty.

All Tariff Sections, Chapters, headings and subheadings and the rates of import duty under Section 104 of Presidential Decree No. 34 and all subsequent amendment issues under Executive Orders and Presidential Decrees are hereby adopted and form part of this Code.

There shall be levied, collected, and paid upon all imported articles the rates of duty indicated in the Section under this Section except as otherwise specifically provided for in this Code:

Provided, that, the maximum rate shall not exceed one hundred per cent ad valorem.

The rates of duty herein provided or subsequently fixed pursuant to Section four hundred one of this Code shall be subject to periodic investigation by the Tariff Commission and may be revised by the President upon recommendation of the National Economic and Development Authority.

The rates of duty herein provided shall apply to all products whether imported directly or indirectly of all foreign countries, which do not discriminate against Philippine export products. An additional 100% across -the -board duty shall be levied on the products of any foreign country which discriminates against Philippine export products.

The tariff Sections, Chapters, headings and subheadings and the rate of import duty under Section One Hundred Four of this Code shall be as follows:

SECTION 105. Conditionally-Free Importations.

The following articles shall be exempt from the payment of import duties upon compliance with the bed in, or with, the regulations which shall be promulgated by the Commissioner of Customs with Secretary of Finance; Provided, That any article sold, bartered, hired or used for purposes were intended for without prior payment of the duty, tax or other charges which would have been due and payable at the time of entry if the article had been entered without the benefit of this section, shall be subje:7. -c e importation shall constitute a fraudulent practice against customs revenue punishable under Section Thirty-six hundred and two, as amended, of this Code; Provided, further, That a sale pursuant to a judicial order or in liquidation of the estate of a deceased person shall not be subject to the preceding proviso, without prejudice to the payment of duties, taxes and other charges; Provided, finally, That the President may upon recommendation of the Secretary of Finance, suspend, disallow or completely withdraw, in whole or in part, any of the conditionally -free importation under this section:

1. Aquatic products (e.g., fishes, crustaceans, mollusks, marine animals, seaweeds, fish oil, roe), caught or gathered by fishing vessels of Philippine registry: Provided, That they are imported in such vessels or in crafts attached thereto: And provided, further, That they have not been landed in any foreign territory or, if so landed, they have been landed solely for transshipment with - - -T having been advanced in condition;

2. Equipment for use in the salvage of vessels or aircrafts, not available locally, upon identification and the giving of a bond in an amount equal to one and one -half times the ascertained duties, taxes and other charges thereon, conditioned for the exportation thereof or payment of .corresponding duties, taxes and other charges within six (6) months from the date of acceptance of the import entry: Provided, That the Collector of Customs may extend the time for exportation or payment of duties, taxes and other charges for a term not exceeding six (6) months from the expiration of the original period;

3. Cost of repairs, excluding the value of the article used, made in foreign countries upon vessels or aircraft documented, registered or licensed in the Philippines, upon proof satisfactory to the Collector of Customs (1) that adequate facilities for such repairs are not afforded in the Philippines, or (2) that such vessels or aircrafts, while in the regular course of her voyage or flight, was compelled by stress of weather or other casualty to put into a foreign port to make such & repairs in order to secure the safety, seaworthiness or airworthiness of the vessel or aircraft to enable her to reach her port of destination;

Articles brought into the Philippines for repair, processing or reconditioning to be re-exported upon completion of the repair, processing or reconditioning: Provided, That the Collector of Customs shall require the giving of a bond in an amount equal to one and one -half times the ascertained duties, taxes and other charges thereon, conditioned for the exportation thereof or payment of the corresponding duties, taxes and other charges within six (6) months from the date of acceptance of the import entry -,

4. Medals, badges, cups and other small articles bestowed as trophies or prizes, or those received or accepted as honorary distinction;
5. Personal and household effects belonging to residents of the Philippines returning from abroad including jewelry, precious stones and other articles of luxury which were formally declared and listed before departure and identified under oath before the Collector of Customs when exported from the Philippines by such returning residents upon their departure therefrom or during their stay abroad; personal and household effects including wearing apparel, articles of personal adornment (except luxury items), toilet articles, instruments related to one's profession and analogous personal or household effects, excluding vehicles, watercrafts, aircrafts, and animals purchased in foreign countries by residents of the Philippines which were necessary, appropriate and normally used for their comfort and convenience during their stay abroad, accompanying them on their return, or arriving within a reasonable time which, barring unforeseen and fortuitous events, in no case shall exceed sixty (60) days after the owner's return: Provided, That the personal and household effects shall neither be in commercial quantities nor intended for barter, sale o r h ire and t hat t he total dutiable value o f which s hall not exceed Ten Thousand Pesos (P -10,000.00): Provided further, That the returning resident has not previously availed of the privilege under this section within three hundred sixty -five (365) days prior to his arrival: Provided, finally, That a fifty per cent (50%) ad valorem duty across the board shall be levied and collected on the personal and household effects (except luxury items) in excess of Ten Thousand Pesos (4210,000.00). For purposes of this section, the phrase "returning residents" shall refer to nationals who have stayed in a foreign country for a period of at least six (6) months.

    a. In addition to the privilege granted under the immediately preceding paragraph, returning overseas contract workers shall have the privilege to bring in, duty and tax free, used home appliances, limited to one of every kind once in a given calendar year accompanying them on their return, or arriving within a reasonable time which, barring unforeseen and fortuitous events, in no case shall exceed sixty (60) days after the owner's return upon presentation of their original passport at the Port of Entry: Provided, That any excess of Ten Thousand Pesos (P10,000.00) for personal and household effects and/or of the number of duty and tax-free appliances as provided for under this section, shall be subject to the corresponding duties and taxes provided under this Code. For purposes of this section, the following words/phrases shall be understood to mean: (a) Overseas Contract Workers – Holders of Valid passports duly issued by the Department of Foreign Affairs and Certified by the Department of Labor and Employment/Philippine Overseas Employment Agency for overseas employment purposes. It covers all nationals working in a foreign country under employment contracts including Middle East Contract Workers, entertainers, domestic helpers, regardless of their employment status in the foreign country. (b) Calendar Year – shall cover the period from January 1 to December 31.

6. Wearing apparel, articles of personal adornment, toilet articles, portable tools and instrument. theatrical costumes and similar effects accompanying travelers, or tourists, or arriving within a reasonable time before or after their arrival in the Philippines, which are necessary and appropriate for the wear and use of such persons according to the nature of the journey, their comfort and convenience: Provided, That this exemption shall not apply to articles intended for other persons or for barter, sale or hire: Provided, further, That the Collector of Customs may. in his discretion, require either a written commitment o r a bond i n a n a mount equal to one and one -half times the ascertained duties, taxes and other charges conditioned for the exportation thereof or payment of the corresponding duties, taxes and other charges within three (3) months from the date of acceptance of the import entry: And Provided, finally, That t he Collector of Customs may extend the time for exportation or payment of duties, taxes and other charges for a term not exceeding three (3) months from the expiration of the original period;

   a. Personal and household effects and vehicles belonging to foreign consultants and experts hired by, and/or rendering service to, the government, and their staff or personnel and families, accompanying them or arriving within a reasonable time before or after their arrival in the Philippines, in quantities and of the kind necessary and suitable to the profession, rank or position of the person importing them, for their own use and not for barter, sale or hire provided that, the Collector of Customs may in his discretion require either a written commitment or a bond in an amount equal to one and one -half times the ascertained duties, taxes and other charges upon the articles classified under this subsection; conditioned for the exportation thereof or payment of the corresponding duties, taxes and other charges within six (6) months after the expiration of their term or contract; And Provided, finally, That the Collector of Customs may extend the time for exportation or payment of duties, taxes and other charges for term not exceeding six (6) months from the expiration of the original period;

7. Professional instruments and implements, tools of trade, occupation or employment, wearing apparel, domestic animals, and personal and household effects belonging to persons coming to settle in the Philippines or Filipinos and/or their families and descendants who are now residents or citizens of other countries, such parties hereinafter referred to as Overseas Filipinos, in quantities and of the class suitable to the profession, rank or position of the persons importing them, for their own use and not for barter or sale, accompanying such persons, or arriving within a reasonable time, in the discretion of the Collector of Customs, before or after the arrival of their owners, which shall not be later than February 28, 1979 upon the production of evidence satisfactory to the Collector of Customs that such persons are actually coming to settle in the Philippines, that change of residence was bona fide and that the privilege of free entry was never granted to them before or that such person qualifies under the provisions of Letters of Instructions 105, 163 and 210, and that the articles are brought from their former place of abode, shall be exempt from the payment of customs, duties and taxes: Provided, That vehicles, vessels, aircrafts, machineries and other similar articles for use in manufacture, shall not be classified hereunder;
8. Articles used exclusively for public entertainment, and for display in public expositions, or for exhibition or competition for prizes, and devices for projecting pictures and parts and appurtenances thereof, upon identification, examination, and appraisal and the giving of a bond in an amount equal to one and one -half times the ascertained duties, taxes and other charges thereon, conditioned for exportation thereof or payment of the corresponding duties, taxes and other charges within six (6) months from the date of acceptance of the import entry; Provided, That the Collector of Customs may extend the time for exportation or payment of duties, taxes and other charges f or a term not exceeding six (6) months from the expiration of the original period; and technical and scientific films when imported by technical, cultural and scientific institutions, and not to be exhibited for profit: Provided, further, That if any of the said films is exhibited for profit, the proceeds therefrom shall be subject to confiscation, in addition to the penalty provided under Section Thirty -six hundred and ten as amended, of this Code;
9. Articles brought by foreign film producers directly and exclusively used for making or recording motion picture films on location in the Philippines, upon their identification, examination and appraisal and the giving of a bond in an amount equal to one and one -half times the ascertained duties, taxes and other charges thereon, conditioned for exportation thereof or payment of the corresponding duties, taxes and other charges within six (6) months from the date of acceptance of the import entry, unless extended

by the Collector of Customs for another six (6) months ; photographic and cinematographic films, underdeveloped, exposed outside the Philippines by resident Filipino citizens or by producing companies of Philippine registry where the principal actors and artists employed for the production are Filipinos, upon affidavit by the importer a* identification that such exposed films are the same films previously exported from the Philippines As used in this paragraph, the terms "actors " and "artists " include the persons operating the photographic camera or other photographic and sound recording apparatus by which the film is made;

10. mportations for the official use of foreign embassies, legations, and other agencies of foreign governments: Provided, That those foreign countries accord like privileges to corresponding agencies of the Philippines. Articles imported for the personal or family use of the members and attaches of r - -TRW embassies, legations, consular officers and other representatives of foreign governments: Provided, That such privilege shall be accorded under special agreements between the Philippines and the countries which they represent: And Provided, further, That the privilege may be granted only upon specific instructions of the Secretary of Finance in each instance which be issued only upon request of the Department of Foreign Affairs;

11. Imported articles donated to, or for the account of, any duly registered relief organization, not operated for profit, for free distribution among the needy, upon certification by the Departrre -7 if Social Services and Development or the Department of Education, Culture and Sports. as the case may be;

12. Containers, holders and other similar receptacles of any material including kraft paper bags for locally manufactured cement for export, including corrugated boxes for bananas, pineapples and other fresh fruits for export, except other containers made of paper, paperboard and textile fabrics, which are of such character as to be readily identifiable and/or reusable for shipment or transportation of goods shall be delivered to the importer thereof upon identification examination and appraisal and the giving of a bond in an amount equal to one and one -half times the ascertained duties, taxes and other charges within six (6) months from the date of acceptance of the import entry;

13. Supplies which are necessary for the reasonable requirements of the vessel or aircraft in her voyage or flight outside the Philippines, including articles transferred from a bonded warehouse any collection district to any vessel or aircraft engaged in foreign trade, for use or consumption the passengers or its crew on board such vessel o r aircrafts as sea or air stores; o r article purchased abroad for sale on board a vessel or aircraft as saloon stores or air store supplies Provided, That any surplus or excess of

such vessel or aircraft supplies arriving from foreign ports or airports shall be dutiable;

14. Articles and salvage from vessels recovered after a period of two (2) years from the date of filling the marine protest or the time when the vessel was wrecked or abandoned, or parts of a foreign vessel or her equipment, wrecked or abandoned in Philippine waters or elsewhere: Provided That articles and salvage recovered within the said period of two (2) years shall be dutiable;

15. Coffins or urns containing human remain, bones or ashes, used personal and household effects (not merchandise) of the deceased person, except vehicles, the value of which does not exceed Ten Thousand Pesos (P10,000), upon identification as such;

16. Samples of the kind, in such quantity and of such dimension or construction as to render them unsalable or of no appreciable commercial value; models not adapted for practical use; and samples of medicines, properly marked "sample -sale punishable by law", for the purpose of introducing a new article in the Philippine market and imported only once in a quantity sufficient for such purpose by a person duly registered and identified to be engaged in that trade: Provided, That importations under this subsection shall be previously authorized by the Secretary of Finance: Provided, however, That importation of sample medicine shall be previously authorized by the Secretary of Health that such samples are new medicines not available in the Philippines: Provided, finally, That samples not previously authorized and/or properly marked in accordance with this section shall be levied the corresponding tariff duty.

Commercial samples, except those that are not readily and easily identifiable (e.g., precious and semi -precious stones, cut or uncut, and jewelry set with precious or semi -precious stones), the value of any single importation of which does not exceed ten thousand pesos (P -10,000) upon the giving of a bond in an amount equal to twice the ascertained duties, taxes and other charges thereon, conditioned for the exportation of said samples within six (6) months from the date of t he acceptance o f t he import entry or in default t hereof, t he payment o f t he corresponding duties, taxes and other charges. If the value of any single consignment of such commercial samples exceeds ten thousand pesos (P -1 0,000), the importer thereof may select any portion of same not exceeding in value of ten thousand pesos (P10,000) f or entry u rider the consumption, as the importer may elect;

17. Animals (except race horses), and plants for scientific, experimental, propagation, botanical, breeding, zoological and national defense purposes: Provided, That no live trees, shoots, plants, moss, and bulbs, tubers and seeds for propagation purposes may be imported under this section, except by order of the Government or other duly

authorized institutions: Provided, further, That the free entry of animals for breeding purposes shall be restricted to animals of recognized breed. duly registered in the book of record established for that breed, certified as such by the Bureau of Animal Industry: Provided, furthermore, That certificate of such record, and pedigree of such animal duly authenticated by the proper custodian of such book of record, shall be produced and submitted to the Collector of Customs, together with affidavit of the owner or importer, that such animal is the animal described in said certificate of record and pedigree: And Provided, finally, That the animals and plants are certified by the National Economic and Development Authority as necessary for economic development;

18. Economic, technical, vocational, scientific, philosophical, historical, and cultural books and/or publications: Provided, That those which may have already been imported but pending release by the Bureau of Customs at the effectivity of this Decree may still enjoy the privilege herein provided upon certification by the Department of Education, Culture and Sports that such imported books and/or publications are for economic, technical, vocational, scientific, philosophical, historical or cultural purposes or that the same are educational, scientific or cultural materials covered by the International Agreement on Importation of Educational Scientific and Cultural Materials signed by the President of the Philippines on August 2, 1952, or other agreements binding upon the Philippines.

Educational, scientific and cultural materials covered by international agreements or commitments binding upon the Philippine Government so certified by the Department of Education, Culture and Sports. Bibles, missals, prayer books, Koran, Ahadith and other religious books of similar nature and extracts therefrom, hymnal and hymns for religious uses;

19. Philippine articles previously exported from the Philippines and returned without having been advanced in value or improved in condition by any process of manufacture or other means, and upon which no drawback or bounty has been allowed, including instruments and implements, tools of trade, machinery and equipment, used abroad by Filipino citizens in the pursuit of their business, occupation or profession; and foreign articles previously imported when returned after having been exported and loaned for use temporarily abroad solely for exhibition, testing and experimentation, for scientific or educational purposes; and foreign containers previously imported which have been used in packing exported Philippine articles and returned empty if imported by or for the account of the person or institution who exported them from the Philippines and not for sale, barter or hire subject to

identification: Provided, That any Philippine article falling under this subsection upon which drawback or bounty has been allowed shall, upon re -importation thereof, be subject to a duty under this subsection equal to the amount of such drawback or bounty;

20. Aircraft, equipment and machinery, spare parts commissary and catering supplies, aviation gas, fuel and oil, whether crude or refined, and such other articles or supplies imported by and for the use of scheduled airlines operating under Congressional franchise: Provided, That such articles or supplies are not locally available in reasonable quantity, quality and price and are necessary or incidental for the proper operation of the scheduled airline importing the same;

21. Machineries, equipment, tools for production, plants to convert mineral ores into saleable form, spare parts, supplies, materials, accessories, explosives, chemicals, and transportation and communication facilities imported by and for the use of new mines and old mines which resume operations, when certified to as such by the Secretary of Agriculture and Natural Resources upon the recommendation of the Director of Mines, for a period ending five (5) years from the first date of actual commercial production of saleable mineral products: Provided, That such articles are not locally available in reasonable quantity, quality and price and are necessary or incidental in the proper operation of the mine; and aircrafts imported by agro -industrial companies to be used by them in their agriculture and industrial operations or activities, spare parts and accessories thereof;

22. Spare parts of vessels or aircraft of foreign registry engaged in foreign trade when brought into the Philippines exclusively as replacements or for the emergency repair thereof, upon proof satisfactory to the Collector of Customs that such spare parts shall be utilized to secure the safety, seaworthiness or airworthiness of the vessel or aircraft, to enable it to continue its voyage or flight ;

23. Articles of easy identification exported from the Philippines for repair and subsequently reimported upon proof satisfactory to the Collector of Customs that such articles is not capable
 :r being repaired locally: Provided, That the cost of the repairs made to any such article shall pa,., s rate of duty of thirty per cent ad valorem;

24. Trailer chassis when imported by shipping companies for their exclusive use in handling containerized cargo, upon posting a bond in an amount equal to one and one - half times the ascertained duties, taxes and other charges due thereon to cover a period of one year from the date of acceptance of the entry, which period for

meritorious reasons may, be extended by the Commissioner of Customs from year to year, subject to the following conditions:

a. That they shall be properly identified and registered with the Land Transportation Commission;
b. That they shall be subject to customs supervision fee to be fixed by the Collector of Customs and subject to the approval of the Commissioner of Customs;
c. That they shall be deposited in the Customs zone when not in use; and
d. That upon the expiration of the period prescribed above, duties and taxes shall be paid unless otherwise re -exported.

The provisions of Sec. 105 of Presidential Decree No. 34, dated October 27, 1972, to the contrary notwithstanding any officer or employee of the Department of Foreign Affairs, including any attach6, civil or military or member of his staff assigned to a Philippine diplomatic mission abroad by his Department or any similar officer o7 employee assigned to a Philippine consular office abroad, or any personnel of the Reparations Mission in Tokyo or AFP military personnel detailed with SEATO or any AFP military personnel accorded assimilated diplomatic rank or duty abroad who is returning from a regular assignment abroad, for reassignment to his Home office, or who dies. resigns, or is retired from the service, after the approval of this Decree, shall be exempt from the payment of all duties and taxes on his personal and household effects, including one motor car which must have been ordered or purchased prior to the receipt by the mission or consulate of his order of recall, and which must be registered in his name: Provided, however, That this exemption shall apply only to the value of the motor car and to the aggregate assessed value of said personal and household effects the latter not to exceed thirty per centum (30%) of the total amount received by such officer or employee in salary and allowances during his latest assignment abroad but not to exceed four years; Provided, further, That this exemption shall not be availed of oftener than once every four years; And, Provided, finally, That the officer or employee concerned must have served abroad for not less than two years.

The provisions of general and special laws, including those granting fanchises, to the contrary notwithstanding, there shall be no exemptions whatsoever from the payment of customs duties except those provided for in this Code; those granted to government agencies, instrumentalities or government -owned or controlled corporations with existing contracts, commitments, agreements, or obligations (requiring such exemption) with foreign countries; international institutions, associations or organizations entitled to exemption pursuant to agreements or special laws; and those that may be granted by the

President upon prior recommendation of the National Economic and Development Authority in the interest of national economic development.

SECTION 106. Drawbacks.

1. On Fuel Used for Propulsion of Vessels. - On all fuel imported into the Philippines used for propulsion of vessels engaged in trade with foreign countries, or in the coastwise trade, a refund or tax credit shall be allowed not exceeding ninety -nine (99) per cent of the duty imposed by law upon such fuel, which shall be paid or credited u rider such rules and regulations as maybe prescribed by the Commissioner of Customs with the approval of the Secretary of Finance.
2. On Petroleum Oils and Oils Obtained from Bituminous Minerals, Crude Eventually Used for Generation of Electric Power and for the Manufacture of City Gas. - On petroleum oils and oils obtained from bituminous materials, crude oils imported by non -electric utilities, sold directly or indirectly, in the same form or after processing, to electric utilities for the generation of electric power and for the manufacture of city gas, a refund or tax credit shall be allowed not exceeding fifty per cent (50%) of the duty imposed by law upon such oils, which shall be paid or credited under such rules and regulations as may be prescribed by the Commissioner of Customs with the approval of the Secretary of Finance.
3. On Articles made from Imported Materials. - Upon exportation of articles manufactured or produced in the Philippines, including the packing, covering, putting up, marking or labeling thereof either in whole or in part of imported materials for which duties have been paid, refund or tax credit shall be allowed for the duties paid on the imported materials so used including the packing, covering, putting up, marking or labeling thereof, subject to the following conditions:
    a. The actual use of the imported materials in the production of manufacture of the article exported with their quantity, value, and amount of duties paid thereon, having been established;
    b. The duties refunded or credited shall not exceed one hundred (100) per cat of duties paid on the imported materials used;
    c. There is no determination by the National Economic and Development Authority of the requirement for certification on non -availability of locally -produced or manufactured competitive substitutes for the imported materials used at the time of importation:
    d. The exportation shall be made within one (1) year after the importation of materials

used and claim of refund or tax credit shall be filed within six (6) months from the date of exportation;

e. When two or more products result from the use of the same imported materials, an apportionment shall be made on its equitable basis.

For every application of a drawback, there shall be paid to and collected by the Bureau of Customs as filing, processing and supervision fees the sum of Five Hundred Pesos (12500.00) which amount may be increased or decreased when the need arises by the Secretary of Finance upon the recommendation of the Commissioner of Customs.

4. Payment of Partial Drawbacks. - The Secretary of Finance may, upon recommendation of the Commissioner of Customs, promulgate rules and regulations allowing partial payments of drawbacks under this section. –

5. Payment of the Drawbacks. - Claims for refund or tax credit eligible for such benefits shall be paid or granted by the Bureau of Customs to claimants within sixty (60) days after receipt of properly accomplished claims: Provided, That a registered enterprise under Republic Act Number Fifty -one hundred and eighty -six or Republic Act Numbered Sixty -one hundred and thirty five which has previously enjoyed tax credit based on customs duties paid on imported raw materials and supplies, shall not be entitled to drawback under this section, with respect to the same importation subsequently processed and re -exported: Provided, further, That if as a result of the refund or tax credit by way of drawback of customs duties, there would necessarily result a corresponding refund or credit of internal revenue taxes on the same importation, the Collector of Customs shall likewise certify the same to the Commissioner of Customs who shall cause the said refund or tax credit of internal revenue taxes to be paid, refunded or credited in favor of the importer, with advice to the Commissioner of Internal Revenue.

TITLE 11. ADMINISTRATIVE PROVISIONS

PART 1. – BASES OF ASSESSMENT OF DUTY

SECTION 201. Basis of Dutiable Value. -

(A) Method One. - Transaction Value. - The dutiable value of an imported article subject to an ad valorem rate of duty shall be the transaction value, which shall be the price actually paid or payable for the goods when sold for export to the Philippines, adjusted

by adding:
(1) The following to the extent that they are incurred by the buyer but are not included in the price actually paid or payable for the imported goods:
   (a) Commissions and brokerage fees (except buying commissions);
   (b) Cost of containers;
   (c) The cost of packing, whether for labour or materials;
   (d) The value, apportioned as appropriate, of the following goods and services: materials, components, parts and similar items incorporated in the imported goods; tools; dies; moulds and similar items used in the production of imported goods; materials consumed in the production of the imported goods; and engineering, development, artwork, design work and plans and sketches undertaken elsewhere than in the Philippines and necessary for the production of imported goods, where such goods and services are supplied directly or indirectly by the buyer free of charge or at a reduced cost for use in connection with the production and sale for export of the imported goods;
   (e) The amount of royalties and license fees related to the goods being valued that the buyer must pay either directly or indirectly, as a condition of sale of the goods to the buyer;
(2) The value of any part of the proceeds of any subsequent resale, disposal or use of the imported goods that accrues directly or indirectly to the seller;
(3) The cost of transport o f the imported goods from the port of exportation to t he p ort of entry in the Philippines;
(4) Loading, unloading and handling charges associated with the transport of the imported goods from t -e country of exportation to the port of entry in the Philippines; and
(5) The cost of insurance.
   All additions to the price actually paid or payable shall be made only on the basis of objective arc quantifiable data.
   No additions shall be made to the price actually paid or payable in determining the customs value except as provided in this Section: Provided, That Method One s hall not be used in determining the dutiable value o imported goods if:
   (a) There are restrictions as to the disposition or use of the goods by the buyer other than restrictions which:
      (i) Are imposed or required by law or by Philippine authorities;
      (ii) Limit the geographical area in which the goods may be resold; or

(iii) Do not substantially affect the value of the goods.
(b) The sale or price is subject to some condition or consideration for which a value cannot be determined with respect to the goods being valued;
(c) Part of the proceeds of any subsequent resale, disposal or use of the goods by the buyer will accrue directly or indirectly to the seller, unless an appropriate adjustment can be made in accordance with the provisions hereof; or (d) The buyer and the seller are related to one another, and such relationship influenced the price of the goods. Such persons shall be deemed related if:
(i) They are officers or directors of one another's businesses;
(ii) They are legally recognized partners in business;
(iii) There exists an employer -employee relationship between them;
(iv) Any person directly or indirectly owns, controls or holds five percent (5%) or more of the outstanding voting stock or shares of both seller and buyer;
(v) One of them directly or indirectly controls the other;
(vi) Both of them are directly or indirectly controlled by a third person;
(vii) Together they directly or indirectly control a third person; or
(viii) They are members of the same family, including those related by affinity or consanguinity up to the fourth civil degree.

Persons who are associated in business with one another in that one is the sole agent, sole distributor or sole concessionaire, however described, of the other shall be deemed to be related for the purposes of this Act if they fall within any of the eight (8) cases above.

(B) Method Two. - Transaction Value of Identical Goods. - Where the dutiable value cannot be determined under method one, the dutiable value shall be the transaction value of identical goods sold for export to the Philippines and exported at or about the same time as the goods being valued. "Identical goods!" shall mean goods which are the same in all respects, including physical characteristics, quality and reputation. Minor differences in appearances shall not preclude goods otherwise conforming to the definition from. being regarded as identical.

(C) Method Three. - Transaction Value of Similar Goods. - Where the dutiable value cannot be determined under the preceding method, the dutiable value shall be the transaction value of similar goods sold for export to the Philippines and exported at or about the same time as the goods being valued. "Similar goods" shall mean goods which, although not alike in all respects, have like characteristics and like component materials which enable them to perform the same functions and to be commercially interchangeable. The quality of the goods, their reputation and the existence of a trademark shall be among the factors to be considered in determining whether goods are similar.

If the dutiable value still cannot be determined through the successive application of the two immediately preceding methods, the dutiable value shall be determined under method four or, when the dutiable value still cannot be determined under that method, under method five, except that, at the request of the importer, the order of application of methods four and five shall be reversed: Provided, however, That if the Commissioner of Custom deems that he will experience real difficulties in determining the dutiable value using method five, the Commissioner of Customs may refuse such a request in which event the dutiable value shall be determined under method four, if it can be so determined.

(D) Method Four. - Deductive Value. - The dutiable value of the imported goods under this method shall be the deductive value which shall be based on the unit price at which the imported goods or identical or similar imported goods a re s old in the Philippines, I n t he same condition as when imported, in the greatest aggregate quantity, at or about the time of the importation of the goods being valued, to persons not related to the persons from whom they buy such goods, subject to deductions for the following:

(1) Either the commissions usually paid or agreed to be paid or the additions usually made for profit and general expenses in connection with sales in such country of imported goods of the same class or kind;

(2) The usual costs of transport and insurance and associated costs incurred within the Philippines; and

(3) Where appropriate, the costs and charges referred to in subsection (A) (3), (4) and (5); and

(4) The customs duties and other national taxes payable in the Philippines by reason of the importation or sale of the goods.

If neither the imported goods nor identical nor similar imported goods are sold at or about the time of importation of the goods being valued in the Philippines in the conditions as imported, the customs value shall, subject to the conditions set forth in the preceding paragraph hereof, be based on the unit price at which the imported goods or identical or similar imported goods sold in the Philippines in the condition as imported at the earliest date after the importation of the goods being valued but before the expiration of ninety (90) days after such importation.

If neither the imported goods nor identical nor similar imported goods are sold in the

Philippines in the condition as imported, then, if the importer so requests, the dutiable value shall be based on the unit price at which the imported goods, after further processing, are sold in the greatest aggregate quantity to persons in the Philippines who are not related to the persons from whom they buy such goods, subject to allowance for the value added by such processing and deductions provided under Subsections (D)(1), (2), (3) and (4) hereof.

(E) Method Five. - Computed Value. - The dutiable value under this method shall be the computed value which shall be the sum of:
   (1) The cost or the value of materials and fabrication or other processing employed in producing the imported goods;
   (2) The amount for profit and general expenses equal to that usually reflected in the sale of goods of the same class or kind as the goods being valued which are made by producers in the country of exportation for export to the Philippines;
   (3) The freight, insurance fees and other transportation expenses for the importation of the goods;
   (4) Any assist, if its value is not included under paragraph (1) hereof, and
   (5) The cost of containers and packing, if their values are not included under paragraph (1) hereof.

   The Bureau of Customs shall not require or compel any person not residing in the Philippines to produce for examination, or to allow access to, any account or other record for the purpose of determining a computed value.

   However, information supplied by the producer of the goods for the purposes of determining the customs value may be verified in another country with the agreement of the producer and provided they will give sufficient advance notice to the government of the country in question and the latter does not object to the investigation.

(F) Method Six. - Fallback Value. - If the dutiable value cannot be determined under the preceding methods described above, it shall be determined by using other reasonable means and on the basis of data available in the Philippines.

   If the importer so requests, the importer shall be informed in writing of the dutiable value determined under Method Six and the method used to determine such value.

   No dutiable value shall be determined under Method Six on the basis of:
   (1) The selling price in the Philippines of goods produced in the Philippines;
   (2) A system that provides for the acceptance for customs purposes of the higher of two alternative values;
   (3) The price of goods in the domestic market of the country of exportation;

(4) The cost of production, other than computed values, that have been determined for identical or similar goods in accordance with Method Five hereof;
(5) The price of goods for export to a country other than the Philippines;
(6) Minimum customs values; or
(7) Arbitrary or fictitious values.

If in the course of determining the dutiable value of imported goods, it becomes necessary to delay the final determination of such dutiable value, the importer shall nevertheless be able to secure the release of the imported goods upon the filing of a sufficient guarantee in the form of a surety bond, a deposit, cash or some other appropriate instrument in an amount equivalent to the imposable duties and taxes on the imported goods in question conditioned upon the payment of customs duties and taxes for which the imported goods may be liable: Provided, however, That goods, the importation of which is prohibited by law shall not be released under any circumstance whatsoever.

Nothing in this Section shall be construed as restricting or calling into question the right of the Collector of Customs to satisfy himself as to the truth or accuracy of any statement, document or declaration presented for customs valuation purposes. When a declaration has been presented and where the customs administration has reason to doubt the truth or accuracy of the particulars or of documents produced in support of this declaration, the customs administration may ask the importer to provide further explanation, including documents or other evidence, that the declared value represents the total amount actually paid or payable for the imported goods, adjusted in accordance with the provisions of Subsection (A) hereof.

If, after receiving further information, or in the absence of a response, the customs administration still has reasonable doubts about the truth or accuracy of the declared value, it may, without prejudice to an importer's right to appeal pursuant to Article 11 of the World Trade Organization Agreement on customs valuation, be deemed that the customs value of the imported goods cannot be determined under Method One. Before taking a final decision, the Collector of Customs shall communicate to the importer, in writing if requested, his grounds for doubting the truth or accuracy of the particulars or documents produced and give the importer a reasonable opportunity to respond. When a final decision is made, the customs administration shall communicate to the importer in writing its decision and the grounds therefor. (As amended by Republic Act No. 9135 dated 27 April 2001)

SECTION 202. Bases of Dutiable Weight.

On articles that are subject to specific rate of duty, based on weight, the duty shall be ascertained as follows:

(a) When articles are dutiable by the gross weight, the dutiable weight thereof shall be the weight of same, together with the weight of all containers, packages, holders and packing, of any kind, in which said articles are contained, held or packed at the time of importation.
(b) When articles are dutiable by the legal weight, the dutiable weight thereof shall be the weight of same, together with the weight of the immediate containers, holders and/or packing in which such articles are usually contained, held or packed at the time of importation and/or, when imported in retail packages, at the time of their sale to the public in usual retail quantities: Provided, That when articles are packed in single container, the weight of the latter shall be included in the legal weight.
(c) When articles are dutiable by the net weight, the dutiable weight thereof shall be only the actual weight of the articles at the time of importation, excluding the weight of the immediate and all other containers, holders or packing in which such articles are contained, held or packed.
(d) Articles affixed to cardboard, cards, paper, wood or similar common material shall be dutiable together with the weight of such holders.
(e) When a single package contains imported articles dutiable according to different weights, or to weight and value, the common exterior receptacles shall be prorated and the different proportions thereof treated in accordance with the provisions of this Code as to the dutiability or non-dutiability of such packing.

SECTION 203. Rate of Exchange.

For the assessment and collection of import duty upon imported articles and for other purposes, the value and prices thereof quoted in foreign currency shall be converted into the currency of the Philippines at the current rate of exchange or value specified or published, from time to time, by the Central Bank of the Philippines.

SECTION 204. Effective Date of Rates of Import Duty.

Imported articles shall be subject to the rate or rates of import duty existing at the time of entry. or withdrawal from warehouse, in the Philippines, for consumption.

On and after the day when this Code shall go into effect, all articles previously imported, for which no entry has been made, and all articles previously entered without payment of duty and under bond for warehousing, transportation, or any other purpose, for which no permit of delivery to the importer or his agent has been issued, shall be subject to the rates of duty imposed by this Code and to no other duty, upon the entry, or withdrawal thereof from warehouse, for consumption.

On article abandoned or forfeited to, or seized by, the government, and then sold at public auction, the rates of duty and the tariff in force on the date of the auction shall apply: Provided, That duty based on the weight, volume and quantity of articles shall be levied and collected on the weight, volume and quantity at the time of their entry into the warehouse or the date of abandonment, forfeiture and/or seizure.

SECTION 205. Entry, or Withdrawal from Warehouse, for Consumption.

Imported articles shall be deemed "entered " in the Philippines for consumption when the specified entry form is properly filed and accepted, together with any related documents required by the provisions of this Code and/or regulations to be filed with such form at the time of entry, at the port or station by t he customs official designated to receive such entry papers and any duties, taxes, fees and/or other lawful charges required to be paid at the time of making such entry have been paid or secured to be paid with the customs official designated to receive such monies, provided that the article has previously arrived within the limits of the port of entry.

Imported articles shall be deemed 'Withdrawn' from warehouse in the Philippines for consumption when the specified form is properly filed and accepted, together with any related documents required by any provisions of this Code and/or regulations to be filed with such form at the time of withdrawal, by the customs official designated to receive the withdrawal entry and any duties, taxes, fees and/or other lawful charges required to be paid at the time of withdrawal have been deposited with the customs official designated to receive such payment.

PART 2. – SPECIAL DUTIES SECTION 301. Anti –Dumping Duty. –

(a) Whenever any product, commodity or article of commerce imported into the Philippines at an export price less than its normal value in the ordinary course of trade for the like product, commodity or article destined for consumption in the exporting country is causing or is threatening to cause material injury to a domestic industry, or materially retarding the establishment of a domestic industry producing the like product, the Secretary of Trade and Industry, in the case of non -agricultural product, commodity or article, or the Secretary of Agriculture, in the case of agricultural product, commodity or article (both of whom are hereinafter referred to as the Secretary, as the case may be), after formal investigation and affirmative finding of the Tariff Commission (hereinafter referred to as the Commission), shall cause the imposition of an anti-dumping duty equal to the margin of dumping on such product, commodity or article and on like product, commodity or article thereafter imported to the Philippines under similar circumstances, in addition to ordinary duties, taxes and charges imposed by law on the imported product, commodity or article. However, the anti-dumping duty may be less than the margin if such lesser duty will be adequate to remove the injury to the domestic industry. Even when a 11 t he requirements f or t he imposition have been fulfilled, the decision on whether or not to impose a definitive anti-dumping duty remains the prerogative of the Commission. It may consider, among others, the effect of imposing an anti-dumping duty on the welfare of consumers and/or the general public, and other related local industries.

In the case where products are not imported directly from the country of origin but are exported to the Philippines from an intermediate country, the price at which the products are sold from the country of export in the Philippines shall normally be compared with the comparable price in the country of export. However, comparison may be made with the price in the country of origin, if for example, the products are merely transshipped through the country of export, or such products are not produced in the country of export, or there is no comparable price for them in the country of export.

(b) Initiation of Action. An anti-dumping investigation may be initiated upon receipt of a written application from any person whether natural or juridical, representing a domestic industry, which shall include evidence of: a) dumping, b) injury, and c) causal link between the dumped imports and the alleged injury. Simple assertion, unsubstantiated by relevant evidence, cannot be considered sufficient to meet the requirements of this paragraph. The application shall contain such information as is reasonably available to the applicant on the following: 1) the identity of the applicant and a description of the volume and the value of the domestic production of the like product of the applicant; 2) a complete description of the alleged dumped product, the name of the country of origin or export under consideration, the identity of each known exporter or foreign producer, and a list of known persons importing the product under consideration; 3) information on the normal value of the product under consideration in the country of origin or export; and 4) information on the evolution of the volume of the alleged dumped imports, the effect of these imports on the price of the like product in the domestic market, and the consequent impact of the imports on the domestic industry.

Philippine Trade, Agriculture or Finance Attaches and other Consular Officials or Attachs in the concerned exporting member countries are mandated to furnish the applicant pertinent information or documents to support his complaint within a period not exceeding thirty (30) days from receipt of a request.

The application shall be filed with the Secretary of Trade and Industry in the case of non -agricultural product, commodity or article, or with the Secretary of Agriculture in the case of agricultural product, commodity or article. The Secretary shall require the petitioner to post a surety bond in such reasonable amount as to answer for any and all damages which the importer may sustain by reason of the filing of a frivolous petition. He shall immediately release the surety bond upon making an affirmative preliminary determination.

The application shall be considered to have been made "by or on behalf of the domestic industry" if it is supported by those domestic producers whose collective output constitutes more than fifty percent (50%) of the total production of the like product produced by that portion of the domestic industry expressing either support for or opposition to the application. In cases involving an exceptionally large number of producers, the degree of support and opposition may be determined by using a statistically valid sampling technique or by consulting their representative organizations. However, no investigation shall be initiated when domestic producers expressly supporting the application account for less than twenty -five percent (25%) of total production of the like product produced by the domestic industry.

in exceptional circumstances, the Philippines may be divided into two or more competitive markets and the producers within each market may be regarded as a separate industry if (a) the producers within such market have the dominant market share; and (b) the demand in that market is not substantially supplied by other producers elsewhere in the Philippines.

if, in special circumstances, the Secretary decides to initiate an investigation without having received a written application by or on behalf of a domestic industry for the initiation of such investigation, he shall proceed only if he has sufficient evidence of dumping, injury and a causal link, to justify the initiation of an investigation.

Within five (5) working days from receipt of a properly documented application, the Secretary shall examine the accuracy and adequacy of the petition to determine whether there is sufficient evidence to justify the initiation of investigation. If there is no sufficient evidence to justify initiation, the Secretary shall dismiss the petition and properly notify the Secretary of Finance, the Commissioner of Customs, and other parties concerned regarding such dismissal. The Secretary shall extend legal, technical, and other assistance to the concerned domestic producers and their organizations at all stages of the anti-dumping action.

(c) Notice to the Secretary of Finance. - Upon receipt of the application, the Secretary shall, without delay, notify the Secretary of Finance and furnish him with a complete copy 6f the application, or information in case the initiation is made o n h is own motion including its annexes, if any. The Secretary o f Finance s hall immediately inform the Commissioner of Customs regarding the filing and pendency of the application or information and instruct him to gather and to furnish the Secretary within five (5) days from receipt of the instructions of the Secretary of Finance copies of all import entries and relevant documents covering such allegedly dumped product, commodity or article which entered the Philippines during the last twelve (12) months preceding the date of application. The Commissioner of Customs shall also make such similar additional reports on the number, volume, and value of the importation of the allegedly dumped product, commodity or article to the Secretary every ten (110) days thereafter.

(d) Notice to Exporting Member -Country. - Upon receipt of a properly documented application and before proceeding to initiate an investigation, the Secretary shall notify the government of the exporting country about the impending anti-dumping investigation. However, the Secretary shall refrain from publicizing the application for the initiation of the investigation before a decision has been made to initiate an investigation.

(e) Notice to Concerned Patties and Submission of Evidences. - Within two (2) days from initiation of the investigation and after having notified the exporting country, the Secretary shall identify all interested parties, i.e., protestee -importer, exporter and/or foreign producer, notify and require them to submit within thirty (30) days from receipt of such notice evidences and information or reply to the questionnaire to dispute the allegations contained in the application. At this point, the respondent is given the opportunity to present evidences to prove that he is not involved in dumping. He shall furnish them with a copy of the application and its annexes subject to the requirement to protect confidential information. The notice shall be deemed to have been received five (5) days from the date on which it was sent to the respondent or transmitted to the appropriate diplomatic representative of the exporting member, or an official representative of the exporting territory. If the respondent fails to submit his answer, he shall be declared in default, in which case, the Secretary shall make such preliminary determination of the case on the basis of the information available, among others, the facts alleged in the petition and the supporting information and documents supplied by the petitioner.

(f) Preliminary Determination. - Not later than thirty (30) working days from receipt of the answer of the respondent importer, exporter, foreign producer, exporting member-country, and other interested parties, the Secretary shall, on the basis of the application of the aggrieved party and the answer of the respondent/s and their respective supporting documents or information, make a preliminary determination of the application for the imposition of an anti-dumping duty.

in the preliminary determination, the Secretary shall essentially determine the following:

(1) Price difference between the export p rice and t he normal value of the article in question in the country of export or origin;

(2) The presence and extent of material injury or threat of injury to the domestic industry producing like product or the material retardation of the establishment of a domestic industry; and

(3) The causal relationship between the allegedly dumped product, commodity or article and the material injury or threat of material injury to the affected domestic industry or material retardation of the establishment of the domestic industry.

The preliminary finding of the Secretary, together with the records of the case shall, within three (3) days, be transmitted b y t he Secretary to the Commission for its immediate formal investigation. In case his preliminary finding is affirmative, the burden of proof is shifted to the respondent to rebut the preliminary finding. The Secretary shall immediately issue, through the Secretary of Finance, written instructions to the Commissioner of Customs to impose within three (3) days from receipt of instructions a cash bond equal to the provisionally estimated anti-dumping duty but not greater than the provisionally estimated margin of dumping in addition to any other duties, taxes and charges imposed by law on like articles. The cash bond shall be deposited with the government depository bank and shall be held in trust for the respondent. Moreover, the posting of the cash bond shall only be required no sooner than sixty (60) days from the date of initiation of the investigation. The date of initiation of the investigation is deemed to be the date the Secretary publishes such notice in two (2) newspapers of general circulation. The Secretary shall cause such publication immediately after a decision to initiate the investigation has been made. The provisional anti-dumping duty may only be imposed for a four (4)-month period which may be extended to six (6) months upon request by the exporters representing a significant percentage of the trade involved. However, a provisional anti-dumping duty lower than the provisionally estimated margin of dumping can be imposed for a period of six (6) to nine (9) months, if it is deemed sufficient to remove or prevent the material injury.

(g) Termination of Investigation. - The Secretary or the Commission as the case may be, shall motu proprio terminate the investigation at any stage of the proceedings if the provisionally estimated margin of dumping is less than two percent (2%) of export price or the volume of dumped imports or injury is negligible. The volume of dumped imports from a particular country shall normally be regarded as negligible if it accounts for less than three percent (3%) of the imports of the like article in the Philippines unless countries which individually account for less than three percent (3%) of the imports of the like article in the Philippines collectively account for more than seven percent (7%) of the total imports of that article.

(h) Investigation of the Commission. - Within three (3) working days upon its receipt of the records of the case from the Secretary, the Commission shall start the formal investigation and shall accordingly notify in writing all parties on record and, in addition, give public notice of the exact initial date, time and place of the formal investigation through the publication of such particulars and a concise summary of the petition in two (2) newspapers of general circulation.

In the formal investigation, the Commission shall essentially determine the following:

(1) If the article in question is being imported into, or sold in the Philippines at a price less than its normal value; and the difference, if any, between the export price and the normal value of the article.

(2) The presence and extent of material injury or the threat thereof to the domestic industry, or the material retardation of the establishment of a domestic industry;

(3) The existence of a casual relationship between the allegedly dumped product, commodity or article and the material injury or threat of material injury to the affected domestic industry, or material retardation of the establishment of a domestic industry;

(4) The anti-dumping duty to be imposed; and

(5) The duration of the imposition of the anti-dumping duty.

The formal investigation shall be conducted in a summary manner. No dilatory tactics or unnecessary or unjustified delays shall be allowed and the technical rules of evidence used in regular court proceedings shall not be applied.

In case any and all of the parties on record fail to submit their answers to questionnaires/position papers within the prescribed period, the Commission shall base its findings on the best available information.

The Commission shall complete the formal investigation and submit a report of its findings, whether favorable or not, to the Secretary within one hundred twenty (120) days from receipt of the records of the case: Provided, however, That the Commission shall, before a final determination is made, inform all the interested parties in writing of the essential facts under consideration which from the basis for the decision to apply definitive measures. Such disclosure should take place in sufficient time for the parties to defend their interests.

(i) Determination of Material Injury or Threat Thereof. - The presence and extent of material injury to the domestic industry, as a result of the dumped imports shall be determined on the basis of positive evidence and shall require an objective examination of, but shall not be limited to the following:

   (1) The rate of increase and amount of imports, either in absolute terms or relative to production or consumption in the domestic market;

   (2) The effect of the dumped imports on the price in the domestic market for like product, commodity or article, that is, whether there has been a significant price undercutting by the dumped imports as compared with the price of like product, commodity or article in the domestic market, or whether the effect of such imports is otherwise to depress prices to a significant - degree or prevent price increases, which otherwise would have occurred, to a significant degree; and

   (3) The effect of the dumped imports o n t he domestic producers or the resulting retardation o f the establishment of a domestic industry manufacturing like product, commodity or article, including an evaluation of all relevant economic factors and indices having a bearing on the state of the domestic industry concerned, such as, but not limited to, actual or potential decline in output, sales, market share, profits, productivity, return on investments, or utilization of capacity; factors affecting domestic prices; the magnitude of dumping; actual and potential negative effects on cash flow, inventories, employment, wages, growth, and ability to raise capital or investments.

The extent of injury of the dumped imports to the domestic industry shall be determined by the Secretary and the Commission upon examination of all relevant evidence. Any known factors other than the dumped imports which at the same time

are injuring the domestic industry shall also be examined and the injuries caused by these factors must not be attributed to the dumped imports. The relevant evidence m ay include, but shall not be limited to, the following:
(1) The volume and value of imports not sold at dumping prices;
(2) Contraction in demand or changes in consumption pattern;
(3) Trade restrictive practices and competition between foreign and domestic producers;
(4) Developments in technology; and
(5) Export performance and productivity of the domestic industry.

A determination of threat of material injury shall be based on facts and not merely on allegation, conjecture or remote possibility. The change in circumstances which will create a situation in which the dumping will cause injury must be clearly foreseen and imminent. In making a determination regarding the existence of a threat of material injury, the following shall be considered, inter lia, collectively:

(1) A significant rate of increase of the dumped imports in the domestic market indicating the likelihood of substantially increased importation;

(2) Sufficient freely disposable, or an imminent, substantial increase in capacity of the exporter indicating the likelihood of substantially increased dumped exports to the domestic market, taking into account the availability of other export markets to absorb any additional exports;

(3) Whether imports are entering at prices that will have a significant depressing or suppressing effect on domestic prices and will likely increase demand for further imports; and

(4) Inventories of the product being investigated.

(j) voluntary price undertaking executed by the exporter or foreign producer under oath and accepted by the affected industry that he will increase his price or will cease exporting to the Philippines at a dumped price, thereby eliminating the material injury to the domestic industry producing like product. Price increases under such undertakings shall not be higher than necessary to eliminate the margin of dumping.

A price undertaking shall be accepted only after a preliminary affirmative determination of dumping and injury caused by such dumping has been made. No price undertaking shall take effect unless it is approved by the Secretary after a recommendation by the Commission.

Even if the price undertaking is acceptable, the investigation shall nevertheless be continued and completed by the Commission if the exporter or foreign producer so desires or upon advice of the Secretary. The undertaking shall automatically lapse in case of a negative finding. In case of any affirmative finding, the undertaking shall continue, consistent with the provisions of Article VI of the GATT 1994.

(k) Cumulation of Imports. - When imports of products, commodities or articles from more than one country are simultaneously the subject of an anti-dumping investigation, the Secretary or the Commission may cumulatively assess the effects of such imports only if the Secretary and the Commission are convinced that:

(1) The margin of dumping established in relation to the imports from each country is more than de minimis as defined in Subsection G;

(2) The volume of such imports from each country is not negligible, also as defined in Subsection G; and

(3) A cumulative assessment of the effects of such imports is warranted in the light of the conditions of competition between the imported products, commodities or articles, and the conditions of competition between the imported products and the like domestic products, commodities or articles.

(i) Imposition of the Anti-Dumping Duty. - The Secretary shall, within ten (10) days from receipt of the affirmative final determination by the Commission, issue a Department Order imposing an anti-dumping duty on the imported product, commodity or article, unless he has earlier accepted a price undertaking from the exporter or foreign producer. He shall furnish the Secretary of Finance with the copy of the order and request the latter to direct the Commissioner of Customs to collect within three (3) days from receipt thereof the definitive anti-dumping duty.

in case a cash bond has been filed, the same shall be applied to the anti-dumping duty assessed. If the cash bond is in excess of the anti-dumping duty assessed, the remainder shall be returned to the importer immediately including interest earned, if any: Provided, That no interest shall be payable by the government on the amount to be returned. If the assessed anti-dumping duty is higher than the cash bond filed, the difference shall not be collected.

Upon determination of the anti-dumping duty, the Commissioner of Customs shall submit to the Secretary, through the Secretary of Finance, certified reports on the disposition of the cash bond and the amounts of the anti-dumping duties collected.

In case of a negative finding by the Commission, the Secretary shall issue, after the lapse of the period for the petitioner to appeal to the Court of Tax Appeals, through the Secretary of Finance, an order for the Commissioner of Customs for the immediate release of the cash bond to the importer. In addition, all the parties concerned shall also be properly notified of the dismissal of the case.

(m) Period Subject to Anti-Dumping Duty. - An anti-dumping duty may be levied retroactively from the date the cash bond has been imposed and onwards, where a final determination of injury is made, or in the absence of provisional measures, a threat of injury has led to actual injury. Where a determination of threat of injury or material retardation is made, anti-dumping duties may be imposed only from the date of determination thereof and any cash bond posted shall be released in an expeditious manner. However, an anti-dumping duty may be levied on products which were imported into the country not more than ninety (90) days prior to the date of application of the cash bond, when the authorities determine for the dumped product in question that:

(1) There is a history of dumping which caused injury or that the importer was, or should have been, aware that the exporter practices dumping and that such dumping would cause injury; and

(2) The injury is caused by massive dumped imports of a product in a relatively short time which in light of the timing and the volume of the dumped imports and other circumstances (such as rapid build-up of inventories of the imported product) is likely to seriously undermine the remedial effect of the definitive antidumping duty to be applied: Provided, That the importers concerned have been given an opportunity to comment.

No duties shall be levied retroactively pursuant to herein subsection on products entered for consumption prior to the date of initiation of the investigation. "(n) Computation of Anti-Dumping Duty. - If the normal value of an article cannot be determined, the provisions for choosing alternative normal value under Article Vi of GATT 1994 shall apply.

If possible, an individual margin of dumping shall be determined for each known exporter or producer of the article under investigation. In cases where the number of exporters, producers, importers or types of products involved is so large as to make such determination impracticable, the Secretary and the Commission may limit their examination either to a reasonable number of interested parties or products by using samples which are statistically valid on the basis of information available to them at the time of the selection, or to the largest percentage of volume of exports from the country in question which can reasonably be investigated.

However, if a non-selected exporter or producer submits information, the investigation must extend to that exporter or producer unless this will prevent the timely completion of the investigation.

New exporters or producers who have not exported to the Philippines during the period of investigation will be subject to an accelerated review. No anti-dumping duties shall b a imposed during the review. Cash bonds may be requested to ensure that in case of affirmative findings, anti-dumping duties can be levied retroactively to the date of initiation of the review.

(o) Duration and Review of the Anti-Dumping Duty. - As a general rule, the imposition of an antidumping duty shall remain in force only as long as and to the extent necessary to counteract dumping which is causing or threatening to cause material injury to the domestic industry or material retardation of the establishment of such industry.

However, the need for the continued imposition of the anti-dumping duty may be reviewed by the Commission when warranted motu proprio, or upon the direction of the Secretary, taking into consideration the need to protect the existing domestic industry against dumping.

Any interested party with substantial positive information may also petition the Secretary for a review of the continued imposition of the anti-dumping duty: Provided, That a reasonable period of time has elapsed since the imposition of the anti-dumping duty. Interested parties shall have the right to request the Secretary to examine:1) whether the continued imposition of the anti-dumping duty is necessary to offset dumping; and 2) whether the injury would likely continue or recur if the anti-dumping duty were removed or modified, or both.

if the Commission determines that the anti-dumping duty is no longer necessary or warranted, the Secretary shall, upon its recommendation, issue a department order immediately terminating the imposition of the anti-dumping duty. All parties concerned shall be notified accordingly of such termination, including the Secretary of Finance and the Commissi6ner of Customs.

The duration of the definitive anti-dumping duty s hall not exceed five (5) years from the date of its imposition (or from the date of the most recent review if that review has covered both dumping and injury) unless the Commission has determined in a review initiated before that date on their own initiative or upon a duly substantiated request made by or on behalf of the domestic industry within a reasonable time period prior to the termination date that the termination of the anti-dumping duty will likely lead to the continuation or recurrence of dumping and injury.

The provisions of this Section regarding evidence and procedures shall apply to any review carried out under this Subsection and any such review should be carried out expeditiously and should be conducted not later than one hundred fifty (150) days from the date of initiation of such review.

(p) Judicial Review. - Any interested party in an anti-dumping investigation who is adversely affected by a final ruling in connection with the imposition of an anti-dumping duty may file with the Court of Tax Appeals, a petition for the review of such ruling within thirty (30) days from his receipt of notice of the final ruling: Provided, however, That the filing of such petition for review shall not in any way stop, suspend, or otherwise hold the imposition or collection, as the case may be, of the anti-dumping duty on the imported product, commodity or article. The rules of procedure of the court on the petition for review filed with the Court of Tax Appeals shall be applied.

(q) Public Notices. - The Secretary or the Commission shall inform in writing all interested parties on record and, in addition, give public notices by publishing in two (2) newspapers of general circulation when:

(1) Initiating an investigation;

(2) Concluding or suspending investigation;

(3) Making any preliminary or final determination whether affirmative or negative;

(4) Making a decision to accept or to terminate an undertaking; and

(5) Terminating a definitive anti-dumping duty. Commissioner of Customs a list of imported products susceptible to unfair trade practices.

The Commissioner of Customs is hereby mandated to submit to the Secretary monthly reports covering importations of said products, including but not limited to the following:

(1) Commercial invoice;

(2) Bill of lading;

(3) Import entries; and

(4) Pre-shipment reports.

Failure to comply with the submission of such report as provided herein shall hold the concerned officials liable and shall be punished with a fine not exceeding the equivalent of six (6) months salary or suspension not exceeding one (1) year.

(s) Definition of Terms. - For purposes of this Act, the following definitions shall apply:

(1) Anti-dumping duty refers to a special duty imposed on the importation of a product, commodity or article of commerce into the Philippines at less than its normal value when destined for domestic consumption in the exporting country, which is the difference between the export price and the normal value of such product, commodity or article.

(2) Export price refers to (1) the ex-factory price at the point of sale for export; or (2)

the F.O.B. price at the point of shipment. In cases where (1) or (2) cannot be used, then the export price may be constructed based on such reasonable basis as the Secretary or th6 Commission may determine.
(3) Normal value refers to a comparable price at the date of sale of the like product, commodity or article in the ordinary course of trade when destined for consumption in the country of export.
(4) Domestic industry refers to the domestic producers as a whole of the like product or to those of them whose collective output of the product constitutes a major related to the exporters or importers or are themselves importers of the allegedly dumped product, the term 'domestic industry' may be interpreted as referring to the rest of the producers.
(5) Dumped import product refers to any product, commodity or article of commerce introduced into the Philippines at an export price less than its normal value in the ordinary course of trade, for the like product, commodity or article destined for consumption in the exporting country, which is causing or is threatening to cause material injury to a domestic industry, or materially retarding the establishment of a domestic industry producing the like product.
(6) Like product refers to a product which is identical or alike in all respects to the product under consideration, or in the absence of such a product, another product which, although not alike in all respects, has characteristics closely resembling those of the product under consideration.
(7) Non -selected exporter or producer refers to an exporter or producer who has not been initially chosen as among the selected exporters or producers of the product under investigation.
(t) Administrative Support. - Upon the effectivity of this Act, the Departments of Trade and Industry, Agriculture and the Tariff Commission, shall ensure the efficient and effective implementation of this Act by creating a special unit within their agencies that will undertake the functions relative to the disposition of antidumping cases. All anti-dumping duties collected shall be earmarked for the strengthening of the capabilities of these agencies to undertake their responsibilities under this Act. (As amended by Republic Act No. 8752 dated 12 August 1999)

SECTION 302. Countervailing Duty. -

Whenever any product, commodity or article of commerce is granted directly or indirectly by the government in the country or origin or exportation, any kind or form of specific subsidy upon the production, manufacture or exportation of such product, commodity or article, and the importation of such subsidized product, commodity or article has caused or threatens to cause material injury to a domestic industry or has materially retarded the growth or prevents the establishment of a domestic industry as determined by the Tariff Commission (hereinafter referred to as the 'Commission'), the Secretary of Trade and Industry, in the case of nonagricultural product, commodity or article, or the Secretary of Agriculture, in the case of agricultural product, commodity or article (both of whom are hereinafter simply referred to as 'the Secretary,' as the case may be) shall issue a department order imposing a countervailing duty equal to the ascertained amount of the subsidy. The same levy shall be imposed on the like product, commodity or article thereafter imported to the Philippines charges imposed by law on such imported product, commodity or article.

(A) Initiation of Action. - A countervailing action may be initiated by the following:

(1) Any person, whether natural or juridical, who has an interest to protect, by filing a verified petition for the imposition of a countervailing duty by or on behalf of the domestic industry;

(2) The Secretary of Trade and Industry or the Secretary of Agriculture, as the case may be, in special circumstances where there is sufficient evidence of an existence of a subsidy, injury and causal link.

(B) Requirements. - A petition shall be filed with the Secretary and shall be accompanied by documents, if any, which are reasonably available to the petitioner and which contain information supporting the facts that are essential to establish the presence of the elements for the imposition of a countervailing duty, and shall further state, among others:

(1) The domestic industry to which the petitioner belongs and the particular domestic product, commodity or article or class of domestic product, commodity or article being prejudiced;

(2) The number of persons employed, the total capital invested, the production and sales volume, and the aggregate production capacity of the domestic industry that has been materially injured or is threatened to be materially injured or whose growth or establishment has been materially retarded or prevented;

(3) The name and address of the known importer, exporter, or foreign producer, the country of origin or export, the estimated aggregate or cumulative quantity, the port and the date of arrival, the import entry declaration of the imported product, commodity or article, as well as the nature, the extent and the estimated amount of

the subsidy thereon; and

(4) Such other particulars, facts or allegations as are necessary to justify the imposition of countervailing duty on the imported product, commodity or article. "A petition for the imposition of a countervailing duty shall be considered to have been made 'by or on behalf of the domestic industry' if it is supported by those domestic producers whose collective output constitutes more than fifty percent (50%) of the total production of the like product produced by that portion of the domestic industry expressing either support for or opposition to the application. However, an investigation shall be initiated only when domestic producers supporting the application account for at least twenty -five percent (25%) of the total production of the like product produced by the domestic industry. In cases involving an exceptionally large number of producers, degree of support or opposition may be determined by using statistically valid sampling techniques or by consulting their representative organizations.

Within ten (10) days from his receipt of the petition or information, the Secretary shall review the accuracy and adequacy of the information or evidence provided in the petition to determine whether there is sufficient basis to justify the initiation of an investigation. If there is no sufficient basis to justify the initiation of an investigation, the Secretary shall dismiss the petition and shall properly notify the Secretary of Finance, the Commissioner of Customs and other parties concerned regarding such dismissal. The Secretary shall extend legal, technical and other assistance to the concerned domestic producers and their organizations at all stages of the countervailing action.

(C) Notice to the Secretary of Finance. - Upon his receipt of the petition, the Secretary shall, without delay, furnish the Secretary of Finance with a summary of the essential facts of the petition, and request the latter to immediately inform the Commissioner of Customs regarding such petition and to instruct him to gather and secure all import entries covering such allegedly subsidized product, commodity or article without liquidation. The Commissioner of Customs shall submit to the Secretary a complete report on the number, volume, and value of the importation of the allegedly subsidized product, commodity or article within ten (10) days from his receipt of the instruction from the Secretary of Finance, and to make similar additional reports every ten (10) days thereafter.

(D) Notice to and Answer of Interested Parties. - Within five (5) days from finding of the basis to initiate an investigation, the Secretary shall notify all interested parties, and shall furnish them with a copy of the petition and its annexes, if any. The interested parties shall, not later than thirty (30) days from their receipt of the notice, submit their answer, including such relevant evidence or information as is reasonably available to them to controvert the allegations of the petition. If they fail to submit their answer, the Secretary shall make such preliminary determination of the case on the basis of the facts and/or information available.

The Secretary shall avoid, unless a decision has been made to initiate an investigation, any publicizing of the petition. However, after receipt of a properly documented petition and before proceeding to initiate an investigation, he shall notify the government of the exporting country about the impending investigation.

(E) Preliminary Determination. - Within twenty (20) days from his receipt of the answer of the interested parties, the Secretary shall, on the basis of the petition of the aggrieved party and the answer of such interested parties and their respective supporting documents or information, make a preliminary determination on whether or not a prima facie case exists for the imposition of a provisional countervailing duty in the form of a cash bond equal to the provisionally estimated amount of subsidy. Upon finding of a prima facie case, the Secretary shall immediately issue, through the Secretary of Finance, a written instruction to the Commissioner of Customs to collect the cash bond, in addition to the corresponding ordinary duties, taxes and other charges imposed by law on such product, commodity or article. The posting of a cash bond shall be required not earlier than sixty (60) days from the date of initiation of the investigation. The cash bond shall be deposited with a government depository bank and shall be held in trust for the respondent importer. The application of the cash bond shall not exceed four (4) months.

The Secretary shall immediately transmit his preliminary findings together with the records of the case to the Commission for its formal investigation.

(F) Termination of Investigation by the Secretary or the Commission. - The Secretary or the Commission, as the case may be, shall motu proprio terminate the investigation at any stage of the proceedings if the amount of subsidy is de minimis as defined in existing international trade agreements of which the Republic of the Philippines is a party; or where the volume of the subsidized imported product, commodity or article, actual or potential, or the injury is negligible.

(G) Formal Investigation by the Commission. - Immediately upon its receipt of the records of the case from the Secretary, the Commission shall commence the formal investigation and shall accordingly notify in writing all interested parties and, in addition, give public notice of such investigation in two (2) newspapers of general circulation.

In the formal investigation, the Commission shall essentially determine:

(1) The nature and amount of the specific subsidy being enjoyed by the imported product, commodity or article in question;

(2) The presence and extent of the material injury or the threat thereof to, or the material retardation of the growth, or the prevention of the establishment of, the affected domestic industry; and

(3) The existence of a causal relationship between the allegedly subsidized imported product, commodity or article and the material injury or threat thereof to, or the material retardation of the growth, or the prevention of the establishment of, the affected domestic industry.

The Commission is hereby authorized to require any interested party to allow it access to, or otherwise provide, necessary information to enable the Commission to expedite the investigation. In case any interested party refuses access to, or otherwise does not provide, necessary information within a reasonable period of time or significantly impedes the investigation, a final determination shall be made on the basis of the facts available.

The formal investigation shall be conducted in a summary manner. No dilatory tactics nor unnecessary or unjustified delays shall be allowed, and the technical rules or evidence s hall not be applied strictly.

(H) Determination of the Existence of Subsidy. - A subsidy is deemed to exist:

(1) When the government or any public body in the country of origin or export of the imported product, commodity or article extends financial contribution to the producer, manufacturer or exporter of such product, commodity or article in the form of:

(a) Direct transfer of funds such as grants, loans or equity infusion; or

(b) Potential direct transfer of funds or assumption of liabilities such as loan guarantees; or

(c) Foregone or uncollected government revenue that is otherwise due from the producer, manufacturer o r exporter of the product, commodity or article: Provided, That the exemption of any exported product, commodity or article from duty or tax imposed on like product, commodity or article when destined for consumption in the country of origin and/or export or the refunding of such duty or tax, shall not be deemed to constitute a grant of a subsidy: Provided, further,

That should a product, commodity or article be allowed drawback by the country of origin or export, only the ascertained or estimated amount by which the total amount of duties and/or internal revenue taxes was discounted or reduced, if any, shall constitute a subsidy; or

(d) Provision of goods or services other than general infrastructure; or

(e) Purchases of goods from the producer, manufacturer or exporter;

(f) Payments to a funding mechanism; or

(g) Other financial contributions to a private body to carry out one or more of the activities mentioned in subparagraphs (a) to (0 above; or

(2) When there is a benefit conferred.

(I) Determination of Specific Subsidy. - In the determination of whether or not a subsidy is specific, the following principles shall apply:

(1) Where the government or any public body in the country of origin or export of the imported product, commodity or article explicitly limits access to a subsidy to certain enterprises, such subsidy shall be specific;

(2) Where such government or public body through a law or regulation establishes objective criteria and conditions governing the eligibility for, and the amount of, a subsidy, specificity shall not exist: Provided, That the eligibility is automatic and that such criteria or conditions are strictly adhered to. Objective criteria shall mean those which are neutral, do not favor certain enterprises over others, and are economic in nature and horizontal in application, such as number of employees or size of enterprise;

(3) In case a subsidy appears to be non -specific according to subparagraphs (1) and (2) above, but there are reasons to believe that the subsidy may in fact be specific, factors that may be considered are: use of a subsidy program by a limited number of certain enterprises for a relatively longer period; granting of disproportionately large amounts of subsidy to certain enterprises; and exercise of wide and unwarranted discretion for granting a subsidy; and

(4) A subsidy which is limited to certain enterprises located within a designated geographical region within the territory of the government or public body in the country of origin or export shall be specific.

(J) Determination of Injury. - The presence and extent of material injury or threat thereof to a domestic industry, or the material retardation of the growth, or the prevention of the establishment of a nascent enterprise because of the subsidized imports, shall be determined by the Secretary or the Commission, as the case may be, on the basis of

positive evidence and shall require an objective examination of:
(1) The volume of the subsidized imports, that is, whether there has been a significant increase either absolute or relative to production or consumption in the domestic market;
(2) The effect of the subsidized imports on prices in the domestic market for the like product, commodity or article, that is, whether there has been a significant price undercutting, or whether the effect of such imports is otherwise to depress prices to a significant degree or to prevent price increases, which otherwise would have occurred to a significant degree;
(3) The effect of the subsidized imports on the domestic producers of the like product, commodity or article, including an evaluation of all relevant economic factors and indices having a bearing on the state of the domestic industry concerned, such as, but not limited to, actual and potential decline in output, sales, market share, profits, productivity, return on investments, or utilization of capacity; factors affecting domestic prices; actual or potential negative effects on the cash flow, inventories, employment, wages, growth, ability to raise capital or investments and, in the case of agriculture, whether there has been an increased burden on the support programs of the national government; and
(4) Factors other than the subsidized imports which at the same time are injuring the domestic industry, such as: volumes and prices of non -subsidized imports of the product, commodity or article in question; contraction in demand or changes in the patterns of consumption; trade restrictive practices of and competition between the foreign and domestic producers; developments in technology and the export performance and productivity of the domestic industry.

In determining threat of material injury, the Secretary or the Commission, as the case may be, shall decide on the basis of facts and not merely allegation, conjecture or remote possibility. The change in circumstances which would create a situation in which the subsidized imports would cause injury should be clearly foreseen and imminent considering such relevant factors as:
(1) Nature of the subsidy in question and the trade effects likely to arise therefrom;
(2) Significant rate of increase of subsidized imports into the domestic market indicating the likelihood of substantially increased importations;
(3) Sufficient freely disposable, or an imminent substantial increase in, capacity of the exporter of such subsidized imported product, commodity or article indicating the likelihood of substantially increased subsidized imports to the domestic market,

taking into account the availability of other markets to absorb the additional exports;
(4) Whether these subsidized imports are entering at prices that will have a significant depressing or suppressing effect on domestic prices, and will likely increase demand for further imports; and
(5) Inventories of the product, commodity or article being investigated.

In the case where the effect of the subsidized import will materially retard the growth or prevent the establishment of a domestic industry, information on employment, capital investments, production and sales, and production capacity of said domestic industry can be augmented or substituted by showing through a factual study, report or other data that an industry which has potential to grow domestically is adversely affected by the subsidized import. For this purpose, the Department of Trade and Industry for non -agricultural products, and the Department of Agriculture for agricultural products, shall conduct continuing studies to identify and determine the specific industries, whether locally existing or not, which have the potential to grow or to be established domestically and whose growth or establishment will be retarded or prevented by a subsidized import.

(K) Cumulation of Imports. - When imports of products, commodities or articles from more than one (1) country are simultaneously the subject of an investigation for the imposition of a countervailing duty, the Secretary or the Commission, as the case may be, may cumulatively assess the effects of such imports only if:
(1) The amount of subsidization established in relation to the imports from each country is more than de minimis as defiridd in existing international trade agreements of which the Republic of the Philippines is a party; and
(2) The volume of such imports from each country is not negligible; and
(3) A cumulative assessment of the effects of such imports is warranted in the light of the conditions of competition between the imported products, commodities or articles, and the conditions of competition between the imported products, commodities or articles and the like domestic products, commodities or articles.

(L) Public Notices and Consultation Proceedings. - The Secretary or the Commission, as the case may be, shall make public notices and conduct consultation with the government of the exporting country when:
(1) Initiating an investigation;
(2) Concluding or suspending an investigation;
(3) Making a preliminary or final determination;
(4) Making a decision to accept an undertaking or the termination of an undertaking; and

(5) Terminating a definitive countervailing duty.

(M) Voluntary Undertaking. - When there is an offer from any exporter of subsidized imports to revise its price, or where the government of the exporting country agrees to eliminate or limit the subsidy or take other measures to that effect, the Commission shall determine if the offer is acceptable and make the necessary recommendation to the Secretary. If the undertaking is accepted, the Secretary may advise the Commission to terminate, suspend or continue the investigation. The Secretary may also advise the Commission to continue its investigation upon the request of the government of the exporting country. The voluntary undertaking shall lapse if there is a negative finding of the presence of a subsidy or material injury. In the event of a positive finding of subsidization and material injury, the undertaking will continue, consistent with its terms and the provisions of this section.

(N) Final Determination and Submission of Report by the Commission. - The Commission shall complete the formal investigation and submit a report of its findings to the Secretary within one hundred twenty (120) days from receipt of the records of the case: Provided, however, That it shall, before a final determination is made, inform all the interested parties of the essential facts under consideration which form the basis for the decision to impose a countervailing duty. Such disclosure should take place in sufficient time for the parties to defend their interests.

(O) Imposition of Countervailing Duty. - The Secretary shall, within ten (10) days from his receipt of an affirmative final determination by the Commission, issue a department order imposing the countervailing duty on the subsidized imported product, commodity or article. He shall furnish the Secretary of Finance with the copy of the order and request the latter to direct the Commissioner of Customs to cause the countervailing duty to be levied, collected and paid, in addition to any other duties, taxes and charges imposed by law on such product, commodity or article.

In case of an affirmative final determination by the Commission, the cash bond shall be applied to the countervailing duty assessed. If the cash bond is in excess of the countervailing duty assessed, the remainder shall be returned to the importer immediately: Provided, That no interest shall be payable by the government on the amount to be returned. If the cash bond is less than the countervailing duty assessed, the difference shall not be collected.

If the order of the Secretary is unfavorable to the petitioner, the Secretary shall, after the lapse of the period for appeal to the Court of Tax Appeals, issue through the Secretary of Finance a department order for the immediate release of the cash bond to the importer.

(P) Duration and Review of Countervailing Duty. – As a general rule, any imposition of countervailing duty shall remain in force only as long as and to the extent necessary to counteract a subsidization which is causing or threatening to cause material injury. However, the need for the continued imposition of the countervailing duty may be reviewed by the Commission when warranted, motu proprio or upon direction of the Secretary.

Any interested party may also petition the Secretary for a review of the continued imposition of the countervailing duty: Provided, That at least six (6) months have elapsed since the imposition of the countervailing duty, and upon submission of positive information substantiating the need for a review. Interested parties may request the Secretary to examine: (1) whether the continued imposition of the countervailing duty is necessary to offset the subsidization; and/or (2) whether the injury will likely continue or recur if the countervailing duty is removed or modified.

If the Commission determines that the countervailing duty is no longer necessary or warranted, the Secretary shall, upon its recommendation, immediately issue a department order terminating the imposition of the countervailing duty and shall notify all parties concerned, including the Commissioner of Customs through the Secretary of Finance, of such termination.

Notwithstanding the provisions of the preceding paragraphs of this subsection, any countervailing duty shall be terminated on a date not later than five (5) years from the date of its imposition (or from the date of the most recent review if that review has covered both subsidization and material injury), unless the Commission has determined, in a review initiated at least six (6) months prior to the termination date upon the direction of the Secretary or upon a duly substantiated request by or on behalf of the domestic industry, that the termination of the countervailing duty will likely lead to the continuation or recurrence of the subsidization and material injury.

The procedure and evidence governing the disposition of the petition for the imposition of countervailing duty shall equally apply to any review carried out under this subsection. Such review shall be carried out expeditiously and shall be concluded not later than ninety (90) days from the date of the initiation of such a review.

(Q) Judicial Review. - Any interested party who is adversely affected by the department order of the Secretary on the imposition of the countervailing duty may file with the Court of Tax Appeals a petition for review of such order within thirty (30) days from his receipt of notice thereof: Provided, however, That the filing of such petition for review shall not in any way stop, suspend or otherwise toll the imposition and collection of the countervailing duty on the imported product, commodity or article.

The petition for review shall comply with the same requirements, follow the same rules of procedure, and be subject to the same disposition as in appeals in connection with adverse rulings on tax matters to the Court of Tax Appeals.

(R) Definition of Terms. - For purposes of this subsection, the term:
   (1) 'Domestic industry' shall refer to the domestic producers as a whole of the like product, commodity or article or to those of them whose collective output of the product, commodity or article constitutes a major proportion of the total d domestic production of those products, except that when producers a re related to the exporters or importers or are themselves importers of the allegedly subsidized product or a like product from other countries, the term 'domestic industry' may be interpreted as referring to the rest of the producers. In case the market in the Philippines is divided into two or more competitive markets, the term 'domestic industry' shall refer to the producers within each market although their production does not constitute a significant portion of the total domestic industry: Provided, That there is a concentration of subsidized imports into such a separate market: and Provided, further, That the subsidized imports are causing injury to the producers of all or almost all of the production within such market.
   (2) 'Interested parties' shall include: (a) An exporter or foreign producer or the importer of a product subject to investigation, or the government of the exporting country or a trade or business association a majority of the members of which are producers, exporters or importers of such product;
      (b) A producer of the like product in the Philippines or a trade and business association a majority of the members of which produce the like product in the Philippines; and
      (c) Labor unions that are representative of the industry or coalitions of producers and/or labor unions.
   (3) 'Like product' shall mean a product, commodity or article which is identical, i.e., alike in all respects to the product, commodity or article or in the absence of such product, commodity or article, another product, commodity or article which, although not alike in all respects, has characteristics closely resembling those of the imported product, commodity or article under consideration.
(S) An inter-agency committee composed of the Secretaries of Trade and Industry, Agriculture, and Finance, the Chairman of the Tariff Commission, and the Commissioner

of Customs shall promulgate all rules and regulations necessary for the effective implementation of this section." (As amended by Republic Act No. 8751 dated 07 August 1999)

SECTION 303. Marking of Imported Articles and Containers.

a. Marking of Articles. - Except as hereinafter provided, every article of foreign origin (or its container, as provided in subsection "b" hereof) imported into the Philippines shall be marked in any official language of the Philippines and in a conspicuous place as legibly, indelibly and permanently as the nature of the article (or container) will permit in such manner as to indicate to an ultimate purchaser in the Philippines the name of the country of origin of the article. The Commissioner of Customs shall, with the approval of the department head, issue rules and regulations to -

1. Determine the character of words and phrases or abbreviation thereof which shall be acceptable as indicating the country of origin and prescribe any reasonable method of marking, whether by printing, stenciling, stamping, branding, labelling or by any other reasonable method, and a conspicuous place on the article or container where the marking shall appear.
2. Require the addition of any other words or symbols which may be appropriate to prevent deception or mistake as to the origin of the article or as to the origin of any other article with which such imported article is usually combined subsequent to importation but before delivery to an ultimate purchaser; and
3. Authorize the exception of any article from the requirements of marking if:
    a. Such article is incapable of being marked;
    b. Such article cannot be marked prior to shipment to the Philippines without injury;
    c. Such article cannot be marked prior to shipment to the Philippines, except at an expense economically prohibitive of its importation;
    d. The marking of a container of such article will reasonably indicate the origin of such article;
    e. Such article is a crude substance;
    f. Such article is imported for use by the importer and not intended for sale in its imported or any other form;
    g. Such article is to be processed in t he Philippines b y t he importer o r f or h is account otherwise than for the purpose of concealing the origin of such article and in such manner that any mark contemplated by this section would necessarily be obliterated, destroyed or permanently concealed;

    h. An ultimate purchaser, by reason of the character of such article or by reason of the circumstances of its importation must necessarily k now t he country o f origin o f such article even though it is not marked to indicate its origin;

    I. Such article was produced more than twenty years prior to its importation into the Philippines; or

    j. Such article cannot be marked after importation except at an expense which is economically prohibitive, and the failure to mark the article before importation was not due to any purpose of the importer, producer, seller or shipper to avoid compliance with this section.

b. Marking of Containers. - Whenever an article is excepted under subdivision (3) of subsection "a" of this section from the requirements of marking, the immediate container, if any, of such article, or such other container or containers of such article as may be prescribed by the Commissioner of Customs with the approval of the department head, shall be marked in such manner as to indicate to an ultimate purchaser in the Philippines the name of the country of origin of such article in any official language of the Philippines, subject to all provisions of this section, including the same exceptions as are applicable to articles under subdivision (3) of subsection "a".

c. Marking Duty for Failure to Mark. - If at the time of importation any article (or its container, as provided in subsection "b" hereof), is not marked in accordance with the requirements of this section, there shall be levied, collected and paid upon such article a marking duty of 5 per cent ad valorem, which shall be deemed to have accrued at the time of importation, except when such article is exported or destroyed under customs supervision and prior to the final liquidation of the corresponding entry.

d. Delivery Withheld Until Marked. - No imported article held in customs custody for inspection, examination or appraisement shall be delivered until such article and/or its containers, whether released or not from customs custody, shall have been marked in accordance with the requirements of this section and until the amount of duty estimated to be payable under subsection "c" of this section shall have been deposited. Nothing in this section shall be construed as excepting any article or its container from the particular requirements of marking provided for in any provision of law.

e. The failure or refusal of the owner or importer to mark the articles as herein required within a period of thirty days after due notice shall constitute as an act of abandonment of said articles and their disposition shall be governed by the provisions of this Code relative to abandonment of imported articles.

SECTION 304. Discrimination by Foreign Countries.

a. The President. when he finds that the public interest will be served thereby, shall by proclamation specify and declare new or additional duties in an amount not exceeding one hundred (100) per cent ad valorem upon articles wholly or in part the growth or product of, or imported in a vessel of, any foreign country whenever he shall find as a fact that such country -

   1. Imposes, directly or indirectly, upon the disposition or transportation in transit through or re-exportation from such country of any article wholly or in part the growth or product of the Philippines, any unreasonable charge, exaction, regulation or limitation which is not equally enforced upon the like articles of every foreign country; or
   2. Discriminates in fact against the commerce of the Philippines, directly or indirectly, by law or administrative regulation or practice, by or in respect to any customs, tonnage, or port duty, fee, charge, exaction, classification, regulation, condition, restriction or prohibition, in such manner as to place the commerce of the Philippines at a disadvantage compared with the commerce of any foreign country.

b. If at any time the President shall find it to be a fact that any foreign country has not only discriminated against the commerce of the Philippines, as aforesaid, but has, after the issuance of a proclamation as authorized in subsection "a " of this section, maintained or increased its said discrimination against the commerce of the Philippines, the President is hereby authorized, if he deems it consistent with the interests of the Philippines, to issue a further proclamation directing that such product of said country or such article imported in its vessels as he shall deem consistent with the public interests, shall be excluded from importation into the Philippines.

c. Any proclamation issued by the President under this section shall, if he deems it consistent with the interest of the Philippines, extend to the whole of any foreign country or may be confined to any subdivision or subdivisions thereof; and the President shall, whenever he deems the public interests require, suspend, revoke, supplement or amend any such proclamation.

d. All articles imported contrary to the -provisions of this section shall be forfeited to the Government of the Philippines and shall be liable to be seized, prosecuted and condemned in like manner and under the same regulations, restrictions and provisions as may from time to time be established for the recovery, collection, distribution and remission or forfeiture to the government by the tariff and customs laws. Whenever the provision of this section shall be applicable to importations into the Philippines of articles wholly or in part the growth or product of any foreign country, they shall be applicable thereto, whether such articles are imported directly or indirectly.

e. It shall be the duty of the Commission to ascertain and at all times to be informed whether any of the discriminations against the commerce of the Philippines enumerated in subsections "a" and "b" of this section are practiced by any country; and if and when such discriminatory acts are disclosed, it shall be the duty of the Commission to bring the matter to the attention of the President, together with recommendations.

f. The Secretary of Finance shall make such rules and regulations as are necessary for the execution of such proclamation as the President may issue in accordance with the provisions of this section.

PART 3. – FLEXIBLE TARIFF
SECTION 401. Flexible Clause.

a. In the interest of national economy, general welfare and/or national security, and subject to the limitations herein prescribed, the President, upon recommendation of the National Economic and Development Authority (hereinafter referred to as N EDA), is hereby empowered: (1) to increase, reduce or remove existing protective rates of import duty (including any necessary change in classification). The existing rates may be increased or decreased to any level, in one or several stages but in no case shall the increased rate of import duty be higher than a maximum of one hundred (100) per cent ad valorem; (2) to establish import quota or to ban imports of any commodity, as may be necessary; and (3) to impose an additional duty on all imports not exceeding ten (10) per cent ad valorem whenever necessary: Provided : That upon periodic investigations by the Tariff Commission and recommendation of the NEDA, the President may cause a gradual reduction of protection levels granted in Section One Hundred and Four of this Code, including those subsequently granted pursuant to this section.

b. Before any recommendation is submitted to the President by the NEDA pursuant to the provisions of this section, except in the imposition of an additional duty not exceeding ten (10) per cent ad valorem, the Commission shall conduct an investigation in the course of which they shall hold public hearings wherein interested p arties s hall b e afforded reasonable opportunity to b e p resent, produce evidence and to be heard. The Commission shall also hear the views and recommendations of any government office, agency or instrumentality concerned. The Commission shall submit their findings and recommendations to the NEDA within thirty (30) days after the termination of the public hearings.

c. The power of the President to increase or decrease rates of import duty within the limits fixed in subsection "a" shall include the authority to modify the form of duty. In modifying the form of duty, the corresponding ad valorem or specific equivalents of the duty with respect to imports from the principal competing foreign country for the most recent representative period shall be used as bases.
d. The Commissioner of Customs shall regularly furnish the Commission a copy of all customs import entries as filed In t he B ureau o f Customs. The Commission or its duly authorized representatives shall have access to, and the right to copy all liquidated customs Import entries and other documents appended thereto as finally filed in the Commission on Audit.
e. The NEDA shall promulgate rules and regulations necessary to carry out the provisions of this section.
f. Any Order issued by the President pursuant to the provisions of this section shall take effect thirty (30) days after promulgation, except in the , imposition of additional duty not exceeding ten (10) per cent ad valorem which shall take effect at the discretion of the President.

SECTION 402. Promotion of Foreign Trade.

a. For the purpose of expanding foreign markets for Philippine products as a means of assistance in the economic development of the country, in overcoming domestic unemployment, in increasing the purchasing power of the Philippine peso, and in establishing and maintaining better relations between the Philippines and other countries, the President, is authorized from time to time: (1) To enter into trade agreements with foreign governments or instrumentalities thereof; and

(2) To modify import duties (including any necessary change in classification) and other import restrictions, as are required or appropriate to carry out and promote foreign trade with other countries: Provided, however, That in modifying import duties or fixing import quota the requirements prescribed in subsection "a " of Section 401 shall be observed: Provided, further, That any modification of import duties and any fixing of import quotas made pursuant to the agreement on ASEAN Preferential Trading Arrangements ratified on August 1, 1977 shall not be subject to the limitations of aforesaid section "a" of Section 401.

b. The duties and other import restrictions as modified in subsection "a " above, shall apply to articles which are the growth, produce or manufacture of the specific country, whether imported directly or indirectly, with which the Philippines has entered into a trade agreement: Provided, That the President may suspend the application of any concession to articles which are the growth, produce or manufacture of such country because of acts (including the operations of international cartels) or policies which in his opinion tend to defeat the purposes set in this section; and the duties and other import restrictions as negotiated shall be in force and effect from and after such time as specified in the Order.

c. Nothing in this section shall be construed to give any authority to cancel or reduce in any manner any of the indebtedness of any foreign country t o t he Philippines or any claim of the Philippines against any foreign country.

d. Before any trade agreement is concluded with any foreign government or instrumentality thereof, reasonable public notice of the intention to negotiate an agreement with such government or instrumentality shall be given in order that any interested person may have an opportunity to present his views to the Commission which shall seek information and advice from the Department of Agriculture, Department of Natural Resources, Department of Trade and Industry, Department of Tourism, the Central Bank of the Philippines, the Department of Foreign Affairs, the Board of Investments and from such other sources as it may deem appropriate.

e. (1) In advising the President, as a result of the trade agreement entered into, the Commission shall determine whether the domestic industry has suffered or is being threatened with injury and whether the wholesale prices at which the domestic products are sold are reasonable, taking into

   (2) The NEDA shall evaluate the report of the Commission and submit recommendations to the President.

   (3) Upon receipt of the report of the findings and recommendations of the NEDA, the President may prescribe such adjustments in the rates of import duties, withdraw, modify or suspend, in whole or in part, any concession under any trade agreement, establish import quota, or institute such other import restrictions as the NEDA recommends to be necessary in order to fully protect domestic industry and the consumers, subject to the condition that the wholesale prices of the domestic products concerned shall be reduced to, or maintained at, the level recommended by the NEDA unless for good cause shown, an increase thereof, as recommended by the NEDA, is authorized by the President. Should increases be made without such authority, the NEDA shall immediately notify the President, who shall allow the importation of competing products in such quantities as to project the public from the unauthorized increase in wholesale prices.

f. This section shall not prevent the effectivity of any executive agreement or any future preferential trade agreement with any foreign country.

g. The NEDA and the Commission are authorized to promulgate such reasonable procedure, rules and regulations as they may deem necessary to execute their respective functions under this section.

PART 4. – TARIFF COMMISSION SECTION 501. Chief Officials of the Tariff Commission.

The Officials of the Tariff Commission shall be the Chairman and two (2) Member Commissioners to be appointed by the President of the Philippines.

SECTION 502. Qualifications.

No person shall be eligible for appointment as Chairman and Tariff Commissioners unless they are natural -born citizens of the Philippines, of good moral character and proven integrity, and who by experience and academic training are possessed of qualifications requisite for developing expert knowledge of tariff problems. They shall not, during their tenure in office, engage in the practice of any profession, or intervene directly or indirectly in the management or control of any private enterprise which may, in any way, be affected by the functions of their office nor shall be, directly or indirectly, financially interested in any contract with the Government, or any subdivision or instrumentality thereof.

SECTION 503. Appointment and Compensation of Officials and Employees.

All employees of the Commission shall be appointed by the Chairman in accordance with the Civil Service Law except the private secretaries to the Chairman, Commissioners and Executive Director.

The Tariff Commission shall be reorganized in accordance with the requirements of its reorganized functions and responsibilities. The Chairman of the Commission, subject to the approval of the Director -General of the National Economic and Development Authority, shall determine the new positions -designations and salary scales of the officials and employees of the Commission by taking into account the degree of responsibilities of each position: Provided, That the Office of Compensation and Position Classification shall be furnished a copy of the new plantilla of positions incorporating the new designations to be automatically included in its manual of positions: Provided, further, That the reorganization shall not in any way affect whatever benefits the officials and employees of the

Commission are allowed under existing law and/or authority.

SECTION 504. Official Seal.

The Commission is authorized to adopt an official seal.

SECTION 505. Functions of the Commission.

The Commission shall investigate -

(a) the administration of, and the fiscal and industrial effects of, the tariff and customs laws of this country now in force or which may hereafter be enacted; (b) the relations between the rates of duty on raw materials and the finished or partly finished

(c) the effects of ad valorem and specific duties and of compound specific and ad valorem duties;

(d) all questions relative to the arrangement of schedules and classification of articles in the several sections of the tariff law;

(e) the tariff relations between the Philippines and foreign countries, commercial treaties, preferential provisions, economic alliances, the effect of export bounties and preferential transportation rates;

(f) the volume of importations compared with domestic production and consumption;

(g) conditions, causes and effects relating to competition of foreign industries with those of the Philippines, including dumping and cost of production;

(h) in general, to investigate the operation of customs and tariff laws, including their relation to the national revenues, their effect upon the industries and labor of the country, and to submit reports of its investigations as hereinafter provided; and

(i) the nature and composition of, and the classification of, articles according to tariff commodity classification and heading number for customs revenue and other related purposes which shall be furnished to NEDA, Board of Investments, Central Bank of the Philippines, and Secretary of Finance.

SECTION 506. Assistance to the President and Congress of the Philippines.

In order that the President and the Congress may secure information and assistance, it shall be the duty of the Commission to -

(a) Ascertain conversion costs and costs of production in the principal growing, producing or manufacturing centers of the Philippines, whenever practicable;

(b) Ascertain conversion costs and costs of production in the principal growing, producing or manufacturing centers of foreign countries of articles imported into the Philippines whenever such conversion costs or costs of production are necessary for comparison with those in the Philippines;

(c) Select and describe representative articles imported into the Philippines similar to, or comparable with, those locally produced; select and describe articles of the Philippines similar to, or comparable with, such imported article; and obtain and file samples of articles so selected whenever advisable;

(d) Ascertain import costs of such representative articles so selected;

(e) Ascertain the grower's, producer's or manufacturers selling prices in the principal growing, producing or manufacturing centers of the Philippines, of the articles of the Philippines, so selected;

(f) Ascertain all other facts which will show the difference in, or which affect competition between, articles of the Philippines and those imported in the principal markets of the Philippines;

(g) Ascertain conversion costs and costs of production including effects of tariff modifications or import restrictions on prices in the principal growing, producing or manufacturing centers of the Philippines, whenever practicable; and

(h) Submit annual reports of these to the President of the Philippines, copy of which shall be furnished to the NEDA, Central Bank of the Philippines, Department of Finance and the Board of Investments.

SECTION 507. Reports of the Commission.

The Commission shall place at the disposal of the President and any member of the Congress of the Philippines or its member thereof all information at its command; shall make such investigation and report as may be required by the President and the Congress of the Philippines and shall report to the President and Congress on the first Monday of December of each year hereafter a statement of methods adopted and a summary of all reports made during the year.

The Commission or its duly authorized representative shall have access to any document, paper or record, pertinent to the subject matter under investigation, in the possession of any person, firm, co-partnership, corporation or association engaged in the production, importation or distribution of any article under investigation, and shall have power to summon witnesses, take testimony, administer oaths, and to issue subpoena duces tecum requiring the production of books, papers or documents relating to the matter under investigation. The Commission may also request the views, recommendations and/or assistance of any government office, agency or instrumentality, and such office, agency or instrumentality shall cooperate fully with the Commission.

SECTION 509. Sworn Statements.

The Commission may order the taking of sworn statements at any stage of any proceeding or investigation before it. Such sworn statements may be taken before any person having power to administer oaths.

SECTION 510. Verified Statements.

The Commission is authorized to require any importer, grower, producer, manufacturer or seller to file with the Commission a statement, under oath, giving his selling prices in the Philippines of any article imported, grown, produced, fabricated or manufactured by him.

SECTION 511. Rules and Regulations of the Commission.

The Commission shall adopt and promulgate such rules and regulations as may be necessary to carry out the provisions of this Code.

SECTION 512. Appropriation.

In addition to its current appropriation the amount of Six Hundred Thousand Pesos is hereby appropriated to carry out the purpose of sections five hundred one and five hundred three of this Code.

TITLE III. EXPORT TARIFF AND PREMIUM DUTY

SECTION 514. Export Products Subject to Duty and Rates.

There shall be levied, assessed and collected an export duty on the gross F.O.B. value at the time of shipment based on the prevailing rate of exchange, of the following products in accordance with the schedule specified in the column Export Duty.

In addition to the export duties, herein referred to as basic rate, there shall be levied, assessed and collected a premium duty on the difference between the current price as established by the Bureau of Customs and the base price of the products in accordance with the schedule specified under the column Premium Duty; Provided, That should the current price or any export product be below the established base price, then only the basic rate shall be applied: Provided, further, That, initially, the base price upon which the premium duty shall be levied eighty per centum (80%) of the F.O.B. value of exports established by the Bureau of Customs for February 1974. The National Economic and Development Authority shall, from time to time, review and establish such base prices taking into account, among others, the cost conditions in various industries.

EXPORT PRODUCTS   EXPORT DUTY 1/

Wood Products

1. Logs   20%
2. Lumber
3. Veneer
4. Plywood

Mineral Products

1. Metallic ores and concentrates
    a) Copper
    b) Iron
    c) Chromite
2. Gold

EXPORT PRODUCTS   EXPORT DUTY 2/

3. Non-Metallic
    a) Clinker, cement
    b) Portland cement
4. Mineral fuel
    a) Bunker fuel oil
    b) Petroleum pitch
5. Silver

Plant and Vegetable Products

1. Abaca (stripped hemp, unmanufactured)
2. Banana
3. Coconut
    a) Copra
    b) Coconut oil
    c) Copra meal/cake
    d) Desiccated coconut
4. Pineapple
    a) Pineapple sliced or crushed
    b) Pineapple juice or juice concentrate

5. Sugar and Sugar Products
   a) Centrifugal sugar
   b) Molasses
6. Tobacco
   a) Tobacco leaf
   b) Scrap tobacco Animal Products
   1. Shrimps and Prawns
   For purposes of computing the duty, the cost of packaging and crating materials shall be deductible from the export value, provided such materials are domestically manufactured using a substantial portion of local raw materials, as determined by the Board of Investments.

SECTION 515. Flexible Clause.

The President, upon recommendation of the National Economic and Development Authority, may subject any of the above products to higher or lower rates of duty provided in this Title, include additional products, exclude or exempt any product from this Title, or additionally subject any product to an export quota. In the exercise of this authority the President shall take into account: (1) the policy of encouraging domestic processing; (2) the prevailing prices of export products in the world market; (3) the advantages obtained by export products from international agreements to which the Philippines is a signatory; (4) the preferential treatment granted to our export products by foreign governments; and (5) the need to meet domestic consumption requirements.

SECTION 516. Assessment and Collection of the Duty.

The duty shall be assessed by the Bureau of Customs and collected by the Bureau thru authorized agent banks of the Central Bank not later than 30 days from the date of shipment.

SECTION 517. Deficiency and Surcharges.

In case the duty is not fully paid a t the time specified hereof, the deficiency s hall be increased by an amount equivalent to twenty -five per centum (25%) thereof, the total to be collected in the same manner as the duty. Where the deficiency is the result of false or fraudulent statements or representations attributable to the exporter, the surcharge shall be fifty per centum (50%).

SECTION 518. Allotment and Disposition of the Proceeds

The proceeds of this duty shall accrue to the General Fund and shall be allotted for development projects; except that one per centum (1%) annually shall be set aside for the Export Assistance Fund to be administered by the Board of Investments and expended in accordance with the General Appropriation Act to finance export promotion projects; however, thirty per cent of this 1% shall accrue to the Bureau of Customs which shall constitute as its intelligence fund to be disbursed by the Commissioner of Customs in the implementation of this Title, such as but not limited to the purchase of equipment, hiring of personnel if necessary and for such other operational expenses in the promotion of the export industry.

SECTION 519 Rules and Regulations.

The Commissioner of Customs shall promulgate the rules and regulations necessary for the implementation of this Title, subject to the approval of the Secretary of Finance.
1/ Export duties on all export products except logs abolished under Executive Order No. 26 dated July 1, 1986
2/ Export duties on all products except logs abolished under Executive Order No. 26 dated July 1, 1986

TARIFF AND CUSTOMS CODE OF THE PHILIPPINES (TCCP) VOLUME II CONTENTS

BOOK 11 CUSTOMS LAW

TITLE I – THE BUREAU OF CUSTOMS
PART 1 - ORGANIZATION, FUNCTION AND JURISDICTION OF THE BUREAU

Section 601 - Chief Officials of the Bureau of Customs
Section 602 - Functions of the Bureau
Section 603 - Territorial Jurisdiction
Section 604 - Jurisdiction Over Premises Used for Customs Purposes
Section 605 - Enforcement of Port Regulation of. Bureau of Quarantine

Section 606 - Power of the President to Subject Premises to Jurisdiction of Bureau of Customs
Section 607 - Annual Report of Commissioner
Section 608 - Commissioner to Make Rules and Regulations
Section 609 - Commissioner to Furnish Copies of Collector's Liquidated Duplicates

PART 2 - COLLECTION DISTRICT AND PORTS OF ENTRY

Section 701 - Collection Districts and Ports of Entry Thereof
Section 702 - Power of the President to Open and Close Any Port
Section 703 - Assignment of Customs Officers and Employees to Other Duties Section 704 - Seal of Collector of Customs
Section 705 - Authority of Deputy Collectors of Customs
Section 706 - Appointment of Special Duties with Limited Powers
Section 707 - Succession of Deputy Collector to Position of Acting Collector
Section 708 - Designation of Official as Customs Inspector
Section 709 - Authority of Collector to Remit Duties
Section 710 - Records to be Kept by Customs Officials
Section 711 - Port Regulations Section 712 - Reports of Collector to Commissioner

TITLE II – COASTWISE TRADE

Section 906 - Requirement of Manifest in Coastwise Trade
Section 907 - Manifest Required Upon Departure from Port of Entry
Section 908 - Manifests Required Prior to Unloading at Port of Entry
Section 909 - Departure of Vessel Upon Detailed Manifest

TITLE III – VESSELS AND AIRCRAFTS IN FOREIGN TRADE PART 1 – ENTRANCE AND CLEARANCE OF VESSELS

Section 1001 - Ports Open to Vessels Engaged in Foreign Trade - Duty of Vessel to Make Entry
Section 1002 - Control of Customs Official Over Boarding or Leaving of Incoming Vessel and Over Other Vessels Approaching the former
Section 1003 - Quarantine Certificate for Incoming Vessel
Section 1004 - Documents to be Produced by the Master Upon Entry of Vessel Section 1005 - Manifest Required of Vessel from Foreign Port

Section 1006 - Translation of Manifest
Section 1007 - Manifests for Commission on Audit and Collector Section 1008 - Transit Cargo
Section 1009 - Clearance of Foreign Vessels To and From Coastwise Ports Section 1010 - Requirement as to Delivery of Mail
Section 1011 - Production of Philippine Crew
Section 1012 - Record of Arrival and Entry of Vessels
Section 1013 - Arrest of Vessel Departing Before Entry Made
Section 1014 - Discharge of Ballast Section 1015 - Time of Unlading of Cargo Section 1016 - Entrance of Vessel Through Necessity
Section 1017 - Unlading Vessel in Port from Necessity
Section 1018 - Entry and Clearance of Vessels of a Foreign Government
Section 1019 - Clearance of Vessel for Foreign Port
Section 1020 - Detention of Warlike Vessel Containing Arms and Munitions Section 1021 - Manifest of Export Cargo to be Delivered to Chairman, Commission on Audit
Section 1022 - Oath of Master of Departing Vessel
Section 1023 - Extension of Time for Clearance
Section 1025 - Export Product to Conform to Standard Grades

PART 2 - ENTRANCE AND CLEARANCE OF AIRCRAFT IN FOREIGN TRADE Section 1101 - Designation of Airports of Entry

Section 1102 - Advance Notice of Arrival
Section 1103 - Landing at International Airports of Entry
Section 1104 - Report of Arrival and Entry
Section 1105 - Documents Required in Making Entry
Section 1106 - Manifest for Commission on Audit
Section 1107 - Delivery of Mail
Section 1110 - Manifest for Transit Cargo
Section 1111 - Clearance of Aircraft for Foreign Port
Section 1112 - Oath of Person in Charge of Departing Aircraft

TITLE IV - ASCERTAINMENT, COLLECTION, AND RECOVERY OF IMPORT DUTY

PART 1 - IMPORTATION IN GENERAL

Section 1201 - Article to be Imported Only Through Customhouse
Section 1202 - When Importation Begins and Deemed Terminated
Section 1203 - Owner of Imported Articles
Section 1204 - Liability of Importer for Duties
Section 1205 - Importations by the Government
Section 1206 - Jurisdiction of Collector Over Importation of Articles
Section 1207 - Jurisdiction of Collector Over Articles of Prohibited Importation Section 1210 - Disposition of Imported Articles Remaining on Vessel After Time for Unlading
Section 1211 - Handling of Articles on Which Duty Has Not Been Paid

PART 2 - ENTRY AT CUSTOMHOUSE

Section 1301 - Persons Authorized to Make Import Entry
Section 1302 - Import Entries
Section 1303 - Entry of Article in Part for Consumption and in Part for Warehousing
Section 1304 - Declaration of the Import Entry
Section 1305 - BY Whom to be Signed
Section 1306 - Forms and Contents of Import Entry
Section 1307 - Description of Articles
Section 1308 - Commercial Invoice
Section 1309 - (Repealed by E.O. 736)
Section 1310 - (Repealed by P.D. 1679, March 6, 1980)
Section 1311 - (Repealed by P.D. 1679, March 6, 1980)
Section 1312 - (Repealed by P.D. 1679, March 6, 1980)
Section 1313 - Information Furnished on Classification and Value
Section 1314 - Forwarding of Cargo and Remains of Wrecked Vessel or Aircraft Section 1315 - Derelicts and Articles From Abandoned Wrecks

PART 3 - EXAMINATION, CLASSIFICATION AND APPRAISAL OF IMPORTED ARTICLES

Section 1401 - Conditions for Examination
Section 1402 - Ascertainment of Weight and Quantity

Section 1403 - Duties of Customs Officer Tasked to Examine, Classify and Appraise Imported Articles
Section 1404 - (Repealed by R.A. 7650, April 6, 1993)
Section 1405 - Proceeding and Report of Appraisers
Section 1406 - Appraisers' Samples
Section 1407 - Readjustment of Appraisal, Classification or Return
Section 1408 - Assessment of Duty on Less Than Entered Value
Section 1409 - Employment and Compensation of Persons to Assist in Appraisal or Classification of Articles

PART 4 - DELIVERY OF ARTICLES

Section 1501 - Delivery of Articles to Holder of Bill Lading
Section 1502 - Delivery of Articles Without Production of Bill of Lading
Section 1503 - Cash Deposit Upon Delivery of Unexamined Packages
Section 1504 - Delivery Upon Order of Importer
Section 1505 - Witholding Delivery Pending Satisfaction of Lien
Section 1506 - Customs Expenses Constituting Charge on Articles
Section 1507. - Fine or Surcharge on Articles
Section 1508 - Authority of the Collector of Customs to Hold the Delivery or Release of Imported Articles

PART 5 - LIQUIDATION OF DUTIES

Section 1601 - Liquidation and Record of Entries
Section 1602 - Tentative Liquidation
Section 1603 - Finality of Liquidation
Section 1604 - Treatment of Fractions in the Liquidation

PART 6 - ABATEMENTS AND REFUNDS

Section 1701 - Abatement for Damage Incurred During Voyage
Section 1702 - Abatement or Refund of Duty on Missing Package
Section 1703 - Abatement or Refund for Deficiency in Contents of Package Section 1704 - Abatement or Refund of Duties on Articles Lost or Destroyed After Arrival
Section 1705 - Abatement of Duty on Dead or Injured Animals
Section 1706 - Investigation Required in Case of Abatements and Refunds

Section 1707 - Correction of Errors - Refund of Excess Payments
Section 1708 - Claim for Refund of Duties and Taxes and Mode of Payment

PART 7 - ABANDONMENT OF IMPORTED ARTICLES

Section 1801 - Abandonment, Kinds and Effects of Section 1802 - Abandonment of Imported Articles
Section 1803 - (Repealed by R.A. 7651, June 4, 1993)

TITLE V - WAREHOUSING OF IMPORTED ARTICLES
PART 1 - WAREHOUSING IN GENERAL

Section 1901 - Establishment and Supervision of Warehouses
Section 1902 - Responsibility of Operators
Section 1903 - Bonded Warehouses
Section 1904 - Irrevocable Domestic Letter of Credit or Bank Guarantee or Warehousing Bond
Section 1905 - Discontinuance of Warehouses
Section 1906 - Entry of Articles for Warehousing
Section 1907 - Withdrawal of Articles from Bonded Warehouse
Section 1908 - Limit to Period of Storage in Bonded Warehouse
Section 1909 - Charges of Storage in Bonded Warehouse

PART 2 - BONDED MANUFACTURING AND SMELTING WAREHOUSE

Section 2001 - Establishment of Bonded Manufacturing warehouses
Section 2002 - Exemption from Duty
Section 2003 - Procedure for Withdrawal
Section 2004 - Verification by the Commissioner
Section 2005 - Bonded Smelting Warehouses

PART 3 - TRANSPORTATION IN BOND

Section 2101 - Entry for Immediate Transportation
Section 2102 - Bonding of Carrier Transporting Articles Under the Preceding Section
Section 2103 - Articles Entered for Immediate Exportation.

TITLE VI – ADMINISTRATIVE AND JUDICIAL PROCEEDINGS
PART 1 - SEARCH, SEIZURE AND ARREST

Section 2201 - Trespass or Obstruction of Customs Premises

Section 2202 - Special Surveillance for Protection of Customs Revenue and Prevention of Smuggling

Section 2203 - Persons Having Police Authority

Section 2204 - Place Where Authority May Be Exercised

Section 2205 - Exercise of Power of Seizure and Arrest

Section 2206 - Duty of Officer or Official to Disclose Official Character

Section 2207 - Authority to Require Assistance

Section 2208 - Right of Police Officer to Enter Inclosure

Section 2209 - Search of Dwelling House

Section 2210 - Right to Search Vessels or Aircrafts and Persons or Articles Conveyed Therein

Section 2211 - Right to Search Vehicles, Beasts and Persons

Section 2212 - Search of Persons Arriving From Foreign Countries

PART 2 - ADMINISTRATIVE PROCEEDINGS

Section 2301 - Warrant for Detention of Property -Cash Bond

Section 2302 - Report of Seizure to Commissioner and Chairman, Commission on Audit

Section 2303 - Notification to Owner or Importer

Section 2304 - Notification to Unknown Owner

Section 2305 - Description, Appraisal and Classification of Seized Property Section 2306 - Proceedings in Case of Property Belonging to Unknown Parties Section 2307 - Settlement of Case by Payment of Fine or Redemption of Forfeited Property

Section 2308 - Protest and Payment Upon Protest in Civil Matters

Section 2309 - Protest Exclusive Remedy in Protestable Case

Section 2310 - Form and Scope of Protest

Section 2311 - Samples to be Furnished by Protesting Parties

Section 2312 - Decision or Action of Collector in Protest and Seizure Cases

Section 2313 - Review of Commissioner

Section 2314 - Notice of Decision of Commissioner

Section 2315 - Supervisory Authority of Commissioner and Secretary of Finance in Certain Cases

Section 2316 - Authority of Commissioner to Make Compromise
Section 2317 - Government's Right of Compulsory Acquisition

PART 3 - JUDICIAL PROCEEDINGS

Section 2401 - Supervision and Control Over Criminal and Civil Proceedings Section 2402 - Review of Court of Tax Appeals

PART 4 - SURCHARGES, FINES AND FORFEITURES

Section 2501 - Failure to Pay Liquidated Charges
Section 2501 - Unauthorized Withdrawal of Imported Articles From Bonded Warehouse
Section 2502 - (Repealed by P.D. 1679, March 6,1980)
Section 2503 - Undervaluation, Misclassification and Misdeclaration in Entry Section 2504 - Failure or Refusal of Party to Give Evidence or Submit Documents for Examination
Section 2505 - Failure to Declare Baggage
Section 2506 - Breach of Bond
Section 2513 - Vessel or Aircraft Departing Before Entry Made
Section 2514 - Obstruction to Boarding Official
Section 2515 - Unlawful Boarding or Leaving of Vessel or Aircraft
Section 2516 - Failure to Deliver or Receive Mail
Section 2517 - Unlading of Cargo Before Arrival at Port of Destination
Section 2518 - Unlading of Cargo at Improper Time or Place After Arrival Section 2519 - Failure to Exhibit or Deposit Documents
Section 2520 - Bringing of Unmanifested Arms, Explosives or War Equipment Section 2521 - Failure to Supply Requisite Manifests Section 2522 - Disappearance of Manifested Article
Section 2523 - Discrepancy Between Actual and Declared Weight of Manifested Article
Section 2524 - Delivery of Cargo Not Agreeing with the Master's or Pilot's In Command Report
Section 2525 - Breaking of Seal Placed by Customs Official
Section 2526 - Breaking of Lock or Fastening Placed by Customs Officials
Section 2527 - Disappearance of Trunk or Package Specially Noted by Customs Official
Section 2528 - False Statement of Vessel's or Aircraft's Destination Section 2529 - Other Offenses
Section 2530 - Property Subject to Forfeiture Under Tariff and Customs Laws Section 2531 -

Properties Not Subject to Forfeiture in the Absence of Prima Facie Evidence
Section 2532 - Conditions Affecting Forfeiture of Article
Section 2533 - Enforcement of Lien, Administrative Fines, and Forfeitures
Section 2534 - Seizure of Vessel or Aircraft for Delinquency of Owner or Officer Section 2535 - Burden of Proof in Seizure and/or Forfeiture
Section 2536 - Seizure of Other Articles

PART 5 - DISPOSITION OF PROPERTY IN CUSTOMS CUSTODY

Section 2601 - Property Subject to Sale
Section 2602 - Place of Sale or Other Disposition of Property
Section 2603 - Mode of Sale
Section 2604 - Disqualification to Participate in Auction Sale
Section 2605 - Disposition of Proceeds
Section 2606 - Disposition of Surplus from the Proceeds of Sale of Abandoned or Forfeited or Acquired Articles
Section 2607 - Disposition of Articles Liable to Deterioration
Section 2608 - Disposition of Articles Unfit for Use or Sale or Injurious to Public Health
Section 2609 - Disposition of Contraband
Section 2610 - Disposition of Unsold Articles for Want of Bidders
Section 2611 - Treatment of Dangerous Explosives
Section 2612 - Disposition of Smuggled Articles

PART 7 - FEES AND CHARGE S

Section 3301 - Customs Fees and Charges
Section 3302 - Other Charges
Section 3303 - Effect of Failure to Affix Stamp Upon Document
Section 3304 - General Provision on the Authority to Increase or Decrease Fees and Charges

TITLE VII – GENERAL PROVISIONS
PART 1 - CUSTOMS BROKERS

Section 3401 - Qualifications of Applicants for Custom Broker's Certificate
Section 3402 - Examination by the Board of Examiners for Customs Brokers Section 3403 - The Board of Examiners

부록 Ⅳ. TARIFF AND CUSTOMS CODE OF THE PHILIPPINES(TCCP) 147

Section 3404 - Compensation of Members of the Board
Section 3405 - Fee Section 3406 - Annual License Fee
Section 3407 - Issuance, Revocation and Suspension of Certificate
Section 3408 - Roster of Customs Brokers
Section 3409 - Rules and Regulations by the Commissioner of Civil Service

PART 2 - MISCELLANEOUS PROVISIONS

Section 3501 - Duty of Collector to Report Rulings to Commissioner
Section 3502 - Application of Established Ruling or Decision
Section 3503 - Authority of Official to Administer Oaths and Take Testimony Section 3504 - General Bonds Section 3505 - Supervision Over Attorneys -in -Fact Section 3506 - Assignment of Customs Employees to Overtime Work
Section 3510 - Reduction of Testimony to Writing
Section 3511 - Collector Not Liable in Respect of Ruling in Customs Cases Section 3512 - Interest Prohibited to be Held by Customs Employees
Section 3513 - Reward to Persons Instrumental in the Discovery and Seizure of Smuggled Goods
Section 3514 - Requirement to Keep Records
Section 3515 - Compliance Audit or Examination of Records
Section 3516 - Scope of the Audit
Section 3517 - Documents in Foreign Language
Section 3518 - Records to be Kept by Customs
Section 3519 - Words and Phrases Defined

PART 3 - PROVISIONS ON PENALITIES

Section 3601 - Unlawful Importation
Section 3602 - Various Fraudulent Practices Against Customs Revenue
Section 3603 - Failure to Report Fraud
Section 3604 - Statutory Offenses of Officials and Employees
Section 3605 - Concealment or Destruction of Evidence of Fraud
Section 3606 - Affixing Seals
Section 3607 - Removal, Breakage, Alteration of Marks
Section 3608 - Removing or Repacking Goods in Warehouse
Section 3609 - Removing Goods from Customs Custody
Section 3610 - Failure to Keep Importation Records and Give Full Access to Customs

Officers
Section 3611 - Failure to Pay Correct Duties and Taxes on Imported Goods Section 3612 - Violations of Tariff and Customs Laws And Regulations in General

FINAL PROVISIONS

Section 3701 - Repealing Clause
Section 3702 - Transitory Provisions
Section 3703 - Separability Clause
Section 3704 -Effectivity Date

BOOK II - CUSTOMS LAW

TITLE I - THE BUREAU OF CUSTOMS

PART 1 – ORGANIZATION, FUNCTION AND JURISDICTION OF THE BUREAU

SEC. 601. Chief Officials of the Bureau of Customs. –

The Bureau of Customs shall have one chief and four assistant chiefs, to be known respectively as the Commissioner of Customs (hereinafter known as the Commissioner) and four (4) Deputy Commissioners of Customs, each one to head (a) Customs Revenue Collection Monitoring Group; (b) Customs Assessment and Operations Coordinating Group; (c) Intelligence and Enforcement Group; (d) Internal Administration Group, who shall each receive an annual compensation in accordance with the rates prescribed by existing law. The Commissioner and the Deputy Commissioners of Customs shall be appointed by the President of the Philippines. (As amended by E.O. 127 effective 30 January 1987).

In case of temporary and permanent vacancy, one of the Deputy Commissioners shall be designated by the Secretary of Finance to act as Commissioner of Customs, until the incumbent Commissioner reassumes his duties or the position is filled by permanent appointment.

SEC. 602. Functions of the Bureau. –

The general duties, powers and jurisdiction of the bureau shall include:

a. The assessment and collection of the lawful revenues from imported articles and all other dues, fees, charges, fines and penalties accruing under the tariff and customs laws;
b. The prevention and suppression of smuggling and other frauds upon the customs;
c. The supervision and control over the entrance and clearance of vessels and aircraft engaged in foreign commerce;
d. The enforcement of the tariff and custom laws and all other laws, rules and regulations relating to the tariff and customs administration;
e. The supervision and control over the handling of foreign mails arriving in the Philippines, for the purpose of the collection of the lawful duty on the dutiable articles thus imported and the prevention of smuggling through the medium of such mails;
f. Supervise and control all import and export cargoes, landed or stored in piers, airports, terminal facilities, including container yards and freight stations, for the protection of government revenue;
g. Exercise exclusive original jurisdiction over seizure and forfeiture cases under the tariff and customs laws

SEC. 603. Territorial Jurisdiction. –

For the due and effective exercise of the powers conferred by law and to the extent requisite therefore, said Bureau shall have the right of supervision and police authority over all seas within the jurisdiction of the Philippines and over all coasts, ports, airports, harbors, bays, rivers, and inland waters whether navigable or not from the sea.

When a vessel becomes subject to seizure by reason of an act done in Philippine waters in violation of the tariff and customs laws, a pursuit of such vessel began within the jurisdictional waters may continue beyond the maritime zone, and the vessel may be seized on the high seas. Imported articles which may be subject to seizure for violation of the tariff and customs laws may be pursued in their transportation in the Philippines by land, water or air and such jurisdiction exerted over them at any place therein as may be necessary for the due enforcement of the law.

SEC. 604. Jurisdiction Over Premises Used for Customs Purposes. –

The Bureau of Customs shall for customs purposes, have exclusive control, direction and management of customhouses, warehouses, offices, wharves, and other premises in the respective ports of entry, in all cases without prejudice to the general police powers of the city or municipality and the Philippine Coast Guard in the exercise of its functions wherein such premises are situated.

SEC. 605. Enforcement of Port Regulation of Bureau of Quarantine. —

Customs employees shall cooperate with the quarantine authorities in the enforcement of the port quarantine regulations promulgated by the Bureau of Quarantine and shall give effect to the same in so far as connected with matters of shipping and navigation.

SEC. 606.

Power of the President to Subject Premises to Jurisdiction of Bureau of Customs any public wharf, landing place, street or land, not previously under the jurisdiction of the Bureau of C in any port of entry, is necessary or desirable for any proper customs purpose, the President of the Pr may, by executive order, declare such premises to be under the jurisdiction of the Bureau of Custo - thereafter the authority of such Bureau in respect thereto shall be fully effective.

SEC. 607. Annual Report of Commissioner. —

The annual report of the Commissioner to the President shall, among other things, contain a compilation of the (a) quantity and value of the articles imported into the Philippines and the corresponding amount of custom duties, taxes and other charges assessed and collected on imported articles itemized in accordance with the tariff headings and subheadings as appearing the liquidated customs entries provided for in this Code, (b) percentage collection of the peso value of imports, (c) quantity and value of conditionally -free importations, (d) customs valuation over and above letters of credit opened, (e) quantity and value of tax -free imports, and (f) the quantity and value of articles exported from the Philippines as well as the taxes and other charges assessed and collected on them for the preceding year. Copies of such annual report shall be furnished regularly to the Department of Finance. Commission, NEDA, Central Bank of the Philippines. Board of Investments, Department of Budget, and other economic agencies of the government, on or before December 30, of each year.

For more scientific preparation of the annual report, the Commissioner shall cause computerization of the data contained in the liquidated entries filed with the Bureau of Customs.

SEC. 608. Commissioner to Make Rules and Regulations. —

The Commissioner shall, subject tc approval of the Secretary of Finance, promulgate all rules and regulations necessary to enforce the provisions of this Code. He shall also cause the preparation and publication of a customs manual covering up -to -date rules and regulations and decisions of the Bureau of Customs. The manual shall be published and made available to the public at least once every quarter within the first month after the end of every quarter. The Secretary of Finance and/or the Commissioner of Customs shall furnish the Central Bank of the Philippines, Board of Investments, the NEDA and the Tariff Commission with at least three copies each of eve department order, administrative order, memorandum circulars and such rules and regulations which a promulgated from time to time for the purpose of implementing the provisions of the Code.

SEC. 609. Commissioner to Furnish Copies of Collectors' Liquidated Duplicates. –

The Commissioner shall regularly furnish the NEDA, the Central Bank of the Philippines, the Tariff Commission a copy of each of all customs import/export entries as filed with the Bureau of Customs. The Tariff Commission or its duly authorized agents shall have access to and the right to copy all the customs liquidated import entries and other documents appended thereto as finally filed in the Commission on Audit,

PART 2. – COLLECTION DISTRICTS AND PORT OF ENTRY

SEC. 701. Collection Districts and Ports of Entry Thereof. –

For administrative purposes, the Philippines shall be divided into as many collection districts as necessary, the respective limits of which may be changed from time to time by the Commissioner of Customs upon approval of the Secretary of Finance. The principal ports of entry for the respective collection districts shall be Manila, Ninoy Aquino International Airport, Cebu, Iloilo, Davao, Tacloban, Zamboanga, Cagayan de Oro, Surigao, Legaspi, Batangas, San Fernando, Subic and Manila International Container Port.

SEC. 702. Power of the President to Open and Close Any Port. –

The president may open or close any port of entry upon recommendation of the Commissioner and the Secretary of Finance. While a port of entry is closed, its existing personnel shall be reassigned to other duties by the Commissioner subject to the approval of the Secretary of Finance.

SEC. 703. Assignment of Customs Officers and Employees to Other Duties. –

The Commissioner of Customs may, with the approval of the Secretary of Finance, assign any employee of the Bureau of Customs to any port, service, division or office within the

Bureau or assign him duties as the best interest of the service may require, in accordance with the staffing pattern or organizational set-up as may be prescribed by the Commissioner of Customs with the approval of the Secretary of Finance: Provided, That such assignment shall not affect the tenure of office of the employees nor result in the change of status, demotion in rank and/or deduction in salary.

SEC. 704. Seal of Collector of Customs. –

In the office of the Collector of a collection district there shall be kept a seal of such design as the Commissioner shall prescribe, with the approval of the Secretary of Finance with which shall be sealed all documents and records requiring authentication in such office.

SEC. 705. Authority of Deputy Collectors of Customs. –

The deputy collector at a principal port of entry may, in the name of the District Collector and subject to his supervision and control, perform any particular act which might be done by the District Collector himself; at subports, a deputy collector may, in his own name, exercise the general powers of a collector, subject to the supervision and control of the Collector of the subport.

SEC. 706. Appointment of Special Deputies with Limited Powers –

Collectors may, with the approval of the Commissioner, appoint from their force such number of special deputies as may be necessary for the proper conduct of the public business, with authority to sign documents and perform such service as may be specified in writing.

SEC. 707. Succession of Deputy Collector to Position of Acting Collector. –

In the absence or disability of a Collector at any port or in the case of a vacancy in his office, the temporary discharge of his duties shall devolve upon the deputy collector of the port. Where no deputy collector is available, an official to serve in such contingency may be designated in writing by the Collector from his own force. The Collector making such designation shall report the same without delay to the Commissioner and the Chairman, Commission on Audit, forwarding them the signature of the person so designated.

SEC. 708. Designation of Official as Customs Inspector. –

At a coastwise port where no customs official or employee is regularly stationed, the

Commissioner may designate any national, provincial or municipal official of the port to act as an inspector of customs for the purpose of enforcing laws and regulations of the Bureau of Customs in the particular port, but all such designations shall be made with the consent of the proper Department head of the official so design:,'9d.

SEC. 709. Authority of Collector to Remit Duties. —

A Collector shall have discretionary authority to remit the assessment and collection of custom duties, taxes and other charges when the aggregate amount of such duties, taxes and other charges is less than ten pesos, and he may dispense with the seizure of articles of less than ten pesos in value except in cases of prohibited importations or the habitual or the intentional violation of the tariff and customs laws.

SEC. 710, Records to be Kept by Customs Officials. —

District Collectors, deputy collectors, and other customs officials acting in such capacities are required to keep true, correct and permanent records of their official transactions, to submit the same to the inspection of authorized officials at all times, and turn over all records and official papers to their successors or other authorized officials.

SEC. 711. Port Regulations. —

A Collector may prescribe local administrative regulation, not inconsistent with law or the general bureau regulations, for the government of his port or district, the same to be effective upon the approval by the Commissioner.

SEC. 712. Reports of Collector to Commissioner. —

A Collector shall immediately make report to the Commissioner concerning prospective or newly begun litigation in his district touching matters relating to the customs service; and he shall, in such form and detail as shall be required by the Commissioner make regular monthly reports of all transactions in his port and district.

TITLE Ⅱ. - COASTWISETRADE

SEC. 906. Requirement of Manifest in Coastwise Trade. —

Manifests shall be required for cargo and passengers transported from one place or port in the Philippines to another only when ore or both of such places is a port of entry.

SEC. 907. Manifest Required Upon Departure from Port of Entry. –

Prior to departure from a port of entry, the master of a vessel licensed for the coastwise trade shall make out and subscribe duplicate Manifests of the whole cargo and all of the passengers taken on board on such vessels, specifying in the cargo manifests the marks and numbers of packages, the port of destination and names of the consignees, together with such further information as may be required and in the passengers manifest the name, sex, age, residence, port of embarkation, and destination of all passengers, together with such further information may be required. He shall deliver such manifests to the Collector of Customs or other customs authorized, before whom he shall swear to the best of his knowledge and belief, in respect to the cargo manifests, that the goods -therein described, if foreign, were imported legally and that duties, taxes and other charges thereon have been paid or secured to be paid, and with respect to the passenger manifests, that the information therein contained is true and correct as to all passengers taken on board. Thereupon, then said Collector of Customs or customs official, shall certify the same on the manifests, the original of which he shall return to the master with a permit specifying thereon, generally, the landing on board such vessel and authorizing him to proceed to his port of destination retaining the duplicates.

SEC. 908. Manifests Required Prior to Unloading at Port of Entry. –

Upon arrival at a port of entry a vessel engaged in the coastwise trade and prior to the unloading of any port of the cargo, the master shall deliver to the Collector or other proper customs official complete manifests of all the cargo and passengers brought into said port, together with the clearance 18
manifests of cargo and passengers for said port granted port or ports of entry from which said vessel may have cleared during the voyage.

SEC. 909. Departure of Vessel Upon - Detailed Manifest. –

The owner, agents or consignees of vessels are required to present the proper detailed manifest before departure of the vessel: Provided, however, that the Commissioner of Customs may by regulation permit a vessel to depart coastwise port of entry upon the filing of a general manifest by the master thereof.

TITLE Ⅲ. - VESSELS AND AIRCRAFT IN FOREIGN TRADE

SEC. 1001. Ports Open to Vessels Engaged in Foreign Trade. −

Duty of Vessel to Make Entry. - Vessels engaged in the foreign trade shall touch at ports of entry only, except as otherwise specially allowed; and every such vessel arriving within a customs collection district of the Philippines from a foreign port make entry at the port of entry for such district and shall be subject to the authority of the Collector of the while within his jurisdiction.

The master of any war vessel employed by any foreign government shall not be required to report, enter on arrival in the Philippines, unless engaged in the transportation of articles in the way of trade.

SEC. 1002. Control of Customs Official Over Boarding or Leaving of Incoming Vessel and Over Other Vessel Approaching the Former. −

Upon the arrival in port of any vessel engaged in foreign trade, it shall be unlawful for any person (except the pilot, consul, quarantine officials, custom officials or other duly authorized persons) to board or leave the vessel without permission of the customs official in charge; and it shall likewise be unlawful for any tugboat, rowboat or other craft to go along side and take any person aboard such vessel take any person therefrom, except as aforesaid, or loiter near or along side such vessel. Unauthorized and other vessels shall keep away from such vessel engaged in foreign trade at a distance of less than fifty meters.

SEC. 1003. Quarantine Certificate for Incoming Vessel. −

Entry of a vessel from a foreign port or place outside of the Philippines shall not be permitted until it has obtained a quarantine certificate issued the Bureau of Quarantine.

SEC. 1004. Documents to be Produced by the Master Upon Entry of Vessel. −

For the purpose making entry of a vessel engaged in foreign trade, the master thereof shall present the following document duly certified by him, to the customs boarding officials:
a. The original manifest of all cargo destined for the port, to be returned with the endorsement of the boarding officials;
b. Three copies of the same manifest, one of which, upon certification by the boarding official as to the correctness of the copy, shall be returned to the master;
c. A copy of the cargo storage plan;

e. One copy of passenger list;

f. One copy of the crew list;

g. The original of all through cargo manifest, for deposit, while in port, with customs official in charge of the vessel;

h. A passenger manifest of all aliens, in conformity with the requirements of the immigration laws in force in the Philippines;

i. One copy of the original duplicate of bills of lading fully accomplished;

j. The shipping articles and register of the vessel of Philippine registry.

SEC. 1005. Manifest Required of Vessel from Foreign Port. —

Every vessel from a foreign port must have on board a complete manifest of all her cargo. All of the cargo intended to be landed at a port in the Philippines must be described in separate manifests for each port of call therein. Each manifest shall include the port of departure and the port of delivery with the marks, numbers, quantity and description of the packages and the names of the consignees thereof. Every vessel from a foreign port must have on board complete manifests of passengers and their baggage, in the prescribed form, setting forth their destination and all particulars required by immigration laws, and every such vessel shall have prepared for presentation to the proper customs official upon arrival in ports of the Philippines a complete list of all sea stores then on board. If the vessel does not carry cargo or passengers, the manifest must show that no cargo or passenger, as the case may be, is carried from the port of departure to the port of destination in the Philippines.

A cargo manifest shall in no case be changed or altered after entry of vessel, except by means of an amendment by the master, consignee or agent thereof, under oath, and attached to the original manifest: Provided, however, That after the invoice and/or entry covering an importation have been received and recorded in the office of the appraiser, no amendment of the manifest shall be allowed, except when it is obvious that a clerical error or any other discrepancy has been committed in the preparation of the manifest, without any fraudulent intent, discovery of which would not have been made until after examination of the importation has been completed. SEC. 1006. Translation of Manifest. - The cargo manifest and each copy thereof shall be accompanied by a translation into the official language of the Philippines, if originally written in another language.

SEC. 1007. Manifests for Commission on Audit and Collector. —

Papers to be Deposited with Consul. - Immediately after -the arrival of a vessel from a foreign port, the master shall deliver or mail to the Chairman, Commission on Audit, Manila a copy of the cargo manifests properly endorsed by the boarding officer, and the master shall immediately present to the Collector the original copy of the cargo manifests properly endorsed by the boarding officer, and, for inspection, the ship's register or other documents in lieu thereof, together with the clearance and other papers granted to the vessel at the port of departure for the Philippines.

SEC. 1008. Transit Cargo. —

When, transit cargo from a foreign port or other local ports is forwarded from the port of importation separate manifest, in triplicate, shall be presented by each carrier.

SEC. 1009. Clearance of Foreign Vessels To and From Coastwise Ports. —

Passengers or articles arriving from abroad upon a foreign vessel may be carried by the sane vessel through any port of entry to the port of destination in the Philippines or articles intended for export may be carried 'in a foreign vessel through a Philippine port.

Upon such reasonable condition as he may impose, the Commissioner may clear foreign vessels for any port and authorize the conveyance therein of either articles or passengers brought from abroad upon such vessels; and he may likewise, upon such conditions as he may impose, allow a foreign vessel to take cargo and passengers at any port and convey the same, upon such vessel to a foreign port.

SEC. 1010. Requirement as to Delivery of Mail. —

A vessel arriving within a collection district in the Philippines shall not be permitted to make entry or break bulk until it is made to appear, to the satisfaction of the Collector, that the master, consignee or agent of the vessel is ready to deliver to the postmaster of the nearest post office all mail matter on board such vessel and destined for that port. Collectors are authorized to examine and search vessels for mail carried contrary to law.

SEC. 1011. Production of Philippine Crew. —

The master of a Philippine vessel returning form abroad shall produce the entire crew listed in the vessel's shipping articles; and if any member be missing, the master shall produce proof satisfactory to the Collector that such member has died, absconded, has been forcibly impressed into other service, or has been discharged; and in case of discharge in. a foreign country, he shall produce a certificate from the consul, vice consul or consular agent of the Philippines there residing, showing that such discharge was effected with the consent of the representative of the Philippines aforesaid

SEC. 1012. Record of Arrival and Entry of Vessels. —

A record shall be made and kept open to public inspection in every customhouse of the date of arrival and entry of all vessels.

SEC. 1013. Arrest of Vessel Departing Before Entry Made. —

When a vessel arriving within r of a collection district from a foreign port departs or attempts to depart before entry shall have been ma - being thereunto compelled by stress of weather, duress of enemies, or other necessity, the Collector of the port or the commander of any revenue cutter may arrest and bring back such vessel to the most convenient port.

SEC. 1014. Discharge of Ballast. —

When not brought to port as article, the ballast of no commercial value may be discharged upon permit granted by the Collector for such purpose.

SEC. 1015. Time of Unlading Cargo. —

Articles brought in a vessel from a foreign port shall be unladen only during regular working hours or regular work days. Unlading at any other time or day may or be done upon authority of the Collector conditioned on the payment of losses and overtime pay by the interested parties.

SEC. 1016. Entrance of Vessel Through Necessity. —

When a vessel from a foreign port is compelled, by stress of weather or other necessity to put into any other port than that of her destination, the master w& twenty -four hours of arrival, shall make protest under oath setting forth the causes or circumstances of such necessity. This protest, if not made before the Collector, must be produced to him, and a copy thereof lodged with him.
With the same time, the master shall make a report to the Collector if any part of the cargo was unladen from necessity or lost by casualty before arrival, and such fact should be made to appear by sufficient proof to the Collector who shall give his approval thereto and the unlading shall be deemed to have been lawfully effected,

SEC. 1017. Unlading of Vessel in Port from Necessity. —

If the situation is such as to require t, unlading of the vessel pending sojourn in port, the Collector shall, upon sufficient proof of the necessity, grant a permit therefore, and the articles shall be unladen and stored under the supervision of the customs authorities,

At the request of the master of the vessel or the owner thereof, the Collector may grant permission enter and pay duties, taxes and other charges on, and dispose of, such a part of the cargo as may be perishable nature or as may be necessary to defray the expenses attending the vessel. Upon departure, the cargo, or a residue thereof, may be reladen on board the vessel, and the vessel may proceed with the same to her destination, subject only to the charge for storing and safe-keeping of the articles and the fees for entrance and clearance. No port charges shall be collected on vessels entering through stress of weather or other causes above described.

SEC. 1018. Entry and Clearance of Vessels of a Foreign Government. —

The entry and clearance transport or supply ship of a foreign government shall be in accordance with the agreement by and between the Philippines and the foreign government.

SEC. 1019. Clearance of Vessel for Foreign Port. —

Before a clearance shall be granted to any vessel bound to a foreign port, the master, or the agent thereof, shall present to the Collector the following properly authenticated documents:

a. A bill of health from the quarantine official or official of the public health service in the port.
b. Three copies of the manifest of export cargo, one of which, upon certification by the customs official as to the correctness of the copy, shall be returned to the master.
c. Two copies of the passenger list, showing alien and other passengers.
d. The register and shipping articles, if the vessel is of Philippine registry.
e. The consular certificate of entry, if the vessel is of foreign registry, when required.
f. A certificate of the Bureau of Posts to the effect that it received timely notice of the sailing of the Vessel: Provided, That the Collector shall not permit any vessel to sail for a foreign port if the master or agent thereof refuses to receive bags of mail delivered to the same by the Bureau of Posts for transportation for a reasonable compensation, In case the Director of Posts and said master or agent do not come to an agreement concerning

the amount of the compensation to be paid for the carriage of the mail, the matter shall be submitted for decision to a Board of Referees composed of three members appointed, respectively, by the Bureau of Posts, the agency of the company to which the vessel concerned belongs, and the Bureau of Customs, which board shall fix a reasonable rate of compensation.

SEC. 1020. Detention of Warlike Vessel Containing Arms and Munitions. —
Collectors shall detain any vessel of commercial registry manifestly built for warlike purposes and about to depart from the Philippines with a cargo consisting principally of arms and munitions of war, when the number of men shipped on board or other circumstances render it probable that such vessel is intended to be employed by the owner or owners to cruise or commit hostilities upon the subjects, citizens, or property of any foreign prince or state, or of any colony, district, or people with whom the Philippines is at peace, until the decision of the President of the Philippines be had thereon, or until the owner or owners shall give bond or security, in double the value of the vessel and cargo, that she will not be so employed, if in the discretion of the Collector such bond will prevent the violation of the provisions of this section.

SEC. 1021. Manifest of Export Cargo to be Delivered to Chairman, Commission on Audit. —
The master shall, prior -to departure, deliver mail to the Chairman, Commission on Audit, Manila, the returned copy of the manifest of export cargo.

SEC. 1022. Oath of Master of Departing Vessel. —
The master of such departing vessel shall state under oath to the effect:
a. That all cargo conveyed on said vessel, with destination to the Philippines, has been duly discharged or accounted for.
b. That he has mailed or delivered to the Chairman, Commission on Audit a true copy of the outgoing cargo manifest.
c. That he has not received and will not convey any letters or packets not, enclosed in properly stamped envelope sufficient to cover postage, except those relating to the vessel, and that he has delivered at the proper foreign port all mails placed on board his vessel before her last clearance from the Philippines.
d. That if clearing without passenger, the vessel will not carry upon the instant voyage,

from the Philippine port, any passenger of any class, or other person not entered upon the ship's declaration.

SEC. 1023. Extension of Time for Clearance. –

At the time of clearance, the master of a departing vessel shall be required to indicate the time of intended departure, and if the vessel should remain in port forty -eight hours after the time indicated the master shall report to the Collector for an extension of time of departure, and without such extension the original clearance shall be of no effect.

SEC. 1025. Export Product to Conform to Standard Grades. –

A collector shall not permit products for which standard grades have been established by the government to be laden aboard a vessel clearing for a foreign port, unless the shipment conforms to the requirements of law relative to the shipment of such products.

PART 2. – ENTRANCE AND CLEARANCE OF AIRCRAFT IN FOREIGN TRADE

SEC. 1101. Designation of Airports of Entry. –

The Secretary of Finance, upon recommendation the Commissioner and the Director of the Civil Aeronautics Administration is authorized to designate airports of entry for civil aircraft arriving in the Philippines from any place outside thereof and for articles carried such aircraft. Such airport of entry shall be considered as a port of entry for aliens arriving on such aircraft as a place of quarantine inspection.

SEC. 1102. Advance Notice of Arrival. –

(a) Non -scheduled Arrivals. - Before an aircraft comes any area in the Philippines from any place outside thereof, a timely notice of the intended flight shall be furnished to the Collector or other customs officer in charge at or nearest the intended place of first landing such area, and to the quarantine and immigration officers in charge at or nearest such place of landing. If dependable facilities for giving notice are not available before departure, any radio equipment of the p shall be used if this will result in the giving of adequate and timely notice during its approach, otherwise landing shall be made at a place where the necessary facilities do exist before coming into any area in Philippines. If, upon landing in any area, the government officers have not arrived, the pilot -in -command s hold the aircraft and any baggage and article thereon intact and keep the passengers and crew members segregated place until the inspecting officers arrive.

(b) Scheduled Arrivals - Such advance notice will not be required in the case of aircraft scheduled airline arriving in accordance with the regular schedule filed with the Collector for the Customs district in which the place of first landing in the area is situated, and also with the quarantine and immigration officials in charge of such place.

SEC. 1103. Landing at International Airport of Entry. –

Except in the case of emergency or for: landings, aircraft arriving in the Philippines from any foreign port or place shall make the first landing at an international airport of entry, unless permission to land elsewhere than at an international airport of entry is first obtained from the Commissioner. In such cases, the owner, operator, or person in charge of the aircraft shall pay the expenses incurred in inspecting the aircraft, articles, passengers and baggage carried there and such aircraft shall be subject to the authority of the Collector at the airport while within his jurisdiction. Should an emergency or forced landing be made by an aircraft coming into the Philippines from place outside thereof, the pilot -in -command shall not allow any article, baggage, passenger or crew member to be removed or to depart from the landing place without permission of a customs officer, unless such removal or departure is necessary for purposes of safety, communication with customs authorities, or preservation of life, health or property. As soon as practicable, the pilot -in -command, or a member of the c in charge, or the owner of the aircraft, shall communicate with the custom officer at the intended place of landing or at the nearest international airport or other customs port of entry in the area and make a full re~ of the circumstances of the flight and of the emergency or forced landing.

SEC. 1104. Report of Arrival and Entry. –

The pilot -in -command of any aircraft arriving from a fore port or place shall immediately report his arrival to the Collector at the airport of entry or to the customs off detailed to meet the aircraft at the place of first landing. Such aircraft upon arrival shall be boarded by quarantine officer and after pratique is granted shall be boarded by customs officer, and no person shall permitted to board or leave the aircraft without the permission of the customs officer in charge.

The pilot -in -command or any other authorized agent of the owner or operator of the aircraft shall make the necessary entry. No such aircraft shall, without previous permission therefore from the collector, de~ from the place of first landing or discharge articles, passengers or baggage.

SEC. 1105. Documents Required in Making Entry.

a. For the purpose of making entry, there shall be presented to the customs boarding officer f copies of a general declaration which shall contain the following data, unless any of such data is otherwise presented on a separate official form:
   1. Name of owner or operator of aircraft, registration marks and nationality of aircraft, and flight number of identification;
   2. Points of clearance and entry, and date of arrival;
   3. Health and customs clearance at the last airport of departure;
   4. Itinerary of aircraft, including information as to airport of origin and departure dates; Itinerary of aircraft, including information as to airport of origin and departure dates,,
   5. Names and nationality of crew members;
   6. Passenger manifest showing places of embarkation and destination;
   7. Cargo manifest showing information as to airway bill number, the number of packages related to each airway bill number, nature of goods, destination, and gross weight, together with a copy of each airway securely attached thereto; and 8. Store list
b. The general declaration shall be written in English and duly signed by the pilot -in -command or operator of the aircraft, or the authorized agent. The Health Section thereon, however, shall be signed only by the pilot -in -command or when necessary, by a crew member when the general declaration itself has been signed by a non -crew member. If the aircraft does not carry cargo or passengers such facts must be shown in the manifests.
c. Cargo manifest shall in no case be changed or altered after entry of the aircraft, except by means of an amendment by the pilot -in -command or authorized agent thereof, under oath, and attached to the original manifest: Provided, however, That after the invoice and/or entry covering an importation have been received and recorded in the office of the appraiser, no amendment shall be allowed except when it is obvious that a clerical error or any other discrepancy has been committed without any fraudulent intent in the preparation of the manifest, discovery of which could not have been made until after examination of the importation has been completed.

SEC. 1106. Manifest for Commission on Audit. –

The pilot -in -command or authorized agent of an aircraft, upon arrival from a foreign port, shall deliver or mail to the Chairman, Commission on Audit, a copy of the general declaration properly endorsed by the customs Boarding Officer.

SEC. 1107. Delivery of Mail. —

Aircraft arriving within a customs collection district in the Philippines shall not be permitted to make entry until it is shown to the satisfaction of the Collector that the pilot -in-command or authorized agent of the aircraft is ready to deliver to the postmaster of the nearest post office all mail matters on board such aircraft and destined for that port.

SEC. 1110. Manifest for Transit Cargo. —

When transit cargo from a foreign port for other local ports is forwarded from the port of importation, separate manifest, in triplicate, shall be presented by each carrier.

SEC. 1111. Clearance of Aircraft for Foreign Port.

a. Any aircraft bound to a foreign port shall, before departure, clear at an airport of entry or at the same place where such aircraft has been authorized to make its landing by the Commissioner
b. Before clearance shall be granted to an aircraft bound to a foreign port, there shall be presented to the Collector or to the customs officer detailed at the place of departure four copies of a general declaration signed by the pilot -in -command or authorized agent of an aircraft which shall contain the following data:
   1. Name of owner or operator of aircraft, registration marks and nationality of aircraft, and flight number of identification;
   2. Point of clearance, data thereof and destination',
   3. Health and customs clearance;
   4. Itinerary of aircraft, including information as to airport of destination and departure date;
   5. Names and nationality of crew members;
   6. Passenger manifest showing place of destination;
   7. Export cargo manifest showing information as to airwaybill number, the number of packages related to each airwaybill number, nature of goods, destination, and gross weight, together with a copy of each airwaybill securely attached thereto; and
   8. Store list showing stores laden.

SEC. 1112. Oath of Person in Charge of Departing Aircraft. —

The pilot -in -command i agent of such departing aircraft shall also state under oath to the effect that:

a. All cargo conveyed on said aircraft destined to the Philippines has been duly d!i -z. - - accounted for.
b. He has mailed or delivered to the Commission on Audit a true copy of the outward general declaration.
c. He has not received nor will convey any letter or packet not enclosed in proper, envelope sufficient to cover postage, except those relating to the cargo of the aircraft, and that he has delivered to the proper foreign port all mails placed on board said aircraft before clearance from the Philippines.
d. If clearing without passengers, the aircraft will not carry upon departure any passenger.

A record shall be made and kept open to public inspection in every customhouse at an airport the dates of arrival and entry of all aircrafts.

TITLE Ⅳ. - ASCERTAINMENT, COLLECTION AND RECOVERY OF IMPORT DUTY

PART 1. — IMPORTATION IN GENERAL

SEC. 1201. Article to be Imported Only Through Customhouse. —

All articles imported Philippines whether subject to duty or not shall be entered through a customhouse at a port of entry.

SEC. 1202. When Importation Begins and Deemed Terminated. —

Importation begins when the carrying vessel or aircraft enters the jurisdiction of the Philippines with intention to unlade therein. Importation is deemed terminated upon payment of duties, taxes and other charges due upon the articles, or sec be paid, at a port of entry and the legal permit for withdrawal shall have been granted, or in case said are free of duties, taxes and other charges, until they have legally left the jurisdiction of the customs.

SEC. 1203. Owner of Imported Articles. —

All articles Imported into the Philippines shall be held to be the property of the person to whom the same are consigned: and the holder of a bill of lading duly en -by the consignee therein named, or, if consigned to order, by the consignor, shall be deemed the consignee thereof. The underwriters of abandoned articles and the salvors of articles saved from wreck at sea, a coast or in any area of the Philippines may be regarded as the consignees.

SEC. 1204. Liability of Importer for Duties. —

Unless relieved by laws or regulations, the liability for duties, taxes, fees and other charges attaching on importation constitutes a personal debt due from the importer to the government which can be discharged only by payment in full of all duties, taxes, fees and other charges legally accruing. It also constitutes a lien upon the articles imported whish may be enforced while such articles are in custody or subject to the control of the government.

SEC. 1205. Importations by the Government. —

Except those provided for in Section One Hundred and Five of this Code, all importations by the Government for its own use or that of its subordinate branches or instrumentalities, or corporations, agencies or instrumentalities owned or controlled by the government shall be subject to the duties, taxes, fees and other charges provided for in this code.

SEC. 1206. Jurisdiction of Collector Over Importation of Articles. —

The Collector shall cause all articles entering the jurisdiction of his district and destined for importation through his port to be entered a~ customhouse, shall cause all such articles to be appraised and classified, and shall assess and collect the duties, taxes, and other charges thereon, and shall hold possession of all imported articles upon which duties, taxes, and other charges have not been paid or secured to be paid, disposing of the same according to law. SEC. 1207. Jurisdiction of Collector Over Articles of Prohibited Importation, - Where articles are of prohibited importation or subject to importation only upon conditions prescribed by law, it shall be the duty of the Collector to exercise such jurisdiction in respect thereto as will prevent importation or otherwise secure compliance with all legal requirements. SEC. 1210. Disposition of Imported Articles Remaining on Vessel After Time for Unlading. - Imported articles remaining on board any vessel after the expiration of the said period for discharge and not reported for transshipment to another port, may be unladen by the customs authorities and stored at the vessel's expense. Unless prevented by causes beyond the vessel's control, such as port congestion, strikes, riots or civil commotions, failure of vessel's gear, bad weather, and similar causes, articles so stored shall be entered within thirty (30) days, which shall not be extendible, from the date of discharge of the last package from the vessel or aircraft and shall be claimed within fifteen (15) days, which shall not likewise be extendible from the date of posting of the notice to claim in conspicuous places in the Bureau of Customs. If not entered or not claimed, it shall be disposed of in accordance with the provisions of this code (R.A. 7651, June 04, 1993).

SEC. 1211. Handling of Articles on, Which Duty Has Not Been Paid. —

Except when done under customs supervision, all unlading or transshipment of the cargo of vessels from foreign ports, which do not discharge at a wharf, must be by bonded lighters; and likewise, on land imported goods on which duty has not been paid shall be carried about and handled by bonded draymen or cartmen only.

PART 2. — ENTRY AT CUSTOMHOUSE

SEC. 1301. Persons Authorized to Make Import Entry. —

Imported articles must be entered in the customhouse at the port of entry within thirty (30) days, which shall not be extendible, from the date of discharge of the last package from the vessel or aircraft either (a) by the importer, being holder of the bill of lading, (b) by a duly licensed customs broker acting under authority from a holder of the bill or (c) by a person duly empowered to act as agent or attorney -in -fact for each holder: Provided, That where the entry is filed by a party other than the importer, said importer shall himself be required to declare under oath and under the penalties of falsification or perjury that the declarations and statements contained in the entry are true and correct: Provided, further, That such statements under oath shall constitute prima facie evidence of knowledge and consent of the importer of violation against applicable provisions of this Code when the importation is found to be unlawful (R.A. 7651, June 04, 1993

SEC. 1302. Import Entries. —

All imported articles, ex6ept importations admitted free of duty under Subsection "k", Section one hundred and five of this Code, shall be subject to a formal or informal entry, Articles of a commercial nature intended for sale, barter or hire, the dutiable, value of which is Two thousand pesos (P2,000.00) or less, and personal and household effects or articles, not in commercial quantity, imported in passenger's baggage, mail or otherwise, for personal use, shall be cleared on an informal entry whenever duty, tax or other charges are collectible.

The Commissioner may, upon instruction of the Secretary of Finance, for the protection of domestic industry or of the revenue, require a formal entry, regardless of value, whatever be the purpose and nature of the importation.

A formal entry may be for immediate consumption, or under irrevocable domestic letter of credit, bank guarantee or bond for:

a. Placing the article in customs bonded warehouse;
b. Constructive warehousing and immediate transportation to other ports of the Philippines upon proper examination and appraisal; or
c. Constructive warehousing and immediate exportation.

Import entries under irrevocable domestic letter of credit, bank guarantee or bond shall be subject to the provisions of Title V, Book 11 of this Code.

All importations entered under formal entry shall be covered by a letter of credit or any other verifiable document evidencing payment. (R.A. 9135, April 27, 2001)

SEC. 1303. Entry of Article in Part for Consumption and in Part for Warehousing. –

Import entries of articles covered by one bill of lading may be made simultaneously for both consumption and warehousing. Where an intent to export the articles is shown by the bill of lading and invoice, the whole or a part of a bill of lading not less than one package) may be entered for warehousing and immediate exportation. Articles received at any port from another port in the Philippines on any entry for immediate transportation entered at the port of delivery either for consumption or warehousing.

SEC. 1304. Declaration of the Import Entry. –

Except in case of informal entry, no entry of article shall be effected until there shall have been submitted to the collector a written declaration under penalties of falsification or perjury, in such form as shall be prescribed by the Commissioner, containing statements in Substance as follows:

a. That the entry delivered to the Collector contains a full account of the value or price articles, including subject of the entry;
b. That the invoice and entry contain a just and faithful account of the value or price of said articles including and specifying the value of all containers or coverings, and that nothing has been omitted, therefrom or concealed whereby the government of the Republic of the Philippines be defrauded of any part of the duties lawfully due on the

articles;
c. That, to the best of the declarant's information and belief, all the invoke and bills of lading to the articles are the only ones in existence relating to the importation in question and that they are in the state in which they were actually received by him;
d. That, to the best of the declarant's information and belief, the entries, invoices and bill of and the declaration thereon under penalties of falsification of perjury are in all respects ge and true, and were made by the person by whom the same purpose to have been made.

SEC. 1305. By Whom to be Signed. —

The declaration shall be signed, under penalties of falsification or perjury, by the importer, consignee or holder of the bill, by or for whom the entry is effected if such p. is an individual, or in case of a corporation, firm or association, by its manager, or by a licensed customs broker duly authorized to act for either of them.

SEC. 1306. Forms and Contents of Import Entry. —

Import entries shall be in the required number of copies in such forms as prescribed by regulations. They shall be signed by the person making the entry articles, and shall contain the names of the importing vessel or aircraft, port of departure and date of a the number and mark of packages, or the quantity, if in bulk, the nature and correct commodity description of the articles contained therein, and its value as set forth in a proper invoice to be presented in duplicate the entry.

SEC. 1307. Description of Articles. —

The description of the articles in the import entry must sufficient detail to enable the articles to be identified both for tariff classification of terms of the headings subheadings of this code and in the currency of the invoice and the quantity and values of each of the several classes of articles he separately declared according to their respective headings or subheadings and the totals of each heading or subheading shall be duty shown.

SEC. 1308. Commercial Invoice. —

Contents of Commercial invoice of articles imported Philippines shall in all cases set forth all the following:
a. The place where, the date when, and the person by whom and the person to whom the

articles sold or agreed to be sold, or if to be imported otherwise than in pursuance of a purchase place from which shipped, the date when the person to whom and the person by whom the shipped:

b. The port of entry to which the articles are destined:

c. A detailed description of the articles according to the terms of the heading or subheadings, if specifically mentioned in this code, otherwise the description must be in sufficient detail to e, the articles to be identified both for tariff classification and statistical purposes, indicating correct commodity description, in customary terms or commercial designation, including the grade or quality, numbers, marks or symbols under which they are sold by the seller or manufacturer, together with the marks and number of the packages in which the articles are packed;

d. The quantities in the weights and measures of the country or place form which the articles are shipped, and in the weights and measures used in this Code;

e. The purchase price of each article in the currency of the purchase and in the unit of the quantity which the articles were bought and sold in the place of country of exportation, if the articles are shipped in pursuance of a purchase or an agreement to purchase;

f. If the articles are shipped otherwise than in pursuance of the purchase or an agreement to purchase, the value of each article in the unit of quantity in which the articles are usually bought and sold, and in the currency in which the transactions are usually made, or, in the absence of such value, the price in such currency which the manufacturer, seller, shipper or owner would have received, or was willing to receive, for such articles if sold in the ordinary course of trade and the usual wholesale quantities in the country of exportation;

g. All charges upon the articles itemized by name and amount when known to the seller or shipper; or all charges by name (e.g., commission, insurance, freight, cases, containers, coverings and cost of packing) included in invoice prices when the amount for such charges are unknown to the seller or shipper;

h. All discounts, rebates, drawbacks and bounties separately itemized allowed upon the exportation of the articles, all internal and excise taxes applicable to the home market;

I. The current home consumption value or price of which same, like or similar article is offered or for sale for exportation to the Philippines, on the date the invoice is prepared or the date of exportation; and, Any other facts deemed necessary to a proper examination, appraisement and classification of the articles which the Commissioner may require.

SEC. 1309. - Repealed by E.O. 736.

SEC. 1310. - Repealed by P.D. 1679, March 6,1980.

SEC. 1311. - Repealed by P.D. 1679, March 6, 1980.

SEC. 1312. - Repealed by P.D. 1679, March 6, 1980.

SEC. 1313. Information Furnished on Classification and Value.

a. As to classification. - When an article imported or intended to be imported is not specifically classified in this Code, the interested party, imported or foreign exporter may submit to the Tariff Commission a sample together with a full description of its component materials and uses, and request it in writing to indicate the heading under which the article is or shall be dutiable, and the Tariff Commission shall comply with such requests within thirty days from receipt thereof if it is satisfied that the application is made in good faith, in which case classification of the article in question upon the particular importation involved shall be made according to the heading indicated by the Tariff Commission: Provided, however, That such rulings of the Tariff Commission on commodity classification, shall be binding upon the Bureau of Customs. the Secretary shall rule otherwise.

b. As to Value. - Upon written application of owner or his agent, the Collector shall furnish any importer within thirty days from receipt thereof the latest information in his possession as dutiable value of the articles to be entered at his port, after arrival or upon satisfactory evidence that they have been exported and are enroute to the Philippines: Provided, That the information shall be given only if the Collector is satisfied, after questioning the importer and examining pertinent papers presented to him, such as invoices, contracts of sale or purchase, orders other commercial documents that the importer is acting in good faith and is unable to proper information as to the dutiable value of the articles on the date of exportation unusual conditions: And, Provided, further, That the information so given is in no ser appraisal or binding upon the Collector's action on appraisal.

SEC. 1314. Forwarding, of Cargo and Remains of Wrecked Vessel or Aircraft. −

When vessels or aircrafts are wrecked within the Philippines, application must be made to the Commissioner by the c owners or consignees of the cargo, or by the underwriters, in case of abandonment to them, for permission to forward the articles saved from the wreck to the ports of destination, in other conveyance, without entry customhouse in the district in which the article was cast ashore or unladen. On receipt of such permission articles may be so forwarded with particular manifests thereof, duly certified by customs officials in cha the articles. If the owner of the vessel or aircraft wishes to export the remains of the wreck, he may be permit' do so upon proper examination and inspection. The remains of a wrecked vessel shall be considered to be not only the hull and rigging of the same but also all sea stores and articles of equipment, such as sails, ropes, chains, anchors and so forth.

SEC. 1315. Derelicts and Articles from Abandoned Wrecks. –

Derelicts and all articles picked a, or recovered from abandoned wrecks, shall be taken possession of in the port or district where they shall first arrive, and be retained in the custody of the Collector, and if not claimed and entered, as the case may be, by the owner, underwriter or salvor, shall be dealt with as unclaimed property. When such articles are brought into port by lighters or other craft, each of such vessels shall make entry by manifest of her cargo. If, in case of wreck, there be no customhouse at the point where the vessel or aircraft is wrecked, coastguard or customs official nearest the scene of the wreck shall render all possible aid in saving the c -and cargo of the vessel or aircraft, taking charge of the articles saved and giving immediate notice to Collector or the nearest customhouse. In order to prevent any attempt to defraud the revenue the Collector shall be presented at the salvage of the cargo by customs officials detailed for that purpose, who shall examine and countersign the inventory made of such cargo and receive a copy of the same. Derelicts and articles salvaged from foreign vessels or aircrafts picked up at sea, or taken from wreck is prima facie dutiable and may be entered for consumption or warehousing. If claimed to be of Philippine production, and consequently free, proof must be adduced as in ordinary cases of reimportation of articles. Foreign articles landed from a vessel or aircraft in distress is dutiable if sold or disposed of in the Philippines. Before any article which has been taken from a recent wreck shall be admitted to entry, the same shall be appraised, and the owner or importer shall have the same right to appeal as in ordinary importation. No part of a Philippine vessel or aircraft or her equipment, wrecked either in Philippine or foreign waters, shall be subject to duty.

PART 3. – EXAMINATION, CLASSIFICATION AND APPRAISAL OF IMPORTED ARTICLES

SEC. 1401. Conditions for Examination. –

For the protection of government revenue and public interest and to prevent the entry into the country of smuggled or contraband goods, the Commissioner shall, in consultation with

the Oversight Committee and subject to approval of the Secretary of Finance, promulgate the rules and regulations that shall prescribe the procedure in accordance with which the examination shall be undertaken on the importation and the required quantity or percentage thereof: Provided, That the imported articles shall in any case be subject to the regular physical examination when:
(1) The government surveyor's seal on the container has been tampered with or broken or the container shows signs of having been opened or having its identity changed;
(2) The container is leaking or damaged;
(3) The number, weight, and nature of packages indicated in the customs entry declaration and supporting documents differ from that in the manifest;
(4) The shipment is covered by alert/hold order issued pursuant to existing orders;
(5) The importer disagrees with the findings as contained in the government surveyor's report; or
(6) The articles are imported through air freight where the Commissioner or Collector has knowledge that there is a variance between the declared and true quantity, measurement, weight and tariff classification (R.A. 7650, April 06, 1993).

SEC. 1402. Ascertainment of Weight and Quantity. –

Where articles dutiable by weight, and not otherwise specially provided for, are customarily contained in packing, packages, or receptacles of uniform or similar character, it shall be the duty of the Commissioner, from time to time, to ascertain by tests the weight as quantity of such articles, and the weight of the packing, packages or receptacles thereof, respectively, in which the same are customarily imported, and upon such ascertainment, to prescribe rules for estimating the dutiable weight or quantity thereof, and thereafter such articles, imported in such customary packing, packages or receptacles shall be entered, and the duties thereon levied and collected, upon the bases of such estimated dutiable weight or quantity: Provided, That if the importer, consignee or agent shall be dissatisfied, with such estimated dutiable weight or quantity, and shall file with the Collector prior to the delivery of the packages designated for examination a written specification of his objections thereto, or if the Collector shall have reason to doubt the exactness of the prescribed weight or quantity in any instance, it shall be his duty to cause such weights or quantities to be ascertained.

SEC. 1403. Duties of Customs Officer Tasked to Examine, Classify and Appraise Imported Articles. —

The customs officer tasked to examine, classify, and appraise imported articles shall determine whether the packages designated for examination and their contents are in accordance with the declaration in the entry, invoice and other pertinent documents and shall make a return in such a manner to indicate whether the articles have been truly and correctly declared in the entry as regard their quantity, measurement, weight, and tariff classification and not imported contrary to law. He shall submit sample to the laboratory for analysis when feasible to do so and when such analysis is necessary for the proper classification, appraisal, and/or admission into the Philippines of imported articles. Likewise, the customs officer shall determine the unit of quantity in which they are usually bought and sold and appraise the imported articles in accordance with Section 201 of this Code. Failure on the part of the customs officer to comply with his duties shall subject him to the per prescribed under 3604 of this Code (R.A. 7650, April 06, 1993).

SEC. 1404. - Repealed by R.A. 7650, April 06, 1993.

SEC. 1405. Proceedings and Report of Appraisers. —

Appraisers shall, by all reasonable way~ means, ascertain, estimate and determine the value or price of the articles as required by law, any invoice or affidavit thereto or statement of cost, or of cost of production to the contrary notwithstanding, and revising and correcting the report of the examiners as they may judge proper, shall report in writing c face of the entry the value so determined, irrespective of whether such value is equal, higher or lower than the invoice and/or entered value of the articles. Appraisers shall describe all articles on the face of the entry in tariff and such terms as will enable the Collector to pass upon the appraisal and classification of the same, which appraisal and classification shall be subject to his approval or modification, and shall note thereon the measurements and quantities, an disagreement with the declaration.

SEC. 1406. Appraiser's Samples. —

Appraisers shall see that representative and sufficient samples all kinds of articles which may be readily sampled are taken under proper receipt and retained for official purposes; but samples of articles identical in quality, material and values shall not be retained, if their re desired, longer than may be required for use in contested cases. The quantity and value of the samples taken shall be noted on the face of entry. Such samples shall be duly labeled as will definitely identify them with the importation for which they are taken.

SEC. 1407. Readjustment of Appraisal, Classification or Return. —

Such appraisal, classification return as finally passed upon and approved or modified by the Collector shall not be altered or modified in any manner, except:
(a) Within one year after payment of the duties, upon statement of error in conformity with seventeen hundred and seven hereof, approved by the Collector.
(b) Within fifteen days after such payment upon request for reappraisal and/or reclassification addressed to the Commissioner by the Collector, if the appraisal and/or classification is deemed to be low.
(c) Upon request for reappraisal and/or reclassification, in the form of a timely protest addressed to the Collector by the interested party if the latter should be dissatisfied with the appraisal or return.
(d) Upon demand by the Commissioner of Customs after the completion of compliance audit p, to the provisions of this Code." (R.A. 9135, April 27, 21001)

SEC. 1408. Assessment of Duty on Less Than Entered Value. —

Duty shall not be assessed case upon an amount less than the entered value, unless by direction of the Commissioner in cases which the importer certifies at the time of entry that the entered value is higher than the dutiable value and that the articles are so entered in order to meet increases made by the appraiser in similar cases then pending reappraisement; and the lower assessment shall be allowed only when the importer's contention is sustained by the final decision, and shall appear that such action of the importer was taken in good faith after due diligence and inquiry on his part.

SEC. 1409. Employment and Compensation of Persons to Assist in Appraisal or Classification & Articles. —

When necessary, the Collector may request two disinterested persons versed in the matter tc the appraiser in appraising or ascertaining dutiable value of any article. Persons so employed shall L compensation in an amount to be determined by the Commissioner, not exceeding fifty pesos (P 50.oo) for each day of such service.

PART 4. – DELIVERY OF ARTICLES

SEC. 1501. Delivery of Articles to Holder of Bill of Lading. –

A Collector who makes a delivery of a shipment, upon the surrender of the bill of lading, to person who by the terms thereof appears to be the consignee or lawful holder of the bill shall not be liable on account of any defect in the bill or irregularity in its negotiation, unless he has notice of the same.

SEC. 1502. Delivery of Articles Without Production of Bill of Lading. –

No Collector shall deliver imported articles to any person without the surrender by such person of the bill of lading covering said article, except on written order of the carrier or agent of the importing vessel or aircraft, in which case neither the Government nor the Collector shall be held liable for any damages arising from wrongful delivery of the articles: Provided, however, That where delivery of articles is made against such written order of the carrier or agent of the importing vessel or aircraft, the Collector may, for customs purpose s, require the production of an exact copy of the bill of lading therefore.

SEC. 1503. Cash Deposit Upon Delivery of Unexamined Packages. –

To effect immediate delivery of packages not ordered for examination, the Collector shall require a cash deposit, an irrevocable domestic letter of credit, bank guarantee or a bond, in an amount equivalent to one hundred per cent (100 %) of the duties, taxes, fees or other charges sufficient to safeguard the revenue. If such cash deposit, irrevocable domestic letter of credit, bank guarantee or bond is not supplied, all the packages shall be held until the return is made and duties, taxes and other charges paid.

SEC. 1504. Delivery Upon Order of Importer. –

An importer of record may authorize delivery to another person by writing upon the face of the warehouse withdrawal entry his orders to that effect. Such authority to deliver the article entered for warehousing in accordance with section nineteen hundred and four shall not relieve the importer and his cash deposit, irrevocable domestic letter of credit, bank guarantee or bond from liability for the payment of the duties, taxes and other charges due on the said article unless the person to whom the delivery was authorized to be made assumes such liability by complying with the requirements of above mentioned section.

SEC. 1505. Withholding Delivery Pending Satisfaction of Lien. —

When the Collector is duly notified in writing of a lien for freight, lighterage or general average upon any imported articles in his custody, he shall withhold the delivery of the same until he is satisfied that the claim has been paid or secured. In case of a disagreement, as to the amount due between the party filling the lien and the importer regarding the amount of the freight and lighterage based upon the quantity or weights of the articles imported, the Collector may deliver the articles upon payment of the freight and lighterage due on the quantity or weight actually landed as shown by the return of the proper official or by other means to his satisfaction.

SEC. 1506. Customs Expenses Constituting Charges on Articles. —

All expenses incurred by the customs service for the handling or storage of articles and other necessary operations in connection therewith, or incident to its seizure, shall be charged against such articles, and shall constitute a lien upon it.

SEC. 1507. Fine or Surcharge on Articles. —

No article which is liable for any fine or surcharge imposed under the tariff and customs laws shall be delivered until the same shall have been paid or secured by cash deposit, irrevocable domestic letter of credit, bank guarantee or bond.

SEC. 1508. Authority of the Collector of Customs to Hold the Delivery or Release of Imported Articles. —

Whenever any importer, except the government, has an outstanding and demandable account with the Bureau of Customs, the Collector shall hold the delivery of any article imported or consigned to such importer unless subsequently authorized by the Commissioner of Customs, and upon notice as in seizure cases, he may sell such importation or any portion thereof to cover the outstanding account of such importer; Provided, however, That at any time prior to the sale, the delinquent importer may settle his obligations with the Bureau of Customs, in which case the aforesaid articles may be delivered upon payment of the corresponding duties and taxes and compliance with all other legal requirements.

PART 5. – LIQUIDATION OF DUTIES

Sec. 1601. Liquidation and Record of Entries. –

If the Collector shall approve the returns of the appraiser and the report of the weights, gauge or quantity, the liquidation shall be made on the face of the entry showing the particulars thereof, initiated by the customs assessor, approved by the chief customs assessor, and recorded in the record of liquidations. A daily record of all entries liquidated shall be posted in public corridor of the customhouse, name of the vessel or aircraft, the port from which she arrived, the date of her arrival, the name of the importer, and the serial number and the date of the entry. The daily record must also be kept by the collector of all additional duties, taxes and other charges found upon liquidation, and notice shall promptly the interested parties.

SEC. 1602. Tentative Liquidation. –

If to determine the exact amount due under the law in part some future action is required, the liquidation shall be deemed to be tentative as to the item or items affected and shall to that extent be subject to future and final readjustment and settlement within a six (6) months from date of tentative liquidation. The entry in such case shall be stamped liquidation.

SEC. 1603. Finality of Liquidation.

When articles have been entered and passed free of duty or final adjustments of duties made, with subsequent delivery, such entry and passage free of duty or settlements of duties will, after the expiration of three (3) years from the date of the final payment of duties, in the absence of ,fraud or protest or compliance audit pursuant to the provisions of this Code, be final and conclusive upon all parties, unless the liquidation of the import entry was merely tentative." (R.A. 9135, April 27, 2001)

SEC. 1604. Treatment of Fractions in the Liquidation. –

In determining the total amount taxes, surcharges, and/or other charges to be paid on entries, a fraction of a peso less than fifty centavos shall be disregarded, and a fraction of a peso amounting to fifty centavos or more shall be considered as one peso. In case of overpayment or, underpayment of duties, taxes, surcharges and/or other charges entries, where the amount involved is less than ten pesos, no refund or collection shall be made.

PART 6. - ABATEMENTS AND REFUNDS

SEC. 1701. Abatement for Damage Incurred During Voyage. -

Except as herein specially no abatement of duties shall be made on account of damage incurred or deterioration suffered d, voyage of importation; and duties will be assessed on the actual quantity imported, as shown by the return of weighers, gauges, measurers, examiners or appraisers, as the case may be.

SEC. 1702. Abatement or Refund of Duty on Missing Package. -

When any package or p; appearing on the manifest or bill of lading are missing, an abatement or refund of the duty thereon a be made if it is certified, under penalties of falsification or perjury, by the importer or consignee, and upon production of proof satisfactory to the Collector that the package or packages in question have not been imported in to the Philippines contrary to law.

SEC, 1703. Abatement or Refund for Deficiency in Contents of Packages. -

If, upon opening any package, a deficiency or absence of any article or of part of the contents thereof as called for by the shall be found to exist, such deficiency shall be certified, under penalties of falsification or perjury or perjury, to the Collector by the examiner and appraiser; and upon the production of proof satisfactory to the C showing that the shortage occurred before the arrival of the article in the Philippines, the proper rebatement or refund of the duty shall be made.

SEC, 1704. Abatement or Refund of Duties on Articles Lost or Destroyed After Arrival. -

A C may abate or refund the amount of duties accruing or paid, and may likewise make a corresponding allowance on the irrevocable domestic letter of credit, bank guarantee, or the entry bond or other doc upon satisfactory proof of injury, destruction, or loss by theft, fire or other causes of any article as follow:

a. While within the limits of any port of entry prior to unlading under customs supervisions;
b. While remaining in customs custody after unlading;
c. While in transit under irrevocable domestic letter of credit, bank guarantee or bond with formal entry in accordance with section one thousand three hundred two from the port of entry to any port in the Philippines;
d. While released under irrevocable domestic letter of credit, bank guarantee or bond for

export except in case of loss by theft.

SEC. 1705. Abatement of Duty on Dead or Injured Animals. —

Where it is certified, under penalties falsification or perjury, and upon production of proof satisfactory to the Collector that an animal which is the subject of importation dies or suffers injury before arrival, or while in customs custody, the duty shall be correspondingly abated by him, provide the carcass of any dead animal remaining on board or in customs custody be removed in the manner required by the Collector and at the expense of the importer.,

SEC. 1706. Investigation Required in Case of Abatements and Refunds. —

The Collector shall, in al; cases of allowances, abatements, or refunds of duties, cause an examination or report in writing to be made as to any fact discovered during such examination which tends to account for the discrepancy or difference and cause the corresponding adjustment to be made on the import entry: Provided, That no abatement or refund of duties, taxes and other charges shall be allowed on articles lost or destroyed in bonded public or private warehouses outside customs zone.

SEC. 1707. Correction of Errors. - Refund of Excess Payments. —

Manifest clerical errors made in an invoice or entry, errors in return of weight, measure and gauge, when duly certified to, under penalties of falsification or perjury, by the surveyor or examining official (when there are such officials at the port), and errors in the distribution of charges on invoices not involving any question of law and certified to, under penalties of falsification or perjury, by the examining official, may be corrected in the computation of duties, if such errors be discovered before the payments of duties, or if discovered within one year after the final liquidation, upon written request and notice of error from the importer, or upon statement of error certified by the Collector. For the purpose of correcting errors specified in the next preceding paragraph the Collector is authorized to reliquidate entries and collect additional charges, or to make refunds on statement of errors within the statutory time limit.

SEC. 1708. Claim for Refund of Duties and Taxes and Mode of Payment. —

All claims for refund of duties shall be made in writing and forwarded to the Collector to whom such duties are paid, who upon receipt of such claim, shall verify the same by the records of his Office, and if found to be correct and in accordance with law, shall certify the same to the Commissioner with his recommendation together with all necessary papers and documents. Upon receipt by the Commissioner of such certified claim he shall cause the same to be paid if found correct. If a result of the refund of customs duties there would necessarily result a corresponding refund of internal revenue taxes on the same importation, the Collector shall likewise certify the same to the Commissioner who shall cause the said taxes to be paid, refunded, or tax credited in favor of the importer, with advice to the Commissioner of Internal Revenue.

PART 7. − ABANDONMENT OF IMPORTED ARTICLES

SEC. 1801. Abandonment, Kinds and Effects of −

An imported article is deemed abandoned under any of the following circumstances:

a. When the owner, importer, consignee of the imported article expressly signifies in writing to the Collector of Customs his intention to abandon; or

b. When the owner, importer, consignee or interested party after due notice, fails to file an entry within thirty (30) days, which shall not be extendible, from the date of discharge of the last package from the vessel or aircraft, or having filed such entry, fails to claim his importation within fifteen (15) days, which shall not likewise be extendible, from the date of posting of the notice to claim such importation. Any person who abandons an article or who fails to claim his importation as provided for in the preceding paragraph shall be deemed to have renounced all his interests and property rights therein (R.A. 7651, June 04, 1993).

SEC. 1802. Abandonment of Imported Articles. −

An abandoned article shall ipso facto be deemed the property of the Government and shall be disposed of in accordance with the provisions of this Code. Nothing in this section shall be construed as relieving the owner or importer from any criminal liability which may arise from any violation of law committed in connection with the importation of the abandoned article. Any official or employee of the Bureau of Customs or of other government knowledge of the existence of an abandoned article or having control or custody of such abandoned article, fails to report to the Collector within twenty -four (24) hours from the time the article is shall be -punished with the penalties prescribed in Paragraph 1, Section 3604 of this Code (R.A. 7651, June 04, 1993).

SEC. 1803. Repealed by R.A. 7651, June 04, 1993.

TITLE V. - WAREHOUSING OF IMPORTED ARTICLES

PART 1. – WAREHOUSING IN GENERAL

SEC. 1901. Establishment and Supervision of Warehouses. –

When the business c such facilities, The Collector subject to the approval of the Commissioner shall designate and establish warehouses for use as public and private bonded warehouses, sheds or yards, or for other special purposes. All such warehouses and premises shall be subject to the supervision of the Collector, who shall impose such conditions as may be deemed necessary for the protection of the revenue an -stored therein.

SEC. 1902. Responsibility of Operators. –

The operators of bonded warehouse in cast imported articles stored shall be liable for the payment of duties and taxes due thereon. The government assumes no legal responsibility in respect to the safekeeping of article -s customs warehouse, sheds, yards or premises.

SEC. 1903. Bonded Warehouses. –

Application for the establishment of bonded warehouses must be made in writing and filed with the Collector, describing the premises, the location, and capacity and the purpose for which the building is to be used. Upon receipt of such application, the Collector shall cause an examination of the pre reference particularly to its location, construction and means provided for the safekeeping of articles and if found satisfactory, he may authorize its establishment, and accept a bond for its operation and maintenance. The operator of such bonded warehouse shall pay an annual supervision fee in an amount to be fixed by the Commissioner. The bonded warehouse officers and other employees thereof shall be regular employees who shall be appointed in accordance with the Civil Service Law, rules and regulations.

SEC. 1904.

Irrevocable Domestic Letter of Credit or Bank Guarantee or Warehousing B0 articles declared in the entry for warehousing shall have been examined and the duties, taxes charges shall have been determined, the Collector shall require from the importer an irrevocable letter of credit, bank guarantee or bond equivalent to the amount of such duties, taxes and other charges conditioned upon the withdrawal of articles within the period prescribed by section nineteen hundred of this Code and for payment of any duties, taxes and other charges to which the articles shall be the and upon compliance with all legal requirements regarding their importation.

SEC. 1905. Discontinuance of Warehouses. −

The use of any warehouse may be discontinue Collector at any time when conditions so warrant, or, in case of private warehouse, upon receipt c request to that effect from the operator thereof of the premises, provided all the requirements of the regulations have -been complied with by said operator. Where the dutiable article is stored in such premises, the same must be removed at the risk and expense of the operator and the premises shall relinquished, nor discontinuance of its use authorized, until a careful examination of the account warehouse shall have been made. Discontinuance of any warehouse shall be effective upon official notice and approval thereof by the Collector.

SEC. 1906. Entry of Articles for Warehousing. −

The entry of articles for warehousing shall be required number of copies in the prescribed form, and shall be verified as in the entry of the articles for consumption. No warehousing entry shall be accepted for any article if from the entry, supporting documents and/or information such article is imported contrary to any law.

SEC. 1907. Withdrawal of Articles from Bonded Warehouse.

Articles entered under irrevocable domestic letter of credit, bank guarantee or bond may be withdrawn at any time for consumption for transportation to another port, for exportation or for delivery on board a vessel or aircraft engaged in foreign trade for use on board such vessel or aircraft as sea stores or aircraft stores after liquidation of the entry. The withdrawal must be made by a person or firm duly authorized by the former, whose authority must appear in writing upon the face of the withdrawal entry.

SEC. 1908. Limit to Period of Storage in Bonded Warehouse. −

Articles duly entered for warehousing may remain in bonded warehouses for a maximum period of one year from the time of arrival at the port of entry. Articles not withdrawn at the expiration of the prescribed period shall be sold at public auction by the Collector.

SEC. 1909. Charges of Storage in Bonded Warehouse. —

The rates of storage in public or private bonded warehouses shall be subject to arrangement between the importer and the warehouse operator, but such rates shall not be in excess of the customary charges fixed by the Collector of the port for such warehouses.

PART 2. — BONDED MANUFACTURING AND SMELTING WAREHOUSE

SEC. 2001. Establishment of Bonded Manufacturing Warehouses. —

All articles manufactured in whole or in part of imported materials, and intended for exportation without being charged with duty, shall, in order to be so manufactured and exported, be made and manufactured in bonded manufacturing warehouses under such rules and regulations as the Commissioner of Customs with the approval of the Secretary of Finance, shall prescribe: Provided, That the manufacturer of such articles shall first file a satisfactory bond for the faithful observance of all laws, rules and regulations applicable thereto.

SEC. 2002. Exemption from Duty. —

a. Whenever articles manufactured in any bonded manufacturing warehouse established under the provisions of the preceding section shall be exported directly therefrom or shall be duly laden for immediate exportation under the supervision of the proper official, such articles shall be exempt from duty.

b. Any imported material used in the manufacture of such articles, and any package, covering, brand and label used in putting up the same may, under the regulation prescribed by the Commissioner, with the approval of the Secretary of Finance, be conveyed without the payment of duty into any bonded manufacturing warehouse, and imported articles may, under the aforesaid regulations, be transferred without the payment of duty from any bonded warehouse into any bonded manufacturing warehouse, or to duly accredited sub-contractors of manufacturers who shall process the same into finished products for exports and deliver such finished products back to the bonded manufacturing warehouse, therefrom to be exported; but this privilege shall not be held to apply to implements, machinery or apparatus to be used in the construction or repair of any bonded manufacturing warehouse: Provided, however, That the materials transferred or conveyed into any bonded manufacturing warehouse shall be used in the manufacture of articles for exportation within a period of nine (9) months from date of such transfer or conveyance into the bonded manufacturing warehouse, which period may for sufficient reasons be further extended for not more then three (3) months by the Commissioner. Materials not used in the manufacture of articles for exportation within the prescribed period shall pay the corresponding duties: Provided, further, That the operation of embroidery and apparel firms shall continue to be governed by Republic Act Numbered Thirty -one hundred and thirty -seven,

SEC. 2003. Procedure for Withdrawal. ―

Articles received into such bonded manufacturing warehouse or articles manufactured therein may be withdrawn or removed therefrom for direct shipment and for immediate exportation in bond under the supervision of the proper customs officer, who shall certify to such shipment and exportation, or lading for immediate exportation as the case may be, describing the articles by their mark or otherwise, the quantity, the date of exportation, in the name of the vessel of aircraft: Provided, That the waste and by -products incident to the process of manufacture in said bonded warehouse may be withdrawn for domestic consumption upon payment of duty equal to the duty which would be assessed and collected pursuant to law as if such waste or by -products were imported from a foreign country: Provided, further, That all waste materials may be disposed under government supervision. All labor performed and services rendered under these provisions shall be under the supervision of officer and at the expense of the manufacturer.

SEC. 2004. Verification by the Commissioner. ―

A careful account shall be kept by articles delivered by him to any bonded manufacturing warehouse, and a sworn monthly return, verified by the customs officer In-charge, shall be made by the manufacturer containing a detailed statement of all the imported articles used by him in the manufacture of the exported articles. All documents, books and records of accounts concerning the operation of any bonded manufacturing warehouse shall, upon demand, be made available to the Collector or his representative for examination and/or audit. Before commencing business the operator of any bonded manufacturing warehouse shall file Commissioner a list of all the articles intended to be manufactured in such warehouse, and state the formula of manufacture and the names and quantities of the ingredients to be used therein.

SEC. 2005. Bonded Smelting Warehouses. —

The plants of manufacturers engaged in smelting or refining, or both, of ores and crude metals, may, upon the filing of satisfactory bonds, be designated as bonded smelting warehouses. Ores or crude metals may be removed form the vessel or aircraft in which imported, or from the bonded warehouse, into a bonded smelting warehouse without the payment of duties thereon, and there smelted or refined, or both, together with ores or crude metals of home or foreign production: Provided, That the bonds shall be charged with a sum equal in amount to the regular duties which would have been payable on such ores and crude metals if entered for consumption at the importation, and the several charges against such bond shall be cancelled upon the exportation a bonded manufacturing warehouse established under section twenty hundred and one hereof a quality of the same kind of metal equal to the quantity of metal producible from the smelting or refining, or dutiable metal contained in such ores or crude metals, due allowance being made of smelter ascertained from time to time by the Commissioner: Provide, further, That the said metals so producible or any portion thereof, may be withdrawn for domestic consumption or transferred to a bonded warehouse and withdrawn therefrom and the several charges against the bond cancelled upon the payment of the duties chargeable against an equivalent amount of ores or crude metals from which said metal would be in their condition as imported: Provided, further, That on the arrival of the ores or crude meta establishments they shall be sampled and assayed according to commercial methods under the S of proper government officials: Provided, further, That all labor performed and services rendered pursuant to this section shall be under the supervision of the proper customs official and at the expense of the manufacturer: Provided, further, That all regulations for carrying out the provisions of this section shall be prescribed by the Commissioner with the approval of the Department head: And Provided, finally several charges against the bond of any smelting warehouse established under the provisions of this section may be cancelled upon the exportation or transfer to a bonded manufacturing warehouse from bonded smelting warehouse established under this section of a quantity of the same kind of metal, of that covered by open bonds, equal to the amount of metal producible from the smelting or refining or both of the dutiable metal contained in the imported ores or crude metals, due allowance being made of the wastage as ascertained from time to time by the Commissioner with the approval of the department head.

PART 3. – TRANSPORTATION IN BOND

SEC. 2101. Entry for Immediate Transportation. –

Articles entered for constructive warehouse immediate transportation under transit manifest to other ports of the Philippines without appraisement transported under irrevocable domestic letter of credit, bank guarantee or bond, upon proper examination consigned to the Collector at the port of destination, who will allow entry to be made at his port consignee. Articles received at any port from another port of the Philippines on an entry for immediate transportation may be entered at the port of delivery either for consumption or warehousing.

SEC. 2102. Bonding of Carrier Transporting Articles Under the Preceding Section. –

A carrier engaged in conveying imported articles under the preceding section from a port of importation to other shall give security in the nature of a general transportation bond, in a sum not less than ten thousand (P 10,000.00) conditioned that the carrier shall transport and deliver without delay, and in accordance with law and regulations, to the Collector at the port of destination all articles delivered to such carrier and that all proper charges and expenses incurred by the customs authorities or at their instance by reason of -transshipments shall be duly paid.

SEC. 2103. Articles Entered for Immediate Exportation. –

Where an intent to export the articles s shown by the bill of lading, invoice, manifest, or other satisfactory evidence, the whole or a part of a bill (no: less than one package) may be entered for immediate exportation under bond. The Collector shall designate the vessel or aircraft in which the articles are laden constructively as a warehouse to facilitate the direct transfer of the articles to the exporting vessel or aircraft. Unless it shall appear by the bill of lading, invoice, manifest, or other satisfactory evidence, that articles arriving in the Philippines are destined for transshipment, no exportation thereof will be permitted except under entry for immediate exportation under irrevocable domestic letter of credit, bank guaranty or bond in an amount equal to the ascertained duties, taxes and other charges. Upon the exportation of the articles, and the production of proof of landing of same beyond the limits of the Philippines, the irrevocable domestic letter of credit, bank guaranty or bond shall be released.

TITLE VI. - ADMINISTRATIVE AND JUDICIAL PROCEEDINGS.

PART 1. – SEARCH, SEIZURE AND ARREST

SEC. 2201. Trespass or Obstruction of Customs Premises. –

No person other than those with legitimate business with, or employees of, the port or the Bureau of Customs shall be allowed to enter the customs premises without a written permission of the Collector. No person shall obstruct a customhouse, warehouse, office, wharf, street or other premises under the control of the Bureau of Customs, or in any approaches to that house or premises.

SEC. 2202. Special Surveillance for Protection of Customs Revenue and Prevention of Smuggling.

In order to prevent smuggling and to secure the collection of the legal duties, taxes and other charges, the customs service shall exercise surveillance over the coast, beginning when a vessel or aircraft enters Philippine territory and concluding when the article imported therein has been legally passed through the customhouse: Provided, That the function of the Philippine Coast Guard to prevent and suppress illegal entry, smuggling and other customs frauds and violations of the maritime law and its proper surveillance of vessels entering and/or leaving the Philippine territory as provided in section 3 (a) of Republic Act Numbered Fifty -one hundred and seventy -three shall continue to be in force and effect.

SEC, 2203. Persons Having Police Authority. –

For the enforcement of the tariff and customs laws, the following persons are authorized to effect searches, seizures and arrests conformably with the provisions of said laws.
a. Officials of the Bureau of Customs, district collectors, deputy collectors, police officers, agents, inspectors and guards of the Bureau of Customs;
b. Officers of the Philippine Navy and other members of the Armed Forces of the Philippines and national law enforcement agencies when authorized by the Commissioner;
c. Officials of the Bureau of Internal Revenue on all cases falling within the regular performance of their duties, when the payment of internal revenue taxes are involved;
d. Officers generally empowered by law to effect arrests and execute processes of courts, when acting under the direction of the Collector. In order to avoid conflicts, and insure

coordination among these persons having authority to effect searches, seizures and arrests for the effective enforcement of, and conformably with tariff and customs laws, the Secretary of Finance, shall, subject to the approval of the President of the Philippines, define the scope, areas covered, procedures and conditions governing the exercise of such police authority including custody and responsibility for the goods seized. The rules and regulations to this effect shall be furnished to all the government agencies and personnel concerned for their guidance and compliance, and shall be published in a newspaper of general circulation.

SEC. 2204. Place Where Authority May be Exercised. —

All persons conferred with powers in the preceding section may exercise the same at any place within the jurisdiction of the Bureau of Customs.

SEC. 2205. Exercise of Power of Seizure and Arrest. —

It shall be within the official or person authorized as aforesaid, and it shall be his duty, to make seizure of any vessel, aircraft, cargo, article, animal or other movable property, when the same is subject to forfeiture imposed under tariff and customs laws, rules and regulations, such power to be exercise the law and the provisions of this Code: Provided, That the powers of the Fisheries C arrests, searches and seizures as provided in section four paragraphs "g" and "I" of Rep Thirty -five hundred and twelve, and the Philippine Coast Guard under Republic Act hundred and seventy -three shall continue to be in force and effect.

SEC. 2206. Duty of Officer or Official to Disclose Official Character. —

It Shall person exercising authority as aforesaid, upon being questioned at the time of the exercise thereof, to make known his official character as an officer or official of the Government, and if his authority is derived from special authorization in writing to exhibit the same for inspection, if demanded.

SEC. 2207. Authority to Require Assistance. —

Any person exercising police authority under the customs and tariff laws may demand assistance of any police officer when such assistance shall be necessary to effect any search, seizure or arrest which may be lawfully made or attempted c. the duty of any police officer upon whom such requisition is made to give such lawful assistance in the matter as may be required.

SEC. 2208. Right of Police Officer to Enter Inclosure. —

For the more effective discharge of his official duties, any person exercising the powers herein conferred, may at any time enter, pass through, or search any land or inclosure or any warehouse, store or other building, not being a dwelling house. A warehouse, store or other building or inclosure used for the keeping or storage of a become a dwelling house within the meaning hereof merely by reason of the fact that the person as watchman lives in the place, nor will the fact that his family stays there with him alter the case.

SEC. 2209. Search of Dwelling House. —

A dwelling house may be entered and search only upon warrant issued by a Judge of the Court or such other responsible officers as may be authorize -sworn application showing probable cause and particularly describing the place to be searched a thing to be seized.

SEC. 2210.

Right to Search Vessels or Aircrafts and Persons or Articles Conveyed Thebe lawful for any official or person exercising police authority under the provisions of this Code to go abroad any vessel or aircraft within the limits of any collection district, and to inspect, search and examine or aircraft and any trunk, package, box or envelope on board, and to search any person on bcc vessel or aircraft if under way, to use all necessary force to compel compliance; and if it shall appear that any breach or violation of the customs and tariff laws of the Philippines has been committed, whereby or in consequence of which such vessels or aircrafts, or the article, or any part thereof, on board of or imported by such vessel or aircraft, is liable to forfeiture to make seizure of the same or any part thereof. The power of search hereinabove given, shall extend to the removal of any false bottom bulkhead or other obstruction, so far as may be necessary to enable the officer to discover W dutiable or, forfeitable articles may be concealed therein. No proceeding herein shall give rise to any claim for the damage thereby caused to article or vessel or aircraft.

SEC. 2211. Right to Search Vehicles, Beasts and Persons. —

It shall also be lawful for exercising authority as aforesaid to open and examine any box, trunk, envelope or other container, found when he has reasonable cause to suspect the presence therein of dutiable or prohibited article introduced into the Philippines contrary to law, and likewise to stop, search and examine any vehicle person reasonably suspected of holding or conveying such article as aforesaid.

SEC. 2212. Search of Persons Arriving From Foreign Countries. –

All persons coming Philippines from foreign countries shall be liable to detention and search by the customs authorities under such regulations as may be prescribed relative thereto. Female inspectors may be employed for the examination and search of persons of their own sex.

PART 2. – ADMINISTRATIVE PROCEEDINGS

SEC. 2301. Warrant for Detention of Property -Cash Bond. –

Upon making any, seizure, the Collector shall issue a warrant for the detention of the property; and if the owner or importer desires to secure the release of the property for legitimate use, the Collector shall, with the approval of the Commissioner of Customs, surrender it upon the filing of a cash bond, in an amount to be fixed by him, conditioned upon the payment of the appraised value of the article and/or any fine, expenses and costs which may be adjudged in the case: Provided, That such importation shall not be released under any bond when there is prima facie evidence of fraud in the importation of the article: Provided, further, That articles the importation of which is prohibited by law shall not be released under any circumstance whomsoever, Provided, finally, That nothing in this section shall be construed as relieving the owner or importer from any criminal liability which may arise from any violation of law committed in connection with the importation of the article (R.A. 7651, June 04, 1993).

SEC. 2302. Report of Seizure to Commissioner and Chairman, Commission on Audit. –

When a seizure is made for any cause, the Collector of the district wherein the seizures is effected shall immediately make report thereof to the Commissioner and Chairman of the Commission on Audit.

SEC. 2303. Notification~ to Owner or Importer. –

The Collector shall give the owner or importer of the property or his agent a written notice of the seizure and shall give him an opportunity to be heard in reference to the delinquency which was the occasion of such seizure. For the purpose of giving such notice and of all other proceedings in the matter of such seizure, the importer, consignee or person holding the bill of lading shall be deemed to be the "owner" of the article included in the bill. For the same purpose, "agent" shall be deemed to include not only any agent in fact of the owner of the seized property but also any person having responsible possession of the property at the time of the seizure, if the owner or his agent in fact is unknown or cannot be reached.

SEC. 2304. Notification to Unknown Owner. –

Notice to an unknown owner shall be effected by posting for fifteen days in the public corridor of the customhouse of the district in which the seizure was made, and, in the discretion of the Commissioner, by publication in a newspaper or by such other means as he shall consider desirable.

SEC. 2305. Description, Appraisal and Classification of Seized Property. –

The Collector shall also cause a list and particular description and/or classification of the property seized to be prepared and an appraisement of the same, like, or similar article at its wholesale value in the local market in the usual wholesale quantities in the ordinary course of trade to be made by at least two appraising officials, if there are such officials at or near the place of seizure. In the absence of - those officials, then by two competent and disinterested citizens of the Philippines, to be selected by him for that purpose, residing at or near the place of seizure, which list and appraisement shall be properly attested to by the Collector and the persons making the appraisal.

SEC. 2306. Proceedings in Case of Property Belonging to Unknown Parties. –

If, within fifteen days after the notification prescribed in section twenty -three hundred and four of this Code, no owner or agent can be found or appears before the Collector, the latter shall declare the property forfeited to the government to be sold at auction in accordance with law.

SEC. 2307. Settlement of Case by Payment of Fine or Redemption of Forfeited Property. –

Subject to approval of the Commissioner, the district collector may, while the case is still pending, except when there is fraud, accept the settlement of any seizure case provided that the owner, importer, exporter, or consignee or his agent shall offer to pay to the collector a fine imposed by him upon the property, or in case of forfeiture, the owner, exporter, importer or consignee or his agent shall offer to pay for the domestic market value of the seized article. The Commissioner may accept the settlement of any seizure case on appeal in the same manner. Upon payment of the fine as determined by the district collector which shall be in amount not less than twenty percentum (20%) nor more than eighty percentum (80%) of the landed cost of the seized imported article or the F.O.B. value of the seized article for export, or payment of the domestic market value, the property shall be forthwith released and all liabilities which may or might attach to the property by virtue of the offence which was the occasion of the seizure and all liability which might have been incurred under any cash deposit or bond given by the owner or agent in respect to such property shall thereupon be deemed to be discharged. Settlement of any seizure case by payment of the fine or redemption of forfeited property shall not be allowed in any case where the importation is absolutely prohibited or where the release of the property would be contrary to law.

SEC. 2308. Protest and Payment Upon Protest in Civil Matters. —

When a ruling or decision of the Collector is made whereby liability for duties, taxes, fees or other charges are determined, except the fixing of fines in seizure cases, the partly adversely affected may protest such ruling or decision by present Collector at the time when payment of the amount claimed to be due the government is made, or wit, (15) days thereafter, a written protest setting forth his objection to the ruling or decision in question with the reason's therefore. No protest shall be considered unless payment of the amount due liquidation has first been made and the corresponding docket fee, as provided for in Section 3301.

SEC. 2309. Protest Exclusive Remedy in Protestable, Case. —

In all cases subject to pr interested party who desires to have the action of the Collector reviewed, shall make a protest, other action of the Collector shall be final and conclusive against him, except as to matters collectible for error in the manner prescribed in section one thousand seven hundred and seven hereof.

SEC. 2310. Form and Scope of Protest. —

Every protest shall be filed in accordance prescribed rules and regulations promulgated under this section and shall point out the particular de ruling, of the Collector to which exception is taken or objection made, and shall indicate with re precision the particular ground or grounds upon which the protesting party bases his claim for relief. The scope of a protest shall be limited to the subject matter of a single adjustment independent transaction, but any number of issue may be raised in a protest with reference to the particular item or items constituting the subject matter of the protest.

SEC. 2311. Samples to be Furnished by Protesting Parties. —

If the nature of the articles permit, importers filing protests involving questions of fact must, upon demand, supply the Collector with samples of the articles which are the subject matter of the protest. Such samples shall be verified by the customs official who made the classification against which the protest are filed.

SEC. 2312. Decision or Action of Collector in Protest and Seizure Cases. —

When a protest in proper form is presented in a case where protest is required, the Collector shall issue an order for hearing within fifteen (15) days from receipt of the protest and hear the matter thus presented. Upon the termination of the hearing, the Collector shall render a decision within thirty (30) days, and if the protest is sustained, in whole or in part, he shall make the appropriate order, the entry reliquidated necessary. In seizure cases, the Collector, after a hearing shall in writing make a declaration of forfeiture amount of the fine or take such other action as may be proper.

SEC. 2313. Review of Commissioner. —

The person aggrieved by the decision or Collector in any matter presented upon protest or by his action in any case of seizure may, within days after notification on writing by the Collector of his actions or decisions, file a written notice to the Collector with a copy furnished to the Commissioner of his intention to appeal the action or decision of the Collector to the Commissioner. Thereupon the Collector shall forthwith transmit all the recc, proceedings to the Commissioner, who shall approve, modify or reverse the action or decision of t~~ and take such steps and make such orders as may be necessary to give effect to his decision: Provided, That when an appeal is filed beyond the period herein prescribed, the same shag be deemed dismissed. If in any seizure proceedings, the Collector renders a decision adverse to the Government, such decision shall be automatically reviewed by the Commissioner and the records of the case elevated (5) days from the promulgation of the decision of the Collector. The Commissioner shall render a decision on the automatic appeal within thirty (30) days from receipts of the records of the case. If the Collector'~ is reversed by the Commissioner, the decision of the Commissioner shall be final and executory: K the Collector's decision is affirmed, or if within thirty (30) days from receipt of the record of the ca~ Commissioner no decision is rendered or the decision involves imported articles whose published value is five million pesos (P 5,000,000.00) or more, such decision shall be deemed automatically appealed to the Secretary of Finance and the records of the proceedings shall be elevated within five (5) days promulgation of the decision of the Commissioner or of the Collector under appeal, as the case may be, is affirmed by the Secretary of Finance, or within thirty (30) days from receipt of the proceedings by the Secretary of Finance, no decision is rendered, the decision of the Secretary of Finance, or of the Commissioner, or of the Collector under appeal, as the case may be, shall become final and executory. In any seizure proceeding, the release of imported articles shall not be allowed unless apd until a decision of the Collector has been confirmed in writing by the Commissioner of Customs (R.A. 7651, June 04, 1993).

SEC. 2314. Notice of Decision of Commissioner. –

Notice of the decision of the Commissioner shall be given to the party by whom the case was brought before him for review, and in seizure cases such notice shall be effected by personal service if practicable.

SEC. 2315. Supervisory Authority of Commissioner and Secretary of Finance in Certain Cases. –

If any case involving the assessment of duties, the Collector renders a decision adverse to the Government, such decision shall be automatically elevated to, and reviewed by, the Commissioner; and if the Collector's decision would be affirmed by the Commissioner, such decision shall he automatically elevated to, and be finally reviewed by, the Secretary of Finance: Provided, however, That if within thirty (30) days from receipt of the record of the case by the Commissioner or by. the Secretary of Finance, as the case may be, no decision is rendered by either of them, the decision under review shall be final and executory: Provided, further, That any party aggrieved by either the decision of the Commission or of the Secretary of Finance may appeal to the Court of Tax Appeals within thirty (30) days from receipt of a copy of such decision. For this purpose, Republic Act numbered eleven hundred and twenty -five is hereby amended accordingly. Except as provided in the preceding paragraph, the supervisory authority of the Secretary of Finance over the Bureau of Customs shall not extend to the administrative review of the ruling or decision of the Commissioner in matters appealed to the Court of Tax Appeals.

SEC. 2316. Authority of Commissioner to make Compromise. —

Subject to the approval of the Secretary of Finance, the Commissioner of Customs may compromise any case arising under this Code or other laws or part of laws enforced by the Bureau of Customs involving the imposition of fines, surcharges and forfeitures unless otherwise specified by law.

SEC. 2317. Government's Right of Compulsory Acquisition. —

In order to protect government revenues against the undervaluation of goods subject to ad valorem duty, the Commissioner of Customs may acquire imported goods under question for a price equal to their declared customs value plus any duties already paid on the goods, payment for which shall be made within ten (10) working days from issuance of a warrant signed by the Commissioner of Customs for the acquisition of such goods. An importer who is dissatisfied with a decision of the Commissioner of Customs pertaining to this section may, within twenty (20) working days after the date on which notice of the decision is given, appeal to the Secretary of Finance and thereafter if still dissatisfied, to the Court of Tax Appeals as provided for in Section 2402 of the Tariff and Customs Code of the Philippines, as amended. Where no appeal is made by the importer, or upon reaffirmation of the commissioner's decision during the appeals process, the Bureau of Customs or its agent shall sell the acquired goods pursuant to existing laws and regulations.
Nothing in this Section limits or affects any other powers of the Bureau of Customs with respect to the disposition of the goods or any liability of the importer or any other person with respect to an offense committed in the importation of the goods." (R.A. 9135, April 27, 2001)

PART 3. – JUDICIAL PROCEEDINGS

SEC. 2401. Supervision and Control Over Criminal and Civil Proceedings. —

Civil and criminal actions and proceedings instituted in behalf of the government under the authority of this Code or other law enforced by the Bureau shall be brought in the name of the government of the Philippines and shall be conducted by customs officers but no civil or criminal action for the recovery of duties or the enforcement of any fine, penalty or forfeiture under this Code shall be filed in court without the approval of the Commissioner." (R.A. 9135, April 27, 2001)

SEC. 2402. Review by Court of Tax Appeals. —

The party aggrieved by the ruling of the Commissioner in any matter brought before him upon protest or by his action or ruling in any case of seizure may appeal to the Court of Tax Appeals, in the manner and within the period prescribed by law and regulations. Unless an appeal is made to the Court of Tax Appeals in the manner and within the period prescribe by laws and regulations, the action or ruling of the Commissioner shall be final and conclusive.

PART 4. — SURCHARGES, FEES AND FORFEITURES

SEC. 2501. Failure to Pay Liquidated Charges. —

For failure to pay the amount of liquidated duties taxes and other charges of a Iiquidation within ten (10) working days after the notice of liquidation shall haw been publicly posted in the customhouse, surcharge of ten percent (10%) of the total amount or balance found upon liquidation shall be added thereto and collected therewith, which surcharge shall be increased to twenty-five percent (25%) if the delinquency lasts for more than one year.

SEC. 2501 -A. Unauthorized Withdrawal of Imported Articles From Bonded Warehouse. —

Upon any unauthorized withdrawal of imported articles stored in a custom bonded warehouse, a surcharge of fifty percent (50%) of duties, taxes, custom fees and charges, found to be due and unpaid, shall be added thereto and collected. The surcharge shall be increased by twenty-five percent (25%) annually taxes if the delinquency lasts for more than one year.

SEC. 2502. - Repealed by P.D. 1679. March 6. 1980.

SEC. 2503. Undervaluation, Misclassification and Misdeclaration in Entry. —

When the dutiable value of the imported articles shall be so declared and entered that the duties, based on the declaration of the importer on the face of the entry would be less by ten percent (10%) than importer's description on the face of the entry would less by ten percent (10%) than should be legally collected based on the tariff classification of when (the dutiable weight, measurement or quantity of imported articles is found upon examination to exceed by ten percent (10%) or more than the entered weight, measurement or quantity, a surcharge shall be collected from the importer in an amount of not less than the difference between the full duty and the estimated duty based upon the declaration of the importer, nor more than twice of such difference: Provided, That an undervaluation, misdeclaration in weight, measurement or quantity of more than thirty percent (30%) between the value, weight, measurement or quantity declared in the entry, and the actual value, weight, quantity, or measurement shall constitute a prima facie evidence of fraud penalized under Section 2530 of this Code: Provide, further, That any misdeclaration or undeclared imported article/items found upon examination shall ipso facto be forfeited in favor of the Government to be disposed of pursuant to the provisions of this Code. When the undervaluation, misdescription, misclassification or misdeclaration in the import entry is intentional, the importer shall be subject to penal provision under Section 3602 of this Code (R.A. 7651, June 04, 1993).

SEC. 2504. Failure or Refusal of Party to Give Evidence or Submit Documents for Examination.

When the owner, importer or consignee of any imported articles, or the agent of either, fails or refuses, upon lawful demand in writing by any customs official to appear, make oath or submit himself to examination or to answer any material question or refuses to produce records, accounts or invoices in his possession pertaining to the value, classification or disposition of the article in question and deemed material in appraising the same, the Collector shall assess a surcharge of twenty percentum ad valorem on the article which is the subject of the importation.

SEC. 2505. Failure to Declare Baggage. –

Whenever any dutiable article is found in the baggage of any person arriving in the Philippines which is not included in the baggage declaration, such article shall be seized and the person in whose baggage it is found may obtain release of such article, if not imported contrary to any law upon payment of treble and appraised value of such article plus all duties, taxes and other charges due thereon unless it shall be established to the satisfaction of the Collector that the failure to mention or declare such dutiable article was without fraud. Nothing in this section shall preclude the bringing of criminal action against the offender.

SEC. 2506. Breach of Bond. –

Upon breach of bond required to be filed under the tariff and customs laws, the Collector subject to the approval of ft Commissioner may accept in satisfaction thereof a smaller sum than that mentioned in the penalty clause of the bond, but in no case less than the amount necessary to indemnify the Government for the damage occasioned by such breach.

SEC. 2513. Vessel or Aircraft Departing Before Entry Made. —

Any vessel or aircraft arriving within the limits of a collection district from a foreign port which departs before the entry is made, without being compelled to do so by stress of weather, pursuit or duress of enemies, or other necessity, shall be fined in the sum not exceeding five thousand pesos.

SEC. 2514. Obstruction to Boarding Official. —

If the master or pilot in command or any member of the complement of any vessel or aircraft arriving at the Philippine port obstructs or hinders any official from lawfully going on board such vessel or aircraft for the purpose of enforcing the customs and tariff laws, or international causes any such official to be so obstructed or hindered, the vessel or aircraft shall be fined in a sum not exceeding five thousand pesos.

SEC. 2515. Unlawful Boarding or Leaving of Vessel or Aircraft. —

If upon arrival at the Philippine port, any master of a vessel or pilot in command of an aircraft engaged in a foreign trade permits any person to board or leave the vessel or aircraft without the permission of the customs official in charge, such vessel or aircraft shall be fined In a sum not exceeding five thousand pesos.

SEC. 2516. Failure to Deliver or Receive Mail. —

if the master of a vessel or the pilot in command of an aircraft arriving at the Philippine port fails or refuses to deliver to the postmaster of the nearest post office, as required by law or contract, all mail matters on board such vessel or aircraft and destined for the particular port, the vessel or aircraft shall be fined in a sum not exceeding one thousand pesos. When any vessel or aircraft which is required by law or contract to carry mail matter departs from a port or place where mail should be received, without giving the postmaster or other postal official a reasonable opportunity to deliver to the vessel or aircraft or its proper officer or agent, any mail matter addressed to or destined for the port or place to which the vessel or aircraft is bound, such vessel or aircraft shall be fined in a sum not exceeding one thousand pesos.

SEC. 2517. Unlading of Cargo Before Arrival at Port of Destination. —

If, upon the arrival within the limits of any collection district of the Philippines of any vessel or aircraft engaged in foreign trade, the master or pilot in command thereof permits any part of the cargo to be unladen before her arrival at her port of destination, and without authority from a proper customs official, such vessel or aircraft shall be fined a sum not less than thirty thousand pesos (P 30,000.00) but not exceeding one hundred thousand pesos (P 100,000.00), provided that no fine shall accude, upon satisfactory proof to the proper collector that the unlading was rendered necessary by stress of weather, accident or other necessity.

SEC. 2518. Unlading of Cargo at Improper Time or Place After Arrival. —

Any vessel or aircraft, which after arrival at her port of destination in the Philippines, discharges cargo at any time or place other than that designated by the Collector shall be fined in a sum not less than thirty thousand pesos (P 30,000.00) and not exceeding one hundred thousand pesos (P 100,000.00), provided that no fine shall accrue upon satisfactory proof to the proper collector that the unlading was rendered necessary by stress of weather, accident or other necessity.

SEC. 2519. Failure to Exhibit or Deposit Documents. —

When the master of a vessel or pilot in command of an aircraft engaged in foreign trade fails to exhibit to the Collector at the time of entry of his vessel or aircraft the register or other paper in lieu thereof, together with the clearance and other papers granted by the customs officials to his vessel or aircraft at the last foreign port of departure, or fails to exhibit any certificate or other documents required to be then exhibited, such vessel or aircraft shall be fined in a sum not exceeding five thousand pesos. Such vessel shall be liable for the payment of the aforesaid fine if the master, within forty eight hours, after arrival, shall fail to deliver to the proper consular officer of his nation such document as are required by law to be deposited with him, or, if after having made such deposit, the master shall fail to produce to the Collector the required evidence that the same has been effected.

SEC. 2520. Bringing of Unmanifested Arms, Explosives or War Equipment. —

Any vessel or aircraft arriving at a port in the Philippines having firearms, gunpowder, cartridges, dynamite or any other explosives, munitions or equipment of war concealed on board the vessel or not contained in the manifest of the vessel or aircraft, shall be fined a sum of not less than thirty thousand pesos (P 30,000.00) but not exceeding one hundred thousand pesos (P 100,000.00).

SEC. 2521. Failure to Supply Requisite Manifests. —

If any vessel or aircraft enters or departs from port of entry without submitting the proper manifests to the customs a6thorities, or shall enter or depart conveying unmanifested cargo other than as stated in the next proceeding section hereof, such vessel aircraft shall be fined in a sum not less than ten thousand pesos (P 10,000.00) but not exceeding thirty thousand pesos (P 30,000.00). The same fine shall be imposed upon any arriving or departing vessel or aircraft If the master or pilot in command shall fail to deliver or mail to the Commission on Audit a true copy of the manifest of the incoming or outgoing cargo, as required by law.

SEC. 2522 - Disappearance of Manifested Article. —

When any package or article mentioned in the manifest shall not be duty forthcoming upon the arrival of the vessel or aircraft shall be fined in a sum not exceeding two thousand pesos (P 2,000.00) unless the disappearance of the package or article in question was not due to the negligence of the master of the vessel or pilot in command of an aircraft and explained to the satisfaction of the Collector. The vessel or aircraft shall be liable for the payment of the same fine when a package or article listed in the manifest does not tally materially in character or otherwise with the description thereof in the manifest.

SEC. 2523. Discrepancy Between Actual and Declared Weight of Manifested Article. —

If the gross weight of any article or package described in the manifest exceeds by more than twenty (20) percentum the gross weight as declared in the manifest or bill of lading thereof, and the Collector shall be of the opinion that such discrepancy was due to the carelessness or incompetency of the master or pilot in command, owner or employee of the vessel or aircraft, a fine of not more than fifteen (15) percentum of he value of the package or article in respect to which the deficiency exists, may be imposed upon the importing vessel or aircraft.

SEC. 2524. Delivery of Cargo Not Agreeing with the Master's or Pilot's in Command Report. —

When a vessel or aircraft arriving from a foreign port is compelled by necessity to put into another port than the port than the port of her destination and permission is granted by the Collector for the unlading of the vessel or aircraft or the delivery of any part of her cargo and it shall be found that the delivery of the cargo does not agree with the master's or the pilot's in command report, and the discrepancy is not satisfactory explained, the vessel or aircraft shall be fined in a sum not exceeding five thousand pesos.

SEC. 2525. Breaking of Seal Placed by Customs Officials. –

If any seal place by a customs official upon any vessel or aircraft or compartment thereof, or upon any box, trunk or other package of article on board any vessel or aircraft shall be fined a sum not exceeding ten thousand pesos (P 10,000.00) for each seal so broken or destroyed.

SEC. 2526. Breaking of Lock or Fastening Placed by Customs Officials. –

If any lock or other fastening device place by a customs official upon any hatch door, or other means of communication with the hold of a vessel or aircraft, or other part thereof, for the security of the same during the night time, shall be unlawfully opened, broken or removed, or if any of the articles contained in the hold or in the other compartments so secured shall be clandestinely abstracted and landed, the vessel or aircraft shall be fined in a sum not exceeding ten thousand (P 10,000.00) pesos.

SEC. 2527. Disappearance of Trunk or Package Specially Noted by Customs Official. –

When any box, trunk or other package of article is found by a customs official on any incoming vessel or aircraft separate form the rest of the cargo or in any unusual or improper place on such vessel or aircraft and the same shall be noted by him, with proper description, and the attention of the master or pilot in command or other responsible officer of the vessel or aircraft is called thereto, the vessel or aircraft shall be fined in a sum not exceeding ten thousand pesos (P 10,000.00) for every such package which may subsequently be missing and unaccounted for upon the arrival of the vessel or aircraft at the port of entry.

SEC. 2528. False Statement of Vessel's or Aircraft's Destination. –

When the master or pilot in command of a vessel or aircraft laden with articles shall make a false statement as to the next destination of such vessel or aircraft when information concerning the same is required of him by a customs official, such vessel or aircraft shall be fined in a sum not exceeding ten thousand pesos (P 10,000.00); and the circumstances that a vessel or aircraft after clearing for a certain port of destination goes to some other port, not being impelled to do so by necessity, shall be prima facie proof that the original statement of the vessel's or aircraft's actual destination was false.

SEC. 2529. Other Offences. —

A vessel shall be fined in an amount hereafter fixed for:

1. Anchoring at any dock, pier, wharf, quay, or bulkhead without rat guards, two hundred pesos (P 200.00) for coastwise vessels, and one thousand pesos (P 1,000.00) for overseas vessels;
2. Dumping garbage or slops over the sides within three miles from the nearest coastline, one thousand pesos (P 1,000.00);
3. Dumping or causing to spread crude oil, kerosene or gasoline in the bay or at the piers within three miles from the nearest coastline, one thousand pesos (P 1,000.00) for each offence;
4. Loading gasoline at a place other than that designated by the regulations, one thousand pesos (P 1,000.00) for each offence;
5. Causing the emission and spread of harmful gas, fumes and chemicals, five thousand pesos (P 5,000.00) for each offence.

SEC. 2530. Property Subject to Forfeiture Under Tariff and Customs Laws. —

Any vehicle, vessel or aircraft, cargo, article and other objects shall, under the following conditions be subjected to forfeiture:

a. Any vehicle, vessel or aircraft, including cargo, which shall be used unlawfully in the importation or exportation of articles or in conveying and/or transporting contraband or smuggled articles in commercial quantities into or from any Philippine port or place. The mere carrying or holding on board of contraband or smuggled articles in commercial quantities shall subject such vessel, vehicle, aircraft, or any other craft to forfeiture: Provided, That the vessel, or aircraft or any other craft is not used as duly authorized common carrier and as such a carrier it is not chartered or leased;
b. Any vessel engaging in the coastwise which shall have on board any article of foreign growth, produce, or manufacture in excess of the amount necessary for sea stores, without such article having been properly entered or legally imported;
c. Any vessel or aircraft into which shall be transferred cargo unladen contrary to law prior to the arrival of the importing vessel or aircraft at her port of destination;

d. Any part of the cargo, stores or supplies of a vessel or aircraft arriving from a foreign port which is unladen before arrival at the vessel's or aircraft's port of destination and without authority from the customs officials; but such cargo, ship or aircraft stores and supplies shall not be forfeited if such unlading was due to accident, stress of weather or other necessity and is subsequently approved by the Collector;

e. Any article which is fraudulently concealed in or removed contrary to law from any public or private warehouse, container yard or container freight station under customs supervision;

f. Any article the importation or exportation of which is effected or attempted contrary to law, or any article of prohibited importation or exportation, and all other articles which, in the opinion of the Collector, have been used, are or were entered to be used as instruments in the importation or the exportation of the former;

g. Unmanifested article found on any vessel or aircraft if manifest therefore is required;

h. Sea stores or aircraft stores adjudged by the Collector to be excessive, when the duties assessed by the Collector thereon are not paid or secured forthwith upon assessment of the same,

I. Any package of imported article which is found by the examining official to contain any article not specified in the invoice or entry, including all other packages purportedly containing imported articles similar to those declared in the invoice or entry to be. the contents of the misdeclared package; Provided, That the Collector is of the opinion that the misdeclaration was contrary to law; j. Boxes, cases, trunks, envelopes and other containers of whatever character used as receptacle or as device to conceal article which is itself subject to forfeiture under the tariff and customs laws or which is so designed as to conceal the character of such articles;

k. Any conveyance actually being used for the transport of articles subject to forfeiture under the tariff and customs laws, with its equipage or trappings, and any vehicle similarly used, together with its equipage and appurtenances including the beast steam or other motive power drawing or propelling the same. The mere conveyance of contraband or smuggled articles by such beast or vehicle shall be sufficient cause for the outright seizure and confiscation of such beast or vehicle but the forfeiture shall not be effected if it is established that the owner of the means of conveyance used as aforesaid, is engaged as common carrier and not chartered or leased, or his agent in charge thereof at the time, has no knowledge of the unlawful act;

1. Any article sought to be imported or exported

(1) Without going through a customhouse, whether the act was consummated, frustrated

or attempted;
(2) By failure to mention to a customs official, articles found in the baggage of a person arriving from abroad;
(3) On the strength of a false declaration or affidavit executed by the owner, importer, exporter or consignee concerning the importation of such article;
(4) On the strength of a false invoice or other document executed by the owner, importer, exporter or consignee concerning the importation or exportation of such article; and
(5) Through any other practice or device contrary to law by means of which such articles was entered hrough a customhouse to the prejudice of the government.

SEC. 2531. Properties Not Subject to Forfeiture in the Absence of Prima Facie Evidence. —

The forfeiture of the vehicle, vessel, or aircraft shall hot be effected if it is established that the owner thereof or his agent in charge of the means of conveyance used as aforesaid has no knowledge of or participation in the unlawful act: Provided, however, That a prima facie presumption shall exist against the vessel, vehicle or aircraft under any of the following circumstances:
1. If the conveyance has been used for smuggling at least twice before;
2. If the owner is not in the business for which the conveyance is generally used; and
3. If the owner is not financially in a position to own such conveyance.

SEC. 2532. Conditions Affecting Forfeiture of Article. —

As regards imported or exported article or articles whereof the importation or exportation is merely attempted, the forfeiture shall be effected only when and while the article is in the custody or within the jurisdiction of the customs authorities or in the hands or subject to the control of the importer, exporter, original owner, consignee, agent of other person effecting the importation, entry or exportation in question, or in the hands or subject to the control of some persons who shall receive, conceal, buy, sell or transport the same or aid in any such acts, with knowledge that the article was imported, or was the subject of an attempt at importation or exportation, contrary to law.

SEC. 2533. Enforcement of Lien, Administrative Fines, and Forfeitures. —

Administrative fines and forfeitures shall be enforced by the seizure of the vehicle, vessel or aircraft or other property subject to the fine or forfeiture and by subsequent proceedings in conformity with the provisions of Parts 2 and 3, Title VI, Book 11, of this Code. For the purpose of enforcing the lien for customs duties, fees and other charges on any seized or confiscated article in the custody of the Bureau of Internal Revenue., the Bureau of Internal Revenue is hereby authorized to impose and enforce the said lien.

SEC. 2534. Seizure of Vessel or Aircraft for Delinquency of Owner or Officer. –

When the owner, .agent, master, pilot in command or other responsible officer of any vessel or aircraft becomes liable to be fined under the tariff and customs laws on account of a delinquency in the discharge of a duty imposed upon him with reference to the said vessel or aircraft, the vessel or aircraft itself may be seized and subjected in an administrative proceeding for the satisfaction of the fine for which such person would have been liable.

SEC. 2535. Burden of Proof in Seizure and/or Forfeiture. –

In all proceedings taken for the seizure and/or forfeiture of any vessel, vehicle, aircraft, beast or articles under the provisions of the tariff and customs laws, the burden of proof shall lie upon the claimant: Provided, That probable cause shall be first shown for the institution of such proceedings and that seizure and/or forfeiture was made under the circumstances and in the manner described in the preceding sections of this Code.

SEC. 2536. Seizure of Other Articles. –

The Commissioner of Customs and Collector of Customs any other customs officer, with the prior authorization in writing by the Commissioner, may demand evidence of payment of duties and taxes on foreign articles openly offered for sale or kept in storage, and if no such evidence can be produced, such articles may be seized and subjected to forfeiture proceedings: , however, That during such proceedings the person or entity for whom such articles have been shall be given the opportunity to prove or show the source of such articles and the payment of duties and taxes thereon.

PART 5. – DISPOSITION OF PROPERTY IN CUSTOMS CUSTODY

SEC. 2601. Property Subject to Sale. –

Property iii customs custody shall be subject to sale under the conditions hereinafter provided: a. Abandoned articles; b. Articles entered under warehousing entry not withdrawn nor the duties and taxes paid thereon within the period described under Section 1908 of this Code; c. Seized property, other than contraband, after liability to sale shall have been established by proper administrative or judicial proceedings in conformity with the provisions of this code; and d. Any article subject to a valid lien for customs duties, taxes or other charges collectible by the Bureau of Customs, after the expiration of the period allowed for the satisfaction of the same (R.A. 7651, June 04,1993).

SEC. 2602. Place of Sale or Other Disposition of Property. −

Property within the purview of this Part of this Code shall be sold, or otherwise disposed of, upon the order of the Collector of the port where the property in question is found, unless the Commissioner shall direct its conveyance for such purpose to some other port.

SEC. 2603. Mode of Sale. −

In the absence of any special provision, subject to the provisions of on 2601 above provided, property subject to sale by the customs authorities shall be sold at public on within thirty (30) days after ten (10) days notice of such sale shall have been conspicuously posted at port and such other advertisement as may appear to the Collector to be advisable in the particular case.

SEC. 2604. Disqualification to Participate in Auction Sale. −

No customs official or employee shall be ed to bid directly or indirectly, in any customs action.

SEC. 2605. Disposition of Proceeds. −

The following charges shall be paid from the proceeds of the in the order named: a. Expenses of appraisal, advertisement of sale. b. Duties except in the case of abandoned and forfeited articles. c. Taxes and other charges due the Government. d. Government storage charges. e. Arrastre and private storage charges. f. Freight, lighterage or general average, on the voyage of importation, of which due notice shall have been given to the Collector.

SEC. 2606. Disposition of Surplus from the Proceeds of Sale of Abandoned or Forfeited or Acquired Articles. −

Except in the case of the sale of abandoned or forfeited articles, and articles which are not claimed by payment of duties, taxes and other charges and compliance with all legal requirements within prescribed period, any surplus remaining after the satisfaction of all unlawful charges as aforesaid shall retained by the Collector for ten (10) days subject to the call of the owner. Upon failure of the owner to claim such surplus within this period, the Collector shall deposit such amount in a special trust fund which shall be used solely for the purpose of financing the compulscacquisition of imported goods by the government as provided in Section 2317 hereof. In all such cases the Collector shall report fully his action in the matter, together with all the particulars the Commissioner and to the Chairman on Audit After one year, the unused amounts in such special trust funds, except for an amount necessary to finance forced government acquisitions before the first auction . the succeeding year, shall be turned over to the Bureau of Treasury as customs receipts." (R.A. 9135, April 27, 2001)

SEC. 2607. Disposition of Articles Liable to Deterioration. —

Perishable articles shall be deposited any appropriate bonded warehouse; and, if not immediately entered for export or transportation from the vessel or aircraft in which imported or entered for consumption and the duties and taxes paid thereon, such articles may be sold at auction, after such public notice, not exceeding three days, as the necessities of the case permit. When seizure shall be made of property which, in the opinion of the Collector, is liable to perish or be wasted or to depreciate greatly in value by keeping or which cannot be kept without great disproportionate expense, whether such property consists of live animals or of any article, the appraiser shall so certify in his appraisal, then the Collector may proceed lo advertise and sell the same at auction, upon notice as he shall deem to be reasonable. The same disposition may be made of any warehoused articles when the opinion of the Collector it is likely that the cost of depreciation, damage, leakage, or other causes, may so reduce its value as to be insufficient to pay the duties, taxes and other charges due thereon, if should be permitted to be so kept and be subjected to sale in the usual course.

SEC. 2608. Disposition of Articles Unfit for Use or Sale or Injurious to Public Health. —

When any article, which in the opinion of the Collector, is a menace to public health, is seized or otherwise comes into the custody of the Bureau of Customs, the Collector of the port shall, if the matter is not disposable under the provisions relating to food and drugs, appoint a board of three members to examine the article. Whenever possible, one member shall be a representative of the Department of Health or of local health officer, and the two others shall be responsible officials of the Bureau of Customs at loom one of whom shall be an appraiser. Such board shall examine said article, and if the same is found a be unfit or a menace to the public health, the board shall so report in writing to the Collector, who shall! kn9nWh aide its destruction in such manner as the case may require. Health authorities at port of entry shall collaborate with the collectors in such matters with reasonable dispatch.

SEC. 2609. Disposition of Contraband. —

Article of prohibited importation or exportation, known as contraband, shall, in the absence of special provision, be dealt with as follows:

a. Dynamite, gunpowder, ammunition and other explosives, firearms and weapons of war and parts thereof, shall be turned over to the Armed Forces of the Philippines;
b. If the article in question is highly dangerous to be kept or handled, it shall forthwith be destroyed;
c. Contraband coin or bullion, foreign currencies and negotiable instruments shall accrue to the Stabilization Fund of the Central Bank subject to the payment of the expenses incident to seizure, including the reward to the informer, if any;
d. Other contraband of commercial value and capable of legitimate use may be sold under such restrictions as will insure its use for legitimate purposes only; but if the thing is unfit for use or the Collector is of the opinion that, if sold, it would be used for unlawful purposes, it shall be destroyed in such manner as the Collector shall direct.

SEC. 2610. Disposition of Unsold Articles for Want of Bidders. —

Articles subject to sale at public auction by Customs authorities shall be sold at a price not less than the wholesale value or price in the domestic market of these or similar articles in the usual wholesale quantities and in the ordinary course of trade as determined in accordance with section twenty-three hundred and five of this Code. When any article remains unsold in at WW two public biddings for want of bidders or for the lack of an acceptable bid, and the article is perishable and/or suitable for official use, then the Collector shall report the matter immediately to the Commissioner of Customs who may, subject to the approval of the Secretary of Finance, authorize the official use of that article by the Bureau of Customs to promote the intensive collection of taxes and/or to help prevent or suppress smuggling and other frauds upon the Customs, and if the article is not suitable for such use, then it may be channeled to the official use of other offices of the National Government. If the article is suitable for shelter or consists of foodstuffs, clothing materials or medicines then that article shall be given to government charitable institutions through the Department of Social Services and Development. If the article offered for sale is not suitable either for official use or charity, then the same may be reexported as government property through the Department of Trade or any other government entity through barter or sale. If the article cannot be disposed of as provided above, the Collector shall report the matter immediately to the Commissioner who may, subject to the approval of the Secretary of Finance, dispose of the article to the best advantage of the government in a negotiated private sale which shall be consummated in the presence of a representative of the Commission on Audit, in the manner provided for by this Code.

SEC. 2611. Treatment of Dangerous Explosives. —

Gunpowder or other dangerous or explosive substances, including firecrackers, shall not be deposited in a bonded warehouse, and when not entered for immediate use, transportation or export, shall be subject to such disposition, in the discretion of the Commissioner of Customs, consistent with public safety. Expenses incurred in such disposition shall constitute a lien on the articles and a charge against the owner.

SEC. 2612. Disposition of Smuggled Articles. —

Smuggled articles, after liability to seizure or forfeiture shall have been established by proper administrative or judicial proceedings in conformity with the provisions of this Code, shall be disposed of as provided for in section twenty -six hundred and ten: Provided, That articles whose importation is prohibited under Section One Hundred Two sub -paragraphs b, c, d, e and j shall, upon order to the Collector in writing, be burned or destroyed, in such manner as the case may require as to render them absolutely worthless, in the presence of a representative each from the Commission on Audit, Ministry of Justice, Bureau of Customs, and if possible, any representative of the private sector,

PART 6. — FEES AND CHARGES

SEC. 3301. Customs F9es and Charges. —

For services rendered and documents issued by the Bureau of Customs, the following fees shall be charged and collected, by affixing documentary customs stamps in the correct amount upon the document or any other paper which is the subject of the charge and by the cancellation of such stamps in the manner prescribed by the Commissioner, and no such document or any other paper shall be issued or granted by any customs official until the correct amount of stamps shall have been affixed and cancelled: Provided, however, That fees of twenty pesos or over may be paid in cash.

For each amendment allowed to a foreign inward manifest P 30.00

For each permit to others than passengers to take cigars aboard ship, per thousand cigars 30.00

For each permit (to other than passengers) to take cigarettes aboard ship, per thousand cigarettes, 30.00
For each original import or export entry exceeding fifty pesos in value, 30.00
For each entry for immediate transportation in bond, 30.00
For each original internal revenue entry, 30.00
For each original withdrawal entry from any bonded warehouse, 30.00 For each bond accepted or renewed, 30.00
For each approval of application in respect to transaction covered by general bond, 30.00
For every formal protest filed before the Collector of Customs, 50.00
For each appeal in protest and seizure cases, 50.00
For each -certificate not hereinabove specified, exclusive of such are made in the course of routine administration in the bureau which do not subserve any special pecuniary interest of the party concerned therein, 30.00

SEC. 3302. Other Charges. —

When any article is sold or any service rendered by the Bureau o Customs in any matter for which a charge may be collected legally, no fee therefore having been fixed by law such charge shall be on such amount as may from time to time be fixed by regulations or order of the Commissioner and approved by the Department of Finance, and the payment of such charge may be made by affixing and canceling the documentary customs stamps.

SEC. 3303. Effect of Failure to Affix Stamp upon Document. —

No document or any other paper upon which no documentary customs stamps have been affixed and cancelled shall be received or recognized b~ any customs officials.

SEC. 3304. General Provision on the Authority to Increase or Decrease Fees and Charges. —

The rates of the fees and charges in all ports in the Philippines shag be those now provided for under section thirty -three hundred and one of this Code: Provided. however. That the Secretary of Finance may, upon recommendation of the Commissioner of Customs, increase or decrease the said fees, dues and charges collectible by the Bureau of Customs to protect the interest of the Government.

TITLE VII - GENERAL PROVIISIIONIS

PART 1. — CUSTOMS BROKERS 61

SEC. 3401. Qualifications of Applicants for Customs Broker's Certificate. —

All applicants for customs broker's certificates shall pass a written examination for the purpose.

Applicants for admission to the said examination shall have the following qualifications:

(a) At least 21 years of age;

(b) A citizen of the Philippines;

(c) Of good moral character; and

(d) Has completed at least four -year -collegiate course, where he has creditably taken at least eighteen (18) academic units in tariff and customs and/or taxation, and applicant may be allowed to take the examination provided that for every deficiency of three (3) academic units in tariff and customs and/or taxation shall be substituted by at least three (3) months of actual experience in customs brokerage and/or customs and tariff matters: Provided, That said experience shall be duty certified by the employer or employers of the applicant No corporation, association or partnership shall engage in the customs brokerage business unless at least two (2) of the officers of such corporation or association, or at least two (2) of the members of such partnership have such certificate. No certificate as customs broker shall be granted to any person who has been convicted of a crime involving moral turpitude.

SEC. 3402. Examination by the Board of Examiners for Customs Brokers. —

Examinations for customs broker shall be given by the Board of Examiners for customs broker under the supervision of the Civil Service Commission.

Application for admission to such examination -shall be filed with the Civil Service

Commission. Examination for customs brokers shall be given once every two (2) years or oftener as the need therefore arises which fact shall be certified by the Commissioner of Customs and shall be confined to subjects with which such brokers are required to be conversant, including knowledge of customs and tariff laws and regulations, and of other laws and regulations the enforcement of which is the concern of the Bureau of Customs. The board shall submit within one hundred twenty (120) days after the date of examination the ratings obtained by each candidate to the Commissioner of Civil Service who shall submit such ratings to the President of the Philippines for release. A general average of seventy -five per cent (75%) shall be the passing grade for this examination: Provided, That the examinee shall not have obtained a grade of less than sixty per cent (60%) in any of the examination subjects.

This customs brokers' examination shall be considered as equivalent to the first grade regular examination given by the Civil Service Commission for purposes of appointment to positions in the classified the duties of which involve knowledge of customs and tariff matters. The examination and registration fees shall be subject to Republic Act Numbered four hundred and sixty -five.

SEC. 3403. The Board of Examiners. −

The board of Examiners for Customs Brokers shall be composed of the Commissioner of Customs, as ex -officio chairman, the Tariff Commissioner and three (3) others members who shall be appointed by the President upon the recommendation of the Commissioner of Civil Service. The three (3) members of the Board shall be holders of customs brokers' certificate and shall hold office for a term of two (2) years: Provided, That the term of any incumbent shall not be affected thereby. Vacancies in the Board shall be filled for the expired term.

SEC. 3404. Compensation of Members of the Board. −

The chairman and members of the board shall receive a compensation of ten pesos (P10.00) for each candidate examined.

SEC. 3405. Fees. −

(a) Each applicant for examination shall pay a fee as provided for in Republic Act Numbered four hundred and sixty -five, as amended, which shall be paid to the Civil Service Commission. (b) Each successful candidate shall be issued a certificate as customs broker upon payment of a fee of fifty pesos P50.00) to the Civil Service Commission.

SEC. 3406. Annual License Fee. —

Any person who is a holder of a customs broker's certificate, desiring to establish a customs brokerage business at any port in the Philippines shall apply for an annual cense from the Collector of the port concerned. No such license shall be issued unless the applicant pays the required annual license fee of one hundred pesos (P100) and files the required bonds for customs brokers. Whenever it shall appear that a bond given by a customs broker is inadequate, the Collector shall require additional or substitute bond to be 'led. The additional or substitute bond shall be furnished by the broker within ten (10) days after demand, otherwise his permit shall be suspended or revoked as circumstances may warrant. The bonds posted by the customs broker may be personal bonds guaranteed by at least two (2) sureties satisfactory to the Collector of the port or a surety bond posted by a duly licensed surety company.

SEC. 3407. Issuance, Revocation and Suspension of Certificate. —

A candidate who has passed the customs brokers' examination shall be entitled to the issuance of a certificate as a customs broker: Provided, 7hat (1) persons who qualified as customs broker in accordance with customs regulations existing before the adoption of this Code; (2) Commissioner of Customs who has acted as ex -officio Chairman of the Board of Examiners for Customs brokers and the Tariff Commissioner who has acted as member of the said board; and (3) Collectors of Customs who have served as such in any of the collection districts for a period of at least five years, who desire to have a certificate issued to them may apply for the issuance of such certificate, upon payment of the fees required under paragraph (b) of Section Thirty -four hundred and five of this Code. A customs broker's certificate shall show among other things, the full name of the registrant, shall have a serial number and, shall be signed by all the members of the Board of the Commissioner of Civil Service, and shall bear the official seal of the Board.

A complaint for the suspension or revocation of the certificate of a customs broker shall be filed with the Board of Examiners for Customs Brokers which shall investigate the case and shall submit its findings and recommendations to the Commissioner of Civil Service and shall immediately furnish the respondent customs broker with a copy of his decision. Any person who files an entry or facilitates the processing or release of any shipment shall be liable for smuggling if the ostensible owner, importer or consignee and/or the ostensible given address of the owner, importer or consignee is. fictitious and the shipment is found to be unlawful. If the violator is a customs broker, his license shall be revoked by the Commissioner of Customs (R.A. 7651, June 04, 1993).

SEC. 3408. Roster of Customs Brokers. —

A roster showing the names and addresses of the customs brokers shall be prepared by the Commissioner of Civil Service during the month of July of every Copies of this roster shall be mailed to each person so registered and placed on file with the Office of the President of the Philippines and copies thereof, shall be furnished to the Office of the Secretary of Finance the Commissioner and Collector of Customs and to such other bureaus, government agencies and provincial and municipal authorities as may be deemed necessary, and to the public upon request.

SEC. 3409. Rules and Regulations by the Commissioner of Civil Service. —

The Commissioner of Civil Service, upon recommendation of the Board of Examiners for Customs Brokers, shall promulgate s -: rules and regulations as may be necessary to carry out the provisions of Part 1 of this title.

PART 2. — MISCELLANEOUS PROVISIONS

SEC. 3501. Duty of Collector to Report Rulings to Commissioner. —

When any new or unsettle question shall be determined by a collector, he shall, if the matter is not otherwise appealed for, review in the ordinary course, notify the Commissioner of his decision and submit adequate statement of the facts involved.

SEC. 3502. Application of Established Ruling or Decision. —

A ruling or decision of the Commissioner of Customs which determines the construction or application of any provision of law imposing customs duties and which changes any existing established classification, interpretation or practice shall not take effect until after thirty days public notice shall be given in the form of a published customs tariff decision. When such ruling or decision favors the taxpayers, it shall become effective immediately.

SEC. 3503. Authority of Official to Administer Oaths and Take Testimony. —

The Commissioner Collectors and their deputies, and other customs employees especially deputized by the Collector shall have authority to administer oaths and take testimony in connection with any matter within the jurisdiction of the Bureau of Customs and in connection therewith may require the production of relevant papers, documents, books and records in accordance with law.

SEC. 3504. General Bonds. —

In cases where bonds are required to be given under the provisions of the customs and tariff laws, the Collector, instead of requiring separate special bonds where transactions of a particular party are numerous, may accept general bonds extending over such periods of time and covering such transactions of the party in question as shall be satisfactory to said Collector.

SEC. 3505. Supervision Over Attorneys -in -Fact. —

No person acting as agent or attorney -in -fact of other persons shall be allowed to deal in matters pertaining to customs and/or tariff unless his duly notarized power of attorney has been approved by the Collector of the port. No more than one such continuing power may be accepted or recognized from any one person or acting as agent in the importation of articles unless he be a licensed customs broker Provided, That in ports of entry where there are two or more licensed customs brokers doing business as such customs brokers, no person shall act as agent or attorney -in -fact for any regular importer unless he is a full -time employee or official of such importer or principal receiving fixed compensation or salary as such.

SEC. 3506. Assignment of Customs Employees to Overtime Work. —

Customs employees may be assigned by a Collector to do overtime work at rates fixed by the Commissioner of Customs when the service rendered is to be paid for by importers, shippers or other persons served. The rates to be fixed shall not be less than that prescribed by law to be paid to employees of private enterprise.

SEC. 3510. Reduction of Testimony to Writing. —

When testimony is taken in any proceeding or matter under the authority of the Bureau of Customs, either party may require that the same be reduced to writing, and when so taken it shall be filed in the Office of the Collector and preserved for use or reference until final decision.

SEC. 3511. Collector Not Liable in Respect to Ruling in Customs Cases. —

No Collector or other official of customs shall be in any way personally liable for or an account of any official ruling or decision as to which the person claiming to be aggrieved has the right to obtain either an administrative or judicial review, and except for misdelivery of articles a Collector shall not, in the absence of abuse of authority, be liable to any person for a loss occasioned either by his own official act or the acts of his subordinates.

SEC. 3512. Interest Prohibited to be Held by Customs Employees. —

No person employed under the authority of the government in the collection of duties, taxes, fees and other charges in connection with imports and/or exports, shall own, either in whole or in part, any vessel or aircraft or act as attorney, agent or consignee for the owner of any vessel or aircraft or of any cargo laden on board the same nor shall any such person import or be concerned, directly or indirectly, in the importation of any article for sale into the Philippines.

SEC. 3513. Reward to Persons Instrumental in the Discovery and Seizure of Smuggled Goods.

The provisions of general and special laws to the contrary notwithstanding, a cash reward equivalent to twenty per centum (20%) of the fair market value of the smuggled and confiscated goods shall be given to the officers and men and informers who are instrumental in the discovery and seizure of such goods in accordance with ft rules and regulations to be issued by the Secretary of Finance. The provisions of this section, and not those of Republic Act Numbered Twenty -three Hundred and Thirty - eight shall govern the giving of reward in cases covered by the former.

SEC. 3514. Requirement to Keep Records. —

All importers are required to keep at their principal place of business, in the manner prescribed by regulations to be issued by the Commissioner of Customs and for a period of three (3) years from the date of importation, all the records of their importations and/or books of accounts, business and computer systems and all customs commercial data including payment records relevant for the verification of the accuracy of the transaction value declared by the importers/customs brokers on the import entry. All brokers are required to keep at their principal place of business, in the manner prescribed by regulations to be issued by the Commissioner of Customs and for a period of three (3) years from the date of importation copies of the above mentioned records covering transactions that they handle. (R.A. 9135, April 27, 2001)

SEC. 3515. Compliance Audit or Examination of Records. —

The importers/customs brokers shall allow any customs officer authorized by the Bureau of Customs to enter during office hours any premises or place where the records referred to in the preceding section are kept to conduct audit examination, inspection, verification and/or investigation of those records either in relation to specific transactions or to the adequacy and integrity of the manual or electronic system or systems by which such records are created and stored. For this purpose, a duty authorized customs officer shall have full and free access to all books, records, and documents necessary or relevant for the purpose of collecting the proper duties and taxes.

In addition, the authorized customs officer may make copies of, or take extracts from any such documents. The records or documents must, as soon as practicable after copies of such have been taken, be returned to the person in charge of such documents.

A copy of any such document certified by or on behalf of the importer/broker is admissible in evidence in all courts as if it were the original. An authorized customs officer is not entitled to enter any premises under this Section unless, before so doing, the officer produces to the person occupying or apparently in charge of the premises written evidence of the fact that he or she is an authorized officer. The person occupying or apparently in charge of the premises entered by an officer shall provide the officer with all reasonable facilities and assistance for the effective exercise of powers under this Section.

Unless otherwise provided herein or in other provisions of law, the Bureau of Customs may, in case of disobedience, invoke the aid of the proper regional trial court within whose jurisdiction the matter falls. The court may punish contumacy or refusal as contempt. In addition, the fact that the importer/broker denies the authorized customs officer full and free access to importation records during the conduct of a post-entry audit shall create a presumption of inaccuracy in the transaction value declared for their imported goods and constitute grounds for the Bureau of Customs to conduct a re-assesment of such goods. This is without prejudice to the criminal sanctions imposed by this Code and administrative sanctions that the Bureau of Customs may impose against contumacious importers under existing laws and regulations including the authority to hold delivery or release of their imported articles. (R.A. 9135, April 27, 2001)

SEC. 3516. Scope of the Audit. –

(a) The audit of importers shall be undertaken:
  (1) When firms are selected by a computer -aided risk management system, the parameters of which are to be based on objective and quantifiable data are to be approved by the Secretary of Finance upon recommendation of the Commissioner of Customs. The criteria for selecting firms to be audited shall include, but not be limited to, the following:
    (a) Relative magnitude of customs revenue from the firm;
    (b) The rates of duties of the firm's imports;
    (c) The compliance tract record of the firm; and d) An assessment of the risk to revenue of the firm's import activities.
  (2) When errors in the import declaration are detected;
  (3) When firms voluntarily request to be audited, subject to the approval of the Commissioner of Customs.
(b) Brokers shall be audited to validate audits of their importer clients and/or fill in information gaps revealed during an audit of their importer clients." (R.A. 9135, April 27, 2001)

SEC. 3517. Documents in Foreign Language. –

Where a document in a foreign language is presented to a customs officer in relation to the carrying out of any duty or the exercise of any power of the Bureau of Customs under this Code, said document in a foreign language of this of this country. (RA 9135. P4wd 27,2001)

SEC. 3518. Records to be Kept by Customs. –

The Bureau of Customs shall likewise keep a record of audit results in a database of importer and broker profiles, to include but not be limited to:
(a) Articles of Incorporation;
(b) The company structure, which shall include but not be limited to: (1) Incorporators and Board of Directors; (2) Key officers; and (3) Organizational structure;
(c) Key importations;
(d) Privileges enjoyed;
(e) Penalties; and
(f) Risk category (ies). (R.A. 9135, April 27, 2001)

SEC. 3519. **Words and Phrases Defined.** - As used in this Code:

"Foreign Port" means a port or place outside the jurisdiction of the Philippines.

"Port of Entry" is a domestic port open to both foreign and coastwise trade. The term includes principal ports of entry and subports of entry. A "principal port of entry" is the chief port of entry of the collection district wherein it is situated and is the permanent station of the Collector of such port. Subports of entry are under the administrative jurisdiction of the Collector of the principal port of entry of the district. Whenever the term "Port of Entry" is used herein, it shall include "airport of entry".

"Coastwise ports" are such domestic ports as are open to coastwise trade only. These include all ports, harbors and places not ports of entry.

"Vessels" includes every sort of boat, craft or other artificial contrivance used, or capable of being used, as a means of transportation on water.

"Aircraft" includes any weight-carrying devise or structure for the navigation of the air.

"Bill of Lading" includes airway bill of lading.

"Articles", when used with reference to importation or exportation, includes goods merchandise and in general anything that may be made the subject of importation or exportation.

"Transit cargo" is article arriving at any port from another port or place noted in the carrier's manifest and destined for transshipment to another local port or to a foreign port.

"Seized property" means any property seized or held for the satisfaction of any administrative fine or for the enforcement of any forfeiture under the Tariff and Customs Code.

"Tariff and customs laws" includes not only the provisions of this Code and regulations pursuant thereto but all other laws and regulations which are subject to enforcement by the Bureau of Customs or otherwise within its jurisdiction. "Taxes" includes all taxes, fees and charges imposed by the Bureau of Customs and the Bureau of Internal Revenue.

"Secretary" or "Department head" refers, unless otherwise specified, to the Secretary of Finance.

"Commission' refers to the Tariff Commission. "Person" whether singular or plural refers to an individual, corporation, partnership, association company or any other kind of organization.

"Dutiable value" refers to the value defined in section two hundred one. "Bulk cargo" refers to products in a mass of one commodity not packaged, bundled, bottled or otherwise packed.

"Smuggling" is an act of any person who shall fraudulently import or bring into the

Philippines, or assist in so doing, any article, contrary to law or shall receive, conceal, buy, sell or in any manner facilitate the transportation, concealment, or sale of such article after importation, knowing the same to have been imported contrary to law. It includes the exportation of articles in a manner contrary to law. Articles subject to this paragraph shall be known as smuggled articles.

"Contrabands" are articles of prohibited importation or exportation. "Duly Registered" as used in this Act, refers to a person, natural or juridical, which is registered with the proper government agencies, such as the Bureau of Commerce, Securities and Exchange Commission, NACIDA, Board of Investments, Export Incentives Board or Oil Commission as now or may hereafter be required by law. (R.A. 9135, April 27, 2001)

PART 3. – PROVISIONS ON PENALTIES
SEC. 3601. Unlawful Importation. –

Any person who shall fraudulently import or bring into the Philippines, or assist in so doing, any article, contrary to law, or shall receive, conceal, buy, sell, or in any manner facilitate the transportation, concealment, or sale of such article after importation, knowing the same to have been imported contrary to law, shall be guilty of smuggling and shall be punished with:

1. A fine of not less than fifty pesos nor more than two hundred pesos and imprisonment of not less than five days nor more than twenty days; if the appraised value, to be determined in the manner prescribed under this Code, including duties and taxes, of the article unlawfully imported does not exceed twenty -five pesos;
2. A fine of not less than eight hundred pesos nor more than five thousand pesos and imprisonment of not less than six months and one day nor more than four years, if the appraised value, to be determined in the manner prescribed under this Code, including duties and taxes, of the article unlawfully imported exceeds twenty -five pesos but does not exceed fifty thousand pesos;
3. A fine of not less than six thousand pesos nor more than eight thousand pesos and imprisonment of not less than five years and one day nor more than eight years, if the appraised value, to be determined in the manner prescribed under this Code, including duties and taxes, of the art,,: unlawfully imported is more than fifty thousand pesos but does not exceed one hundred thousand pesos;
4. A fine of not less than eight thousand pesos nor more than ten thousand pesos and imprisonment of not less than eight years and one day nor more than twelve years, if the appraised value to be determined in the manner prescribed under this Code, including

duties and taxes, of the artic unlawfully imported exceeds one hundred fifty thousand pesos;

5. The penalty of prison may or shall be imposed when the crime of serious physical injuries shall have been committed and the penalty of reclusion perpetua to death shall be imposed when the crime of homicide shall have been committed by reason or on the occasion of the unlawful importation. In applying the above scale of penalties, if the offender is an alien and the prescribed penalty is not death, he shall be deported after serving the sentence without further proceedings for deportation. If the offender is a government official or employee, the penalty shall be the maximum as hereinabove prescribe and the offender shall suffer and additional penalty of perpetual disqualification from public office, to vote and to participate in any public election.

When, upon trial for violation of this section, the defendant is shown to have had possession of the article in question, possession shall be deemed sufficient evidence to authorize conviction unless the defendant shall explain the possession to the satisfaction of the court: Provided, however, That payment o; the tax due after apprehension shall not constitute a valid defense in any prosecution under this section.

SEC. 3602. Various Fraudulent Practices Against Customs Revenue. –

Any person who makes or attempts to make any entry of imported or exported article by means of any false or fraudulent invoice, declaration, affidavit, letter, paper or by any means of any false statement, written or verbal, or by any means of any false or fraudulent practice whatsoever, or knowingly effects any entry of goods, wares or merchandise, at less than true weight or Measures thereof or upon. a false classification as to quality or value, or by the payment of less than the amount legally due, or knowingly and willfully files any false or fraudulent entry or claim for the payment of drawback or refund of duties upon the exportation of merchandise, or makes or files any affidavit abstract, record, certificate or other document, with a view to securing the payment to himself or others of any drawback, allowance, or refund of duties on the exportation of merchandise, greater than that legally due thereon, or who shall be guilty of any willful act or omission shall, for each offence, be punished in accordance with the penalties prescribed in the preceding section.

SEC. 3603. Failure to Report Fraud. –

Any master, pilot in command or other officer, owner or agent of any vessel or aircraft trading with or within the Philippines and any employee of the Bureau of Customs who, having cognizance of any fraud on the customs revenue, shah fail to report all information relative thereto to the Collector as by law required, shah be punished by a fine of not more than five thousand pesos and imprisonment for not more than one year. If the offender is an alien, he shall be deported after serving the sentence. If the offender is a public official or employee, he shall suffer additional penalty of perpetual disqualification to hold public office, to vote and to participate, in any election.

SEC. 3604. Statutory Offenses of Officials and Employees. —

Every official, agent or employee of the Bureau or of any other agency of the government charged with the enforcement of the provisions of this Code, who is guilty of any delinquency herein below indicated shall be punished with a fine of not less than Five thousand pesos nor more than Fifty thousand pesos and imprisonment for not less than one year nor more than ten years and perpetual disqualification to hold public office, to vote and to participate in any public election.

(a) Those guilty of extortion or willful oppression under color of law;

(b) Those who knowingly demand other or greater sums than are authorized by law or receive any fee, compensation, or reward except as by law prescribed, for the performance of any duty;

(c) Those who willfully neglect to give receipts, as required by law for any sum collection in the performance of duty, or who willfully neglect to perform any of the duties enjoined by law;

(d) Those who conspire or collude with another or others to defraud the customs revenue or otherwise violate the law;

(e) Those who willfully make opportunity for any person to defraud the customs revenue or who do or fail to do any act with intent to enable any person to defraud said revenue;

(f) Those who negligently or designedly permit the violation of the law by any other person;

(g) Those who make or sign any false entry or entries in any book, or make or sign any false certificate or return in any case where the law requires the making by them of such entry, certificate or return;

(h) Those who, having knowledge or information of a violation of the Tariff and Customs Law or any fraud committed on the revenue collectible by the Bureau, fail to report such knowledge or information to their superior official or to report as otherwise required by law;

(i) Those who, without the authority of law, demand or accept or attempt to collect directly or indirectly as payment of otherwise, any sum of money or other thing of value for the compromise, adjustment, or settlement of any charge or complaint for any violation or alleged violation of law; or

(j) Those who, without authority of law, disclose confidential information gained during any investigation or audit, or use such information for personal gain or to the detriment of the government, the Bureau or third parties. (R.A. 9135, April 27, 2001)

SEC. 3605. Concealment or Destruction of Evidence of Fraud. –

Any person who willfully conceals or destroys, any invoice, book or paper relating to any article liable to duty after an inspection thereof has been demanded by the Collector of any collection district or at any time conceals or destroys any such invoice, book or paper for the purpose of suppressing any evidence of fraud therein contained, shall be punished with a fine of not more than five thousand pesos and imprisonment for not more than two years.

SEC. 3606. Affixing Seals. –

Any person who, without authority affixes or attaches a customs seal, fastening, or mark or any seal, fastening or mark purporting to be a customs seal, fastening or mark to any vessel, vehicle on land, sea or air, warehouse, or package, shall be punished with a fine of not more than twenty thousand pesos or imprisonment of not more than five years, or both. If the offender is an alien, he shall be deported after serving the sentence; and if he is a public official or employee, he shall suffer an additional penalty of perpetual disqualification to hold public office, to vote and participate in any election.

SEC. 3607. Removal, Breakage, Alteration of Marks. –

Any person who without authority, willfully removes, breaks, injures, or defaces or alters any custom seal or other fastening or mark placed upon any vessel, vehicles, on land, sea or air, warehouse or package containing merchandise or baggage in bond or in customs custody, shall be punished with the penalty prescribed in Section 3606 hereof.

SEC. 3608. Removing or Repacking Goods in Warehouse. –

Any person who fraudulently conceals, removes, or repacks merchandise in any warehouse or fraudulently alters, defaces or obliterates any marks or numbers placed upon packages deposited in such warehouse, or shall aid or abet in any such acts or omission, shall be punished with the penalties prescribed in Section 3606 hereof. Merchandise so concealed, removed, or repacked, or packages upon which marks or numbers have been so altered, defaced or obliterated, or the value thereof, shall be forfeited to the government.

SEC. 3609. Removing Goods from Customs Custody. –

Any person who maliciously enters any warehouse, or any vehicle laden with or containing merchandise with intent unlawfully to remove therefrom any merchandise or baggage in such vessels, vehicle or warehouse or otherwise in customs custody or control, or any person who receives or transports any merchandise or baggage unlawfully removed from any such vessel, vehicle or warehouse, or shall aid or abet such removal, shall suffer the penalties provided in Section 3606 hereof.

SEC. 3610. Failure to Keep Importation Records and Give Full Access to Customs Officers. –

Any person who fails to keep all the records of importations and/or books of accounts, business and computer systems and all customs commercial data in the manner prescribed in Part 2, Section 3514 of this Title shall be punished with a fine of not less than One hundred thousand pesos (P 100,000.00) but not more than Two hundred thousand pesos (P 200,000.00) and/or imprisonment of not less than two (2) years and one day but not more than six (6) years. This penalty shall likewise be imposed against importers/brokers who deny an authorized customs officer full and free access to such records, books of accounts, business and computer systems, and all customs commercial data including payment records. This is without prejudice to the administrative sanctions that the Bureau of Customs may impose against the contumacious importers under existing laws and regulations including the authority to hold delivery or release of their imported articles." (R.A. 9135, April 27, 2001)

SEC. 3611. Failure to Pay Correct Duties and Taxes on Imported Goods. –

Any person who, after being subjected to post -entry audit and examination as provided in Section 3515 of Part 2, Title VII hereof found to have incurred deficiencies in duties and taxes paid for imported goods, shall be penalized according to three (3) degrees of culpability subject to any mitigating, aggravating or extraordinary factors that clearly established by the available evidence:

(a) Negligence - When a deficiency results from an offenders failure, through an act or acts omission or commission, to exercise reasonable care and competence to ensure that a statement made correct, it shall be determined to be negligent and punishable by a fine equivalent to not less than one -7(1/2) but not more than two (2) times the revenue loss. 72

(b) Gross Negligence - When a deficiency results from an act or acts of omission or commission done with actual knowledge or wanton disregard for the relevant facts and with indifference to or disregard for offender's obligation under the statute, it shall be determined to be grossly negligent and punishable by a fire equivalent to not less than two and a half (2 %) but not more than four(4) times the revenue loss.

(c) Fraud - When the material false statement or act in connection with the transaction was committed or omitted knowingly, voluntarily and intentionally, as established by clear and convincing evidence, it shall be determined to be fraudulent and be punishable by a fine equivalent ID not less than five (5) times but not more than eight (8) times the revenue loss and imprisonment of not less 111han two (2) years but not more than eight (8) years. The decision of the Commissioner of CAn4orns, upon proper hearing, to impose penalties as prescribed in this Section may be appealed in accordance with Section 2402 hereof." (R.A. 9135, April 27, 2001)

SEC. 3612. Violations of Tariff and Customs Laws and Regulations in General. –

Any person who violates a provision of this Code or regulations pursuant thereto, for which delinquency no specific penalty is provided, shall be punished by a fine of not more than one thousand pesos or by imprisonment for not more than one year, or both. If the offender is an alien he shall be deported after serving the sentence and if the offender is a public official or employee, he shall suffer disqualification to hold public office, to vote and participate in any public election for ten year (RA 9135, April 27, 2001)

FINAL PROVISIONS

SEC. 3701. Repealing Clause. –

Sections 207. 301 (Subsection e, f, & k), 302 (Subsection -b), 513, 1024, 1108, 1109, 1208, 2530 (Subsection 1) and 3705 of Republic Act Numbered Nineteen Hundred and Thirty Seven, as amended by Presidential Decree Numbered Thirty Four are hereby repealed. All Acts, Presidential Decrees, Executive Orders. Rules and Regulations or Ws thereof, in conflict with the provisions of this Code, are hereby likewise repealed.

SEC, 3702. Transitory Provisions. —

All suits, proceedings or prosecutions whether civil or criminal, for causes arising or acts done or committed prior to the effectivity of this Code, shall be commenced and/or prosecuted within the same time in the same manner and with the some effect as if this Code had not been enacted and all rights acquired, offences committed and penalties forfeitures or liabilities waived prior to the said effectivity shall not be affected thereby.

Sections 602 (subsections d, e, 0, 801 to 831, 901 to 905, 910 to 913, 2507 to 2512, 2529 (except subsection h) and 3301 (except subsection I to s) of Republic Act Numbered Nineteen Hundred and Thirty Seven as amended by Presidential Decree Numbered Thirty Four are hereby deleted and the same, are incorporated in Republic Act Numbered Fifty One Hundred and Seventy Three, as amended, for enforcement by the Philippine Coast Guard.

Sections 602 (subsection 1), 1209, 1212, 1213, 2701, to 2703, 2801, 2802, 2901 to 2908, 3001 to 3005, 3101 to 3109, 3201 to 3203 and 3507 to 3509 of Republic Act Numbered Nineteen Hundred and Thirty Seven as amended by Presidential Decree Numbered Thirty Four are hereby deleted and the same are incorporated in Presidential Decree Numbered Eight Hundred Fifty Seven, for enforcement by the Philippine Ports Authority.

SEC. 3703. Separability Clause. —

If any part or parts of this Code should for any reason be held to be invalid or unconstitutional, the remaining parts thereof shall remain in full force and effect.

SEC. 3704. Effectivity Date. —

This Code shall take effect immediately.